SELLING TO INDIA'S CONSUMER MARKET

SELLING TO INDIA'S CONSUMER MARKET

Douglas Bullis

Q

QUORUM BOOKS
Westport, Connecticut • London

Library of Congress Cataloging-in-Publication Data

Bullis, Douglas.
    Selling to India's consumer market / Douglas Bullis.
        p. cm.
    Includes bibliographical references and index.
    ISBN 1–56720–105–9 (alk. paper)
    1. Marketing—India—Management. 2. Target marketing—India.
    3. Advertising—India. 4. Consumption (Economics)—India.
    I. Title.
    HF5415.12.I5B85 1997
    658.8'00954—DC21   97–1704

British Library Cataloguing in Publication Data is available.

Library of Congress Catalog Card Number: 97–1704
ISBN: 1–56720–105–9

First published in 1997

Quorum Books, 88 Post Road West, Westport, CT 06881
An imprint of Greenwood Publishing Group, Inc.

Printed in the United States of America

The paper used in this book complies with the
Permanent Paper Standard issued by the National
Information Standards Organization (Z39.48–1984).

10 9 8 7 6 5 4 3 2 1

Copyright Acknowledgment

The author and publisher gratefully acknowledge *Business Today*, for permission to reprint
from the following articles:

S. Ramesh Kumar, "Analyzing the TV Market," *Business Today*, May 22, 1996; S. Ramesh
Kumar, "Strategies During Times of Slow Growth," *Business Today*, September 22, 1996;
S. Ramesh Kumar, "Making a Clean Break," *Business Today*, May 22, 1996.

Dedicated to
Victoria Tichenor, Paul Koller,
Sally Varna, and Sharon Adelman,
without whose understanding and help
this would have never come to be.

Contents

Acknowledgments   ix

Introduction   xiii

1. The Outlook for India's Consumer Economy   1

2. Targeting India's Consumer Market: The Big Picture   61

3. Some Complexities of Indian Consumerism   99

4. Marketing and Advertising   145

5. Distribution and Sales   211

Appendix A: Useful Terms   239

Appendix B: Useful Addresses   249

Appendix C: Additional Reading   261

Index   267

Acknowledgments

This book has no traditional bibliography because so much information was sourced over the Internet and via e-mail. The magazines, journals, and books listed in Appendix C, "Additional Reading" were also sourced for material. Nonetheless, this is perhaps one of the first books of its type that depended on the Internet and personal interviews far more than traditional publications.

This said, there are still so many thanks to be extended to so many people. Far and away the most important influence for this book came from Barbara Crossette, the former *New York Times* correspondent in India, and author of the landmark book *India: Facing the Twenty-First Century* (Indiana University Press). Her observations on the emerging consumer class of India sparked the inspiration for this book and sowed the seed of the portrait of Raja and Srimati India in Chapter 3. If there is one single book a prospective business visitor to India should read, it is Barbara's.

Business leaders whose information contributed to this book include Tara Sinha of her own Tara Sinha Pvt. Ltd. advertising consultancy; DHL's Head of Marketing Pradeep Bonde; P. B. Sawant, Chairman of the Press Council; Nancy Shroff of Bexim's International USA; S. L. Rao, former director of NCAER and now advisor to the Business India Group; R. C. Bhargava, managing director of Maruti Udyog; Parvinder Singh, chief managing director of Ranbaxy; Anand Mahindra, deputy managing director, Mahindra & Mahindra; Subhash Agrawal, president of consultancy Business Foundations in New Delhi; Microsoft's man in Bangalore, Sanjay

Parthasarathy; Edward Milward-Oliver, director of *Inasia.com* (Intermedia Corporation, Hong Kong); J. Venkatadas, CEO of the Canbank Venture Capital Fund; Thomas Thomas of Indus Venture Management; Vinod Haritwal, senior vice president of IL&FS Venture Corporation; David Loseff, Managing Director of Bank of America's Global Equity Investment Asia Group; G. Sabarinthan of the Technology Development and Information Company of India; Sanjay Bhowmick, vice president of Creditcapital Venture Fund (India); Jonathan Bond, director of HSBC Private Equity Management India; Pradip Shah, managing director of Indocean Venture Advisors Private, Ltd.; Kiran Nadkirni, managing director of Draper International (India) Pvt. Ltd.; Roshan Verghese, chief manager of investment funds of ANZ Grindlays; J. Vishwanathan, senior investment officer at the Investment Corp. of India; Philip Banks, vice president of AT Kearny, Inc.; David Bell, chief executive of the Financial Times Group; Bernd Pichetsrieder of BMW AG; Peter Denis Sutherland, chairman of Goldman Sachs International; attorneys L. Rao Penna and Nisith Desai; environmental activist and attorney M. C. Mehta; Samir Arora, founder of NetObjects; arts consultants Anita Rathnam, Arshiya Lokhandwala, and Shireen Gandhy; and Malaysia's Vinayak Chatterjee of Feedback Ventures Malaysia.

Numerous business writers in India and other parts of Asia also contributed information through their articles and via e-mail. These include *Asian Business* writers Sanjay Kumar, Sid Astbury, James Leung, Brian Mertens; *Asiaweek* writers Shirish Nadkarni, Arjuna Ranawana, Ajay Singh, Matthew Fletcher; *Business India* writers Vikram Doctor, Latha Kuttappan, Neera Bhardwaj, Madhumita Bose, Ganga Subramaniam, Namrata Datt, Devina Dutt, K. G. Kumar, Hormazd Sorabjee, N. Chandra Mohan, I. Satya Sreenivas, Bodhisatva Ganguli, Mayank Bhatt; *Business Today* Internet columnist Vivek Bhatia and writers Jairam Ramesh, S. Ramesh Kumar, Adite Chatterjee, Pareena Kawatra, Archana Rai, Bhakti Chuganee; *Business Week's* Manjeet Kripalani; *Business World* writers Shuchi Bansal, Niranjan Rajadhyaksha, D. N. Mukeiriea, Bhupesh Bhandari, Mahasweta Ghosh, Indranil Ghosh, Mainak De, D. N. Mukeriea, Arun Jethmalani, Nandan Chakraborty, S. V. Kumar, Subramaniam Sharma, P. Hari; the *Economist's* nameless Everybody; *Far Eastern Economic Review* writers Neel Chowdhury, Jonathan Karp, Lincoln Kaye; *Frontline* writers T. K. Rajalakshmi; *India Today* writers Stephen David, Uday Mahurear, Rawash Vinayak, Vijay Menon, Robin Abreu, Saurav Sev, Samar Harlarnkar, Navneet Sharma, Manoj Mitta, Smruti Koppikar; and *The Times of India's* Jug Suraiya.

Finally personal gratitude: My long-time associate editor Diane Freburg in the USA graciously pre-edited much of this manuscript so it wouldn't be such a horrifying mess for Quorum Books' editor Eric Valentine. Colleague and confidante Frank Gorin provided many valuable Web sites and e-mail contacts. Kuala Lumpur Associate Stuart Kempsell and Wong Siewlyn dispensed sage advice that kept me sane during the most vexing times when computers and e-mail systems seemed to conspire against this ever being completed. Sometimes in moments like this that one looks back and realizes just how many good friends one has.

Introduction

In the old days, awareness was the privilege of the rich. Now that gap
no longer exists.

> Bhaskar Rao, director, Centre for Media Studies,
> Delhi, November 6, 1996

India has a long history of masking its subtleties behind too-obvious
facades. After six years living in the Subcontinent region and Southeast
Asia, and residing all those years with private families in both India and
its lovely sister Sri Lanka, I learned more about India doing this book than
in all the others. Give India the benefit of your doubts and the attention
of your quieted mind, and it will become a lifelong teacher.

India has changed dramatically in the last few years. The crisis atmos-
phere of mid-1991, which saw Indians aghast as they watched their nearly
last precious gold reserves disappear into a plane for London, galvanized
them for change that came quickly and dramatically. Forty-five years of
socialism and self-reliance went out the window, and in came market
interdependence, the global economy, satellite TV, and Internet. Progress
was neither easy nor simple, but it was definitive. In five years India
transformed its economic attitudes irreversibly. India is just not the same
any more, and it is very unlikely to turn back.

The 1996 elections brought the same kind of sea change politically that
the 1991 reforms did economically. Forty-five years of Congress one-party
rule ended in a dismal display of corruption, to be replaced by a fractious,

feisty coalition that is sure to provide Delhi-watchers with years of enter-tainment. Yet the change underneath was deeper than the squabbles in the Lok Sabha and the press.

The state coffers are—every single one—nearly or actually broke. People are appalled at the worldliness of the country's many "godmen," trading the nobly historical ascetic serenity of the wandering gurus and yogis of the past for all-too-modern wheeling and dealing, monumental cheating, and the company of arms dealers and stock-market manipulators. The populace has awakened to the world on Star TV, and Rupert Murdoch is not noted for pulling his punches.

The wealth and open business environment generated by the 1991 reforms have produced a new force in India cultural life: the middle class. Though mainly Hindu, it is largely a trans-caste class. Its wealthier urban contingent numbers 100 million; their less-well-off country cousins have fewer absolute rupees with which to display their affluence, but they have the same hankering after consumer contentments. The city folks aspire to Marutis, India's home-grown clone of a somewhat dated Suzuki design, while the country folks are saving up for their mixies (the India-wide nickname for an electrical mixer).

The tourists will still come to see the great art and architecture, for nothing can change the significance and gratification of that. The world's seekers of spiritual solace will still come to the ashrams, for India's religious and philosophical inquiry did indeed produce some of humanity's sublimest perceptions. But now joining them are the world's business people, engi-neers, builders, entrepreneurs, producers. India for them is as tangible and as attractive as it is for culture aesthetes and seekers of spiritual attainment.

What can one possibly tell such a potpourri of newcomers?

If there is a single key fact readers should grasp about Indians, it is that they know what their land looked like 2,500 years ago, 250 years ago, 25 years ago, and two-and-a-half minutes ago. From that sum total of experi-ence sighing out over India's vast span of people and time, they know what they want India to look like in similar time spans to come. They know that the rituals of culture bring longer-lived satisfaction than injections of capital and tools. They regard their physical land and cultural heritage as tangible proof that they are a commonwealth not of themselves but of humanity unexplored.

But they want to look into that future from the contemplative vantage of neither dispiriting excess of wealth nor the spiritlessness of poverty. For too long, they realize, India has been of agony and ecstasy, fabled wealth and storyless starvation, colonizer and colonized. They see that democracy, for all its special interests holding governments to hostage, has produced, on balance, the fewest wars with other governments and the most citizens of the middle class.

Hence it is incumbent on visitors to look to India not as an emerging consumer market of unprecedented dimensions or as a low-cost, value-adding, export manufactory where labor is bitchy but cheap, but rather to what Indians are quietly trying to tell everyone who will listen: Any people which has survived 2,500 years despite several complete destructions of its infrastructure; countless invasions; and the wax and wane of economic theories ranging from agrarian commonwealth to monetarist colonialism to laissez-faire industrialism to state-directed socialism to market-economy globalism—assuredly such a people have important views about what works and what does not.

Listen, certainly, to their words of business and markets, but more important, observe all around the 2,500 years of which they speak. What lies within a people that can bring them to so long and so nobly endure?

Whatever it is, the world could use more of it.

SELLING TO INDIA'S CONSUMER MARKET

1

The Outlook for India's Consumer Economy

INDIA IN THE WORLD ECONOMY

India is one-sixth of humanity, the fifth largest economy in the world, one-quarter of the earth's urban humanity, one-third of the world's populace living in democracy, the second largest among the developing economies, and the first massive, complex society to successfully transit from a socialist economy to a market economy.

India's transition has been bumpy but steady. Economic liberalism is deregulating the economy and stimulating local and foreign investments. Since the inauguration of liberalization in 1991, India has emerged as the most promising and democratic mass market in Asia.

India's institutional structure and national psychology are based on political and economic freedom tempered with much more limited social freedom. The country has a prompt and uninhibited press, a judiciary that often overrules the government, a modern if slow legal system, international standards of accounting, and a growing research and academic infrastructure. India's private sector is the backbone of its economy—private business is 75 percent of the GDP. There is considerable opportunity for partnership, joint, and share-based ventures. India's economic vigor transcends the parochialisms of the country's political parties. With the arrival of international TV, the populace is emerging—sometimes gratefully and sometimes kicking and screaming—from its governmental cocoon of spoon-fed culture.

THE LIBERALIZING MINDSET

Today, private enterprise is encouraged in all but a few industries. The largest infrastructure industries, such as the posts, roads, rails, and ports, still are government administered, yet even there a phased program of public sector divestment and restructuring is underway. Telecommunications already are liberalized—some say a little too liberalized given the amount of corruption associated with it. Foreign investment is considered equal to—and as welcome as—domestic investment. Import barriers have dropped substantially and are in line for yet more cuts. Capital markets freely court foreign investment. Banking controls have been eased. Private investment—supported by India's 1996 personal savings average of 22 percent of GDP—is strongly encouraged. Much of it finds its way into capital markets via shares purchases and unit trusts. The tax structure has been simplified and its rates reduced. The Indian rupee is convertible in both current and capital accounts.

In 1995, the GDP exceeded Rs 700 crore (Rs 7 trillion or US $200 billion).[1] It averaged 4.2 percent annual growth between 1982 and 1991, and 5.8 percent after 1991. Inflation fluctuated between 8 and 13 percent over the same period. Today, foreign exchange reserves are comfortable at $19 billion, as is the general trend of the current account balance at 2.3 percent of GDP. Real per-capita GDP growth has been 2.4 percent annually since 1992, slightly exceeding population growth at 2 percent per year.

In the 1994–1995 fiscal year (the year for which the most complete economic statistics were available before the 1996 elections), India's GDP grew 5 percent as a result of 8 percent industrial growth. Growth is not likely to accelerate through 1996 because of a tighter monetary policy and the political realignments brought about by the 1996 national election. For 1997–1998, assuming continued political stability and no agricultural calamity, growth is expected to reach 5.7 percent by the end of 1998.

India's 1991 restructuring plan produced a reasonably smooth transition from a mostly controlled to a mostly free economy. Economic growth and exports have picked up. Capital markets are flourishing amid the optimism produced by the entrance of major international financial institutions into India. Foreign investment has increased sharply.

Key business and economic statistics reflect India's confidence. As of June 1996, the per-capita GNP was $320 and per capita GDP was $1,300. This is a 4-to-1 ratio, compared with Singapore's 1-to-1 ratio, South Korea's 1.2-to-1, Thailand's 3-to-1, and China's 6-to-1. Foreign exchange reserves were high at $19 billion and the inflation rate dropped from 13.5 percent in 1991 to 9.9 percent in 1996. Inflation is predicted to decline steadily to about 7 percent by 2000. India's high FDI-to-GDP ratio reflects growing investor confidence in the country.

In sum, India's 1991 reforms largely accomplished their goal of rejuvenating the country's business environment and opening the economy to foreign investment. Their success established a change in thinking that is unlikely to be shunted aside by parochial political issues.

The 1996 elections brought into office a thirteen-member coalition under the tutelage of Prime Minister Deve Gowda. The 1991 reforms were confirmed in the 1996 budget by Finance Minister P. Chidambaram. The government has had to juggle two basic economic philosophies:

- Progress between 1991 and 1996 has been remarkable and clearly has shown that the wave of the future is the continuance of market reforms, even if it means serious medium-term social unrest as the inefficient public sector is converted to private enterprise.

- Too much private enterprise will exacerbate India's already serious rich/poor disparities, leaving the poor with no social safety net and turning them into a huge, unhappy, and politically chaotic force.

Both of these issues have merit, although the second one is often minimized by free-marketers who have not lived in India and do not realize how deeply rooted is the value system of everyone being taken care of. India lives with a strong legacy of castes, tribes, clans, and families, all of whose longevity is directly related to their strengths of social protection. Democracy has shifted these attitudes to politicians, who transfer the burden to government. Hence, there is considerable pressure on the government to maintain a "pro-poor" image and increase populist spending. The political imperatives resulting from the 1996 elections are likely to resist economic reforms that endanger public welfare. The government will be sensitive to charges raised by the opposition party (whomever it happens to be at the time). The affect will be government economic policies that are slowed down and "fudged" (popular Indian parlance meaning decisions are made but nothing is done).

The Probable Pace of Reforms from 1996 to 2000

Foreign and private investment will be increasingly welcome. No backtracking on reform is expected. Substantial progress already has been made, although some slowdown is likely through 1997 as the government focuses on other priorities. As is apparent from the efforts to woo foreign capital, no political party is seriously opposed to private or foreign investment, although there may be more selectivity in approving it since party politics use overseas investment as a whipping boy.

Public-sector reform will remain sensitive. The government has balked at large-scale privatization since it would involve the sale of the state-owned public-sector units (PSUs) to the private sector and result in considerable job redundancies. The government prefers the indirect route of privatizing industry by opening up public-sector monopolies to private investment and diluting its stake in PSUs via share sales in the capital market. Up to now, this policy has been used largely to raise funds for budgetary needs and has not resulted in the divestment of government management over these corporations. This situation is unlikely to change in the immediate future.

Labor reform is likely to be slow. There is likely to be little talk of a government exit policy encouraging inefficient enterprises to close down or convert to other enterprises. Plant closures and layoffs of workers will continue to be difficult and controversial. The involvement of state governments here will make reform even more difficult. The multitude of parties in power in different states across the country and their varying political commitments will make any labor reform program a complicated one. Progress is likely to be slow despite the generally reformist charter given by the 1996 elections, and exchange rate reform is likely to stay on the back burner.

While foreign exchange reserves are comfortable, the economic fundamentals are not yet stable enough to support capital-account convertibility. The problems of inflation and a widening current-account deficit need to be tackled before exchange rate reform can proceed to its natural conclusion.

Foreign trade and indirect tax reform are expected to be rapid. The commitment to trade reform remains high. As long as the reserve position remains comfortable, the government should face little trouble in sustaining reform.

Will Reforms Prevail?

The 1991 reforms package was no benevolent gift to India from the wise acumen of Narasimha Rao and Manmohan Singh. They had no option but to do what the International Monetary Fund and the World Bank told them to do. Today, external oversight watches India's economy no less than before. Politicians, for all their posturings from the loudspeaker trucks in the villages, know that these postures do not have much of a vote appeal overseas. India faces $24 billion in external debt that must be paid by the year 2000. Its fiscal position in 1996, in debt terms, was not all that much better than it was in 1991. Spending still exceeds revenues by an average of roughly 3.5 percent of the GDP. Interest payments still consume more than one-half of the Centre's[2] tax revenues, and most states are perilously close to bankruptcy. Dependence on imported oil has increased, and current account deficits are looming ominously as natural handmaidens to foreign capital investment. India has signed the World Trade Organization accord, a commitment that cannot be abrogated.

Indeed, India has little room for maneuvering. Many Indian economists call these "India's external anchor" and tend to appreciate the sobering factor it imposes on domestic partisanship. Just about everyone in the know realizes that reforms have done everyone a lot of good and are here to stay.

There are deeper social forces at work within India that reinforce the positive aspects of reforms. The 1991 reforms expanded the size and voice of the constituency for change. Numerous companies have enhanced their global presence and perspective. A new generation of entrepreneurs comfortable with market economics has arisen. Unemployment and poverty have not spun out of control—indeed, the still modest amount of credible nationwide research information available reveals that economic poverty—as opposed to social poverty caused by ingrained traditions such as the caste system—had decreased. Between 1985 and 1991, the economy saw the creation of more than 5 million additional employment opportunities every year; between 1991 and 1996, this increased to more than 6 million. Poverty ratios have fallen, and wage rates have risen. For the first time in years, the terms of trade have moved sharply in favor of agriculture. Agricultural growth has become more regionally diversified, and the non-farm rural sector has become a dynamic job creator.

India also is changing in subtler ways. Close to 60 percent of the population is below the age of 40. This is the so-called "Post-Independence Generation," which has no ideological baggage to carry, and genuflects to no past. Urban India is in fact the world's third largest country. A communications revolution is sweeping both the cities and the countryside. Almost one in every three Indian households is a TV-owning family; about one in nine are on cable. Indians everywhere are exposed day in and day out to new economic messages.

One of these messages is consumerism. Almost 60 percent of Indians own manufactured consumer goods of one kind or another. Another message is the importance of investment. Over 20 million Indians presently invest in some type of security beyond the savings account. The most important economic message they hear—and live—is that change has been for the better.

The media are filled with debates ranging from the sublime to the fulminous on the Enron and KFC types of situations that serve as lightning rods in times of change. The media are generally for reforms—the debate they inspire often centers on transparency issues, not rolling back the calendar. Even the vernacular regional media—which tend to be pretty dubious about anything imposed from the outside—see a positive aspect to reforms: They bring less government interference in local affairs.

In India, who says what is as important as what is said. How something is said is as important as when it is said. Unlike China, which periodically ravages itself with shrillness, India's reforms, for all their magnitude, have been consistently low-key. More important, they have been consistent, which one certainly cannot say of China. However, parallel to China, in their own ways, the states drive reforms as much as the Centre drives the states.

The foreign press tends to focus too much on individuals in the news. Individuals matter, yes. But far more momentous in India today are fundamental processes. These are to be found in the surveys of research firms like the National Council on Applied Economic Research (NCAER) and Marketing and Research Group (MARG), the exit polls, the switches in brand preferences, and the increasing number of hired thugs in a party politician's audience compared with the dwindling number of women and children. India is marvelously subtle within its vast panoply of events and faces in the crowd. Politicians once thwarted these things with impunity. The 1991 liberalization knelled the doom of that. The 1996 elections showed them that the day had arrived. Reforms will continue, but it takes an eye for the detail and the subtle to see where they are working.

No New Nehrus

For forty-odd years after independence, India's guiding philosophy was that presaged by Mahatma Gandhi and articulated by Jawaharlal Nehru. Its four cornerstones were Socialism, Secularism, Nonalignment, and

Democracy. Over the last decade, and especially since the post-1991 reforms, the Nehruvian principles can be characterized as dwindling down to death in snipped-off loose threads.

The "Breakdown of the Nehruvian Vision" is fastened upon by contending parties during elections as an emblem of what each does, or does not, stand for. A commonly asked but never quite answered question is, "Where did Nehru's ideals go?"

The ideal of nonalignment has shifted from its original West versus the Soviets stance, first to West versus East, and now to North versus South. It is likely to vanish further into academic wrangling as India becomes more consumerist and televisionized.

Socialism, however, is still a much debated issue, often from the starting question, "Where did socialism go wrong?" The answer most often arrived at lies in the embarrassing fact—for socialists anyway—that it achieved very little of its two most important "preconditions for a socialist pattern of society"—universal primary education and world standards of public health, sanitation, and nutrition. India's socialism was sidetracked by an unchecked bureaucracy which allowed it to build a license-based, restrictions-laden Raj that served few of socialism's ideals but encouraged many of its defects—black money, corruption on a massive and blatant scale, and an inefficient public sector coexisting with a pampered private sector.

All of these will kill efficiency no matter what particular economic ideal is being served. Thoughtful Indians now are trying to draw lessons from socialism's breakdown. They want Nehru's secularist legacy to survive without placing it in the hands of the bureaucrats.

As an alternative to socialism, the market economy receives mixed reviews. Ideally, it should foster rational behavior. Some feel that television is a great leveling medium that, if its producers can be induced to more fairly (or at least accurately) represent the realities of casteism, will go a long way toward ameliorating it. Certainly, everyone agrees that TV is better than illiteracy, but what exactly visual literacy is *supposed* to achieve is a very open question. Others feel that a competitive society will only exacerbate communal and caste divisions.

India has few models it can look to in this regard. The market economy has not confronted caste systems in other parts of the world anywhere near as divisive and deeply rooted as India's. The key to substantive social change in India at the behest of the market economy very likely will lie in value system presently being devised by today's young middle class. At present, this generation embraces the market model and betterment by career path and rational choice.

Unfortunately, liberal, enlightened ideals are not always decisive. Whether the middle class's personal aspirations will translate into a sense for the aspirations of others is more likely to be configured by TV and the media than by the blandishments of social reformists. Thus far, seeking justice for minorities and the underprivileged are themes not often seen on television, nor, for that matter, are role models promoting individual moral examples. The competitive society may have arrived, but competitive careers are all too often still circumscribed by caste.

India is a narrow road. To Indians, on one side resides the typical Asian suburbanite to whom career is all important. On the other resides a semiliterate population divided into innumerable camps and communities, each after its own bit of fuel for the cookfire. There is as yet little sign in either of any common movement or ideology capable of urging both sides to be concerned with each other's fate. Hence, a major social trend for marketers to watch is how many of this young generation allow their urge to rise to blunt their instinct of concern. Co-option is more likely to set limits on the influence of the middle class than political parties and their platforms.

WHAT MIDDLE-CLASS INDIANS ARE THINKING

What attitudes do Indians share with other countries about the seemingly endless modernizing forces that shape their lives? What do they feel about the control of their destinies? Disciplining their politicians? Nurturing their children? Changing their economic lives? To what extent is the populace mired in fatalism?

In late 1995, *India Today* magazine summarized a global study conducted in some forty countries around the world by International Research Associates (INRA), which operates throughout the world via thirty-one affiliated companies. The Indian survey was conducted by the Marketing and Research Group (MARG), and polled 1,065 respondents in ten metropolitan areas between the ages of 18 and 55. Over 70 percent of the respondents had at least a secondary level of education. Their minimum income level was Rs 7,500 ($215) per month, which is comfortable by Indian standards. Over one-half of the surveyed households had a refrigerator, close to one-third had a telephone connection, and over 25 percent had a motorcycle or scooter.

Those who had notions that India is trapped in a time warp were in for some startling reappraisals. The bottom line was that the Indians surveyed want their nation to move forward, not look to the past.

Indians' main concerns are about social rather than spiritual conditions. They avidly follow current news events around the world. They want rapid economic growth. They want an end to inflation. They want jobs. They want to fight rising crime rates. They want to travel more.

Surprisingly, the survey showed relatively less concern about corruption in government, and also relative unconcern about quality education. This may be because many of them automatically associate a government job with an extra income from graft, and because the country has yet to demonstrate that education is a sure ticket to employment. This hints that Indians as a whole are more interested in larger social issues and problems like AIDS and drug abuse.

But there are contradictions that still need to be explained. Indians rate keeping abreast of current news developments as the highest on their list of interests (7.4 on a scale of 1 to 10) and have among the highest voter turnouts in the world. Indians are politically hyperactive. One-third of those polled have attended either political rallies, speeches, or town- and school-affairs meetings in the past year, compared with 25 percent in the United States. But only 15 percent of them admit to having engaged in political discussions among themselves during the same period; the comparative figure for the United States is 37 percent.

These altitudes could have a bearing on how India conducts its democratic process. People are more likely to be onlookers and less likely to be active in political debates. Some Indians interpret this as implying that this population sample is susceptible to rhetoric and demagogic manipulation centering on caste and religious differences.

The poll appears to bear out this conclusion in several ways. A large number of Indians believe that religion should play a strong role in society. Translated into politics, this could be the harbinger of a volatile political future. On the other hand, there are moderating influences: The margin between those who believe that the role of religion is good and those who believe the opposite is narrow—46 percent versus 42 percent. There is no benchmark to measure whether this margin has narrowed or widened following the fundamentalist waves that have rocked the nation's politics during the past several years. The point, however, is clear: Dealing with the issue of India's religions in the frameworks of India's secular state promises to remain a vexing problem for those who lead.

Economic Vested Interests

Cleaning out India's economic stables will be no less a task than the Augean stables were to Hercules. Managing India by steering a clearer economic path and bringing the bloated rule of the *babus* to heel will be tricky and difficult. (*Babu* literally means "petty merchant" but is broadly used to refer negatively to any small-minded moneyed interest.)

There is a strong undercurrent of resistance to speedy economic reform and getting government to accept a less domineering role in the lives of people. A majority of the Indians polled felt that a reduced role of the government would be unfortunate. This may be due to a deep-seated suspicion of what the private sector's motives are, and a lingering association of nationalism with Nehruvian socialism.

Reconciling the contradictory Indian attitudes that recession and unemployment are serious concerns with their resistance to cutting down on government spending is likely to prove a headache for the managers of the national economy. Unless they can muster quick proof that economic reforms, despite initial hardships, are a sure-fire way to more jobs, a better quality of life, and the guarantee of civic amenities, reformers are likely to hit some tough social resistance within a few years.

Relations with other countries do not figure very high in the Indian list of concerns. Only 3 percent of those polled were concerned about international relations or aid to poor countries in the Third World. Terrorism, on the other hand, bothers Indians more—15 percent felt that this was a very important issue. This is not surprising considering the disorder in Punjab, Kashmir, and Sri Lanka, and that two prime ministers have been assassinated in the last decade.

Indians feel that Western—and especially American—films and television cast undesirable influences on their culture. While foreign television programs (including those from the United States) did very well initially because they offered welcome relief from Doordarshan's tediousness, Indian programs today have a significantly higher viewership. One reason for this is recent marked improvements in variety and quality.

While Indians list recent news events as their main area of interest, travel emerges as a close second—7.1 on a scale of 1 to 10. With the middle class expanding rapidly, so is the leisure-travel trade. An estimated 30 lakh (3 million) Indians went abroad in 1994, up from 19 lakh in 1991. Within India, the number of those taking holidays went up from 6.7 crore (67 million) in 1991 to 8.9 crore in 1995.

Perhaps the biggest attitudinal difference between the way Indians feel in comparison with other countries is in the values they want to inculcate in their children. Good manners tops at 71 percent, compared to 40 percent for most Western European countries and 45 percent in the United States. Encouraging responsibility among children was not high on the Indian parents' agenda. Only 38 percent of Indian parents thought that this was important, compared with 58 percent for the United States, 45 percent for Western Europe, and 50 percent for Japan. On the other hand, obedience and loyalty were higher on the Indian agenda compared with the United States and Western Europe.

These themes point to a population sample that is bread-and-butter oriented and has an active interest in all that is going on around them. They are susceptible to being exploited by religious antagonisms, vulnerable to rhetoric, devoted to family values in bringing up their children, impatient for rapid economic growth, and afraid of any precipitous moves that may upset the established order.

Indians' Major Concerns

Out of fifteen issues, Indians ranked the following eight as most important:

1. crime and lawlessness;
2. inflation and high prices;
3. recession and unemployment;
4. quality of education;
5. corruption in government;
6. AIDS;
7. environmental pollution;
8. terrorism.

Social and Political Activities

True to its tradition of being political, India has among the world's highest proportion of people who have voted in an election—67 percent. Indians back their interest in politics with a healthy participation in political speeches or rallies, and meetings on community affairs. While few Indians like to run for public office (only 2.6 percent), they are more active (9 percent) at serving on local committees. Indians write more letters to the editor of a newspaper or magazine (8 percent) than citizens of any other country in the world except Australia. That very few (3 percent) call in to live radio or television shows is not surprising given the relatively small number of call-in shows in the country. Fifteen percent of them donated money to political parties—another world record.

Only 15 percent said that they had engaged in a political discussion in the past 12 months. This may point to the fact that Indians are fairly fixed in their attitudes and are not much interested in debating. This may mean that the spread of television programs related to political debate may lead to a more active political-debate culture in the future.

Leisure and Personal Interests

High on the list of leisure and personal interests for Indians is news programming that explains what is happening in the world and why. While social issues like crime and unemployment are important, Indians give them a lower ranking than other interests, like travel.

Closely related to the Indian interest in travel is the steady increase in consumer spending on durables in the country, even among the lower income classes (families with an annual income of less than Rs 20,000 or $572). According to consumer surveys by the National Council of Applied Economic Research (NCAER), while forty-five households out of every 1,000 in the country in this lower income category owned black and white television sets in 1989 and 1990, this more than doubled in 1993 and 1994. The number of families in this class that owned motorcycles also doubled, while those buying mopeds and color television sets increased by 50 percent.

Perhaps as a result of the general level of poverty in the country and the preoccupation with making a living, Indians have a much lower level of interest in nature/animals or the environment as compared to most developed countries. Based on the responses to nineteen interests that people were polled for, INRA has categorized people into "humanists," "pragmatists," and "technologists." While India has among the lowest proportion of humanists in its population as compared to other countries, it is interesting that the broad divisions for India are not too dissimilar to those for the United States, but are very different from those for Western Europe, where the proportion of humanists is very high.

Out of nineteen interests in the poll, Indians listed the following eight in their order of importance:

1. recent news events;
2. travel;
3. environmental issues;
4. social issues;
5. do-it-yourself hobbies;
6. lives of important or famous people;
7. cooking;
8. inventions and new products.

What the Future Holds

When it comes to immigrants and working mothers of young children, Indians, like those in the United States and Western Europe, feel that any increase in these is detrimental. Interestingly, the Chinese, who are supposed to be more traditional than the Indians, felt that more working mothers was good, which is perhaps an indication of how much keener the Chinese are to get ahead.

India differs dramatically from the United States and Western Europe in the way they perceive their government. The majority of Indians felt that a decline in the role of the government would be unfortunate. This underscores the underlying pool of resentment against the general purpose of economic reforms—something that the BJP has exploited quite well. On the attitude toward the role of religion in shaping society, 46 percent of Indians felt that it was beneficial, while 42 percent felt that it was harmful.

Like most countries in the world, Indians feel that U.S. films are likely to adversely influence their culture. More people were against U.S. films than in favor.

Indians believe that, in the future:

1. There will be more immigrants.
2. U.S. films will influence Indian culture.
3. More mothers will work full-time.
4. Government will have a smaller role.
5. People will retire at a later age.
6. The role of religion will be larger.
7. More job-related education will be needed.

Desirable Values for Children

Perhaps the most significant way that the East and the West differ in their value systems lies in the values parents wish to inculcate in their children. While countries like Japan, China, and India felt that "good manners and politeness" were the most important, countries like the United States felt that a "sense of responsibility" was the most important and that "good manners" came next. Indians rank the "value of learning" second in the list. Given the relatively low priority to qualities like independence or imagination, it is likely that this refers more to learning by rote than to developing a spirit of inquiry. A "sense of responsibility" was third on the Indian agenda, only 38 percent. Indians rated obedience and loyalty higher. For all of the religious institutions in India, teaching children tolerance and respect for others were low on the agenda. Conscientiousness at work had a higher priority.

TRADITION AND THE FUTURE OF REFORMS

The challenge to the arriving overseas business person is how to see past the virtues of his or her products to their place in things from the Indian traditional world view.

India's political history was shaped by two traditions: the inflexibility of the rule of law, which favored the survival of strong government, and the placing of the effectiveness of traditions above the effectiveness of the government, which favored the rise of powerful bureaucracies.

Placing the effectiveness of traditions above the effectiveness of the government is quite an archaic tradition. Indians raptly worship the minutia of the characters of their lesser gods while tending to ignore the point of the gods' existence. The fact that tradition conveys legitimacy but legitimacy does not demand effectiveness is an important feature of the political power in India. Political evolution has been kind to strong, centralized power. While India has gone from socialism to capitalism within one decade, this does not mean that we are likely to see India replace its political aristocracy with an economic one. The evidence points to market economics that end up reinforcing the existing elites and their interests.

India's sense of the traditional is partly tribal and partly collective. The sense of social foundations is strong, but the sense for tolerance is weak—it is hard to imagine more clique-filled offices; yet they all manage to get the job done. There is a strong sense of community and collective discipline, but a poor sense of respect for leadership. There is a strong sense for religion but a weak sense for spirituality. The ethic that people espouse often is not the one they practice.

Any business in India must grasp the importance of indigenous tradition in the formulation of political ideas. People from the West assume that modernity, like Coca-Cola, comes in a single, universal form. Indians tend to be more reluctant to define matters in strict, definitive terms. This comes from the long cultural predisposition to avoid conflict by sharply defining minute roles—even though the result of such a practice is a lot of sharp definitions abrading each other.

POWER POLLUTION AND THE SWAMI ROLE

For all of the pomp and perks with which they like to surround themselves, Indian politicians live an unnervingly stressful life. Success in Indian politics requires charm, cunning, acting skills, the ability to articulate visions, and "intellectual malleability"—i.e., having no firm ideas of one's own.

Genuine leaders rarely become decision-making ministers; hangers-on and bootlickers are more likely to get that job. Parties are run along feudal lines. Anyone who shows personal leadership qualities is likely to be mistrusted by the consensus leadership. A natural leader soon learns to mask ability if he or she wants to reach high office. (In India's great dramatic dance and theater of the past, all of the figures are in essence masks, and the political leaders are the most elaborately masked.)

Power is a high-stress job in India. Ministers live in luxury and have many people serving their needs. Many assume the *rajadeva* (god-king) role with his own court, satraps, and supplicating masses lined up for audience and blessing. But the more prominent a politician becomes, the more flak he or she draws. The opposition harries them by fair means and foul. Blatant lies are honorable weapons. India's press has an uncanny knack for sowing a grain of untruth and reaping a harvest of letters to the editor that say everything the editor dares not.

Popular hostility exposes India's politicians to very real dangers. The most damaging are psychological. The Indian male's deepest fear is the ignominy of public loss of face. Virtually no one ends a term of office with more friends and supporters than he or she had before it. Great pretense is made that sanctity and wisdom prevail—hence the thriving trade in rubber-stamp personalities doing the dirty work and press-release priests waving incense at everything a politician says.

These dangers, and the fears they create, cause politicians to seek psychological solace in various ways. The favorite is the swami or spiritual adviser. The ideal swami should have a smattering of religiosity (a little astrology never hurts either). The swami's role is to listen, give sympathy and emotional support, and not betray. Most politicians know their swamis have few spiritual insights, but the faith people have in the term "spiritual adviser" is mesmerizing. Hence the perennial photo-ops of the ascetic with the long hair giving audience to the barefooted politician, and the visits to the grand temple priests in their unique ritual garb.

The obvious smarminess associated with political swamis traces to the ancient historical need for the warrior-king's aggression and taxation to be solemnly absolved by a priest-teacher brahmin. One of the first things the great emperor Asoka did after repenting his bloody takeover of Kalinga (now Orissa) was to seek repentance before Buddhist monks.

ECONOMIC REFORMS AND THE FUTURE OF DEMOCRACY

India is not likely to become an economic tiger. It is much more likely to continue its present growth rate of 5–6 percent. The near bankruptcy of the government and even nearer bankruptcy of most states have produced certain laudable short-term gains.

Yet it is not impossible that India might one day take the easy way out and disengage from sustained reform. If parties continue to compete with each other for populist giveaways, there looms near bankruptcy combined with stagflation. This possibility raises the thinking Indian's evaluation of the relationship between reform and democracy. Some businessmen and reformers already blame democracy for their woes. Since political pressures in India create the largest demand for subsidies and specialized treatment, some analysts feel that Indian democracy may be vulnerable.

Such thinking is unnecessarily alarmist. India has several long-established self-centering mechanisms that keep consensus on the rails—albeit rocking, reeling, and screaming during the downhill plunges. As the post-1996 government amply shows, India allows all parties a chance at power—with sometimes surprising results. It would have seemed unimaginable six months before the votes were counted in 1996 that Deve Gowda's benign face would be smiling from the windows of 1 Janapath Marg, New Delhi.

There has been a consistent record since 1991 of parties attacking reform in opposition and then embracing it once in power. Moreover, the same democracy that competes so vigorously in election-year giveaways also sets limits on the process after the votes are in. Once in office, politicians suddenly become acute to the clap of doom that awaits if they lose control of inflation.

Hence, while India's political system may produce slower growth than some of the authoritarian countries of East Asia, democracy may in the long term provide the surer foundation for India-style growth. In the short term, India's volubly populist democracy may impede growth, but political populism is also directly proportionate to political pluralism. Indian economists may watch inflation and investment rates with one hand on the crystal ball, but the other is on their lens on the past when command economics produce no growth at all.

A QUICKLY CHANGING BUSINESS WORLD

The New Face of Corporate Governance

The pattern of board oversight that grew during India's preliberalization days was one of board members investing little and bossing much. Companies often were run like private fiefdoms, flouting norms of disclosure and transparency. Company directors were known to sleep through crucial meetings, awakening to rubber-stamp their acquiescence on sensitive issues. They often sat on the boards of competing companies. Chairmen and CEOs were often the same person. Many of both were recruited through old-school and cocktail-circuit networks. Other board members' main contribution was their celebrityhood. Production figures were disclosed but profit figures were not. The performance of individual divisions was never broken out from overall performance. Managers regarded their job as safeguarding their job. There was no attitude that operational responsibilities should protect stakeholder interests. Boards did not examine auditing practices. The government avoided any responsibility for ensuring good corporate governance.

Post-1991 liberalization brought a closer look at other methods of board oversight. Today, Indian business people are familiar with, and hotly debating, two broad types of corporate governance:

- The market-driven Anglo-American model, which raises capital from the markets and the stock price acts as an approval rating. If the management performs below expectations, shareholders do the "Wall Street Walk" by selling and exiting. If the management consistently fails, an outsider can take over the company by acquiring majority shares.

- The German and Japanese model, which relegates the importance of the markets to second place, beneath the interests of shareholders, who rely on banks, insurance companies, and institutional investors to monitor companies on their behalf.

There is no argument that one of these will eventually prevail. The debate in India is which is more suited to Indian conditions. This debate hinges on the way capital is raised in India.

In the past, international development agencies provided most of India's growth capital. This vehicle has been largely replaced by a capital market. A theory of corporate governance is evolving which tries to reconcile the distinct demands of capital markets and foreign direct investments. The main issue is how directors themselves are to be governed, not how the consequences of their decisions are to be managed.

The public companies have come under the sharpest scrutiny. Most Indian investors and economists readily agree that something is wrong with the way Indian public companies are directed. Directors still control companies through relatively small stakes and adopt strong management but weak oversight roles in their companies. Their power is not counterbalanced by India's institutional investors, who in the main dislike wielding their voting power; when they do so it is usually at the invitation of the government. Most public-company shareholders still remain ignorant of their rights—the main issue they tend to raise at annual meetings is higher dividends.

The private sector, however, has seen several developments come along that are substantially changing the way this sector is being governed. Company managements are slowly becoming more accountable to the stakeholders of the company, which in India means employees, consumers, and suppliers as well as investors. Among these developments are:

- Financial institutions (FIs) are taking a more activist role in response to the finance ministry's encouragement to protect shareholder interests and discipline management. FIs have responded with a surprising readiness to use their power.

- Important sections of the corporate sector are searching for a better directoral system than the pastiches that exist now. The Confederation of Indian Industry (CII) has inaugurated a think tank named the CII Task Force on Corporate Governance, which analyzes issues related to the roles of company boards and the function that FIs have in modernizing boardrooms.

- Mutual funds, which with the FIs own the largest portfolios of Indian companies, have been given the right to vote on company affairs. Company managements now have a vigilant and knowledgeable shareholder voice they have to listen to.

- The Securities and Exchange Board of India (SEBI) has drafted a new takeover code that makes it easier for an acquirer to take over a company. The previous code—written only in 1994—took major steps to protect ordinary shareholders during takeovers. The revised code set up a share depository system to help make takeovers more transparent.

- Some corporate boards have tried to circumvent threats to their independence by issuing nonvoting shares; although the markets have responded very negatively to nonvoting shares.

- Foreign institutional investors (FIIs) originated a trend toward investor influence over management quality. Local investors were not long in seeing advantages to themselves. The quality of management emerged as a primary consideration in selecting stocks. Financial markets have pounded companies felt to be ignoring investors.

- FIIs are likely to be the largest controllers of large blocks of company stock when the global depository receipts (GDRs) of these companies are converted into domestic equity. While the GDRs carry no voting rights and their holders have little direct say in the affairs of the issuing companies, when they are converted to domestic equity, FIIs acquire a strong oversight voice. The documentation of GDR issues (mainly subscribed to by overseas investors) are far more detailed than the documentation of domestic offers.

- Mutual funds must declare their net asset values every week. Hence they put pressure on companies in which they invest to keep posting high returns. They are also more watchful over management.

These developments show how quickly investor power is growing compared with the power of lenders.

India's lenders are primarily concerned with whether a company is generating enough cash flow to repay its loans. Although most FIs nominate representatives to company boards, there is often no correlation between the experience of the nominee and the needs of the company. Moreover, FIs use board nominations as a pool for favors. Typically, an FI has a hundred or more nominee directors on their shopping list. Of these, about one-half will be officials in other companies (sometimes competitors), while the rest retired executives. Governance by favored friends is how most boards become rubber stamps. Today, FIs are trying to formulate guidelines that define what nominee directors are expected to demand from company management.

FIIs, on the other hand, are not as concerned with cash flows as they are with capital appreciation. The net effect has been to convince Indian investors to become more concerned with portfolio yield. A tainted company will not be able to raise money from the markets for very long, and its managers know that. Most takeovers begin in the capital markets when predator hopefuls, often working with unhappy shareholders, start cornering shares of a company in trouble. The threat of a takeover is very frightening to most managements because it represents an ignominious loss of face in addition to income.

They are just as frightened of investor flight, but in this case for purely financial reasons. FIIs are used to high levels of corporate governance and disclosure, and expect the same from Indian companies. They also have the ability to move their money quickly and are restrained by no geographic or cultural compulsions to invest only in India.

One result is more transparency and disclosure. Indian accounting practices can help management hide as much as it reveals in its annual books. For example, data are rarely given on divisional turnover. How can investors judge whether a decision to commit more money to a company is sustainable unless the comparative performance of its divisions is known?

In response, Indian managers have devised their own takeover defenses. Desubsidiarizing divisions needs only board-level clearance, not shareholder approval; hence management can transfer its most profitable divisions into a separate company. Brands also can be similarly moved around. These really are not poison pills as much as asset gutting, but they have the same effect.

The upshot of all of this is that forces far more fundamental than India's political imbroglios like the Enron, Cogentrix, and telecommunications license debacles are transforming India into an international corporate player using mostly the same rules as everyone else.

Fading Family Fiefdoms

India's family empires are in the throes of the same revolution that is changing the thinking of the country's smaller businesses. When the Rao/Singh reforms began to liberalize the economy, they exposed local businesses to market forces for the first time since the country's independence. At first these favored the big empires, since it was they who foreign companies sought as joint-venture partners.

Now the Indian government is making more subtle but far-reaching changes. A case in point is the takeover code finalized by the Securities and Exchange Board of India, which contains several landmark changes. One is that the SEBI wants to make takeovers—including hostile bids— much easier. Among other things, SEBI will no longer have to approve a bidder's price.

Much more important is SEBI's intent to protect the rights of minority shareholders. Any investor who takes a stake of 10 percent in a company must make an offer for a further 20 percent; after that, any substantial increase has to be by an open offer to all shareholders.

In many countries it is uneventful to oblige an investor with 20–30 percent of a company to bid on the open market if he or she wants to acquire the whole thing. In India, however, the new takeover code is a subtle means to replace the families who control most Indian businesses with more widely held companies. The SEBI measures are in reality a vehicle to de-fang India's powerful family dynasties such as the Tatas, Birlas, Singhanias, and Thapars. The SEBI's tactic is to force them into restructuring their businesses if they are to survive.

In the past, the big families could count on the support of India's financial institutions, which own around 40 percent of most big companies. However, financiers such as the Industrial Credit and Investment Corporation of India (ICICI) now are trying hard to prune nonperforming assets. They have told families such as the Modis that they must sort out their run-down businesses, close them (which is difficult under India's restrictive labor laws), or sell them. Before, families were often benign investors. Now they are likely to be told to bow out if they do not perform.

This does not mean that family empires are being thrown to the wolves, but it does mean that they are being pushed out of nonproductive enterprises. In India's biggest 250 private-sector companies, family businesses account for about 70 percent of the total sales and net profits. Big families have long walled off major industrial sectors for themselves. The Tatas make trucks, the Birlas make cars (those venerable Ambassadors), the Bajaj family makes two- and three-wheelers, and the Mahindras make Jeeps. Until recently, such family empires faced little competition. They diversified into any business they wanted. Financing from public-sector institutions was assured, and corporate law codes made it easy to control subsidiaries via small share holdings. The Tata empire, for example, comprises some seventy companies that produce everything from trucks to tea, yet the parent company's average stake in any one rarely exceeds 15 percent.

The old family empires are increasingly vulnerable on other fronts as well. Their most immediate problem is raising capital in India's more open financial markets. With profits dropping in the face of overseas competition, credit harder to come by in more scrutiny-conscious international money markets, and a too-small local equity market, many family firms are being forced to weed out unprofitable investments that they rushed into in more protected times.

The Mahindra family withdrew from oil drilling and instrumentation to concentrate on autos. The Thapars trimmed Ballapur Industries back to its core paper and chemicals products. A branch of the Modi family pulled out of a joint venture in television with Britain's Carlton Communications because it could not raise the required $20 million. General Electric, which now has sales of nearly $500 million in India, recently bought out its partner in a three-year-old lighting venture because the partner needed its thinly stretched resources elsewhere. Daewoo raised its stake in its auto-building joint venture with DCM, a Shriram family business, from 51 to 75 percent, buying the extra shares when DCM could not raise the $70 million it needed for expansion. Soft-drink bottlers are selling out as their market is transformed by Coca-Cola and PepsiCo. In telecoms, various families are either having to sell their shares in joint ventures or borrow the cash for their equity stakes from foreign partners.

Hence the government's relaxation of the rules requiring bidding for shares on the open market makes it easier for better-financed foreign companies to plot takeovers. In the early stages, a foreign firm needs a local partner's contacts and distribution; but once established, foreign firms notice that local partners contribute little in the way of technology or capital. Today there is an established network of consultancies and banks to guide foreign firms; an Indian partner seems less essential. McKinsey & Co., for example, argues that joint ventures are "hidden takeovers" that can be designed from the outset to move the Indian partner out after a few years. This is most likely to affect the consumer sector as foreign brands move in and sometimes take over.

India's businessmen sit in two camps about these changes. On one hand, many younger members of the leading families have been trained in Western business schools and are quite at home with ideas such as focusing on core competencies and courting nonshareholding stakeholders. The Federation of Indian Chambers of Commerce and Industry (FICCI) says that it sees the point of badly run companies becoming takeover targets, but it does not like healthy companies competing to take over each other. That, it says, is destabilizing just when stability is needed.

A more problematic attitude toward change comes from the twenty or so foreign merchant banks and stockbrokers who have set up in Mumbai and Delhi. With relatively little to excite them in the IPO and shares markets, many are keen to generate corporate-finance business. One joint venture was involved in a controversial takeover battle for Ahmedabad Electricity, which was made over by the popular media into a tale of a foreigner manipulating an aggressive local family firm into becoming a surrogate corporate raider. "The predators have been let loose to pounce on the unwary and the big fish will now swallow the minnows," goes the FICCI's vivid but inexact image.

Given India's talent for defying reform, the real worry is that reform will yet again fail to change. On the other hand, it looks as if family dominance will gradually become a thing of the past.

This has some clear downsides in a country as protectively volatile as India. Foreign companies may blunder severely with full control, seeing it as a chance to impose their own business standards—which in India will hit the newspapers and political back rooms as imposing cultural standards. Families are not families in India; they are gods. Look at the gods in the Hindu temple, each with its visages, vehicles, manifestations, and aspects—families.

A Surge in Nonmanufacturing Companies

Dramatic, though unnoticed, shifts have occurred in the kinds of new companies that are registering themselves in India. The 1990s have seen a remarkable surge in the number of nonmanufacturing (real estate, finance, trading, investment, etc.) companies registering, and a likewise significant drop in the number of manufacturing companies.

The number of manufacturing companies as a ratio of total company registrations has been declining steadily for quite some time, from 54 percent in 1987–1988 to just 28 percent in 1994–1995. On the opposite end of the spectrum, the number of trading and finance companies as a ratio of total company registrations climbed quite sharply, from 41 percent in 1990–1991 to 57 percent in 1995–1996. In 1994–1995, finance or finance-related companies alone accounted for as much as 35 percent of all the companies registered.

This is a highly regionalized phenomenon. In West Bengal, 85 percent of the companies registered in 1994–1995 were classified as investment, trading, or construction-related. In Delhi, the number was 65 percent, as was the figure for Maharashtra. Of the approximately 7,900 companies registered in West Bengal in 1994–1995, only 10 percent were manufacturing enterprises.

Private companies form the majority of the companies registered: just twenty-one government companies were registered in 1989–1990, and twelve in 1994–1995. Most of these were small—those with an authorized capital of up to Rs 5 lakh ($14,285) accounted for a third of all nongovernment private limited companies registered in 1994–1995. If authorized capital of up to Rs 10 lakh ($28,570) is considered, the percentage leaps to 87 percent. Since subscribed capital is usually much smaller than the authorized capital, the tinyness of these companies is noteworthy. It seems that the small sector and individual entrepreneurship flourishes the most in a liberal economic environment—and in the regions where the bulk of financial activity is concentrated. There also has been exponential growth in the sheer number of companies registered. In the first nine months of 1996, 41,000 companies were registered, compared with 1994–1995's 30,000. This number is almost equal to the company population during the entire whole of the 1970s.

Five states accounted for 70 percent of the total companies at work in 1994–1995. These were Maharashtra (22 percent), Delhi (18 percent), West Bengal (14 percent), Tamil Nadu (9 percent), and Gujarat (7 percent). At the other end of the spectrum, Tripura, Manipur, Nagaland, Arunachal Pradesh, Meghalaya, Dadra, and Daman & Diu attracted less than 100 companies—again reinforcing the compartmentalization factor.

Most of these companies are further concentrated in just a few districts within most states, usually close to or at urban centers. Three-fourths of the companies in Andhra Pradesh registered their offices in Hyderabad, Secunderabad, and the nearby Ranga Reddy districts. In Maharashtra, Greater Mumbai, and Thane, 85 percent of all firms are registered in the state. In Pune, the figure could go up to 93 percent.

State governments have not really begun to grasp the consequences of so much regional compartmentalization of finance.

India's Stock Exchanges

India has twenty-two stock exchanges. The two largest are the venerable 111-year-old Bombay Stock Exchange (BSE) and the fledgling National Stock Exchange (NSE). For decades, the BSE (which has not changed its name, even though the city is now known as Mumbai) has not had to worry about a serious competitor. However, the upstart NSE now has garnered a sizable market share with policies that are quite different than the BSE.

The NSE's progress since its birth in 1993 has been striking. Its average daily turnover overtook that of the BSE and has since soared. In June 1996, the average daily turnover on the NSE was almost 15 billion rupees ($428 million), compared with just 5.9 billion on the BSE. The two exchanges each cover over 90 percent of India's market capitalization because the shares of the country's biggest firms are quoted on both. The BSE provides quotes for a total of 6,000 companies (3,500 of which are actively traded), whereas the NSE just provides quotes for 1,500 of the largest ones.

The two rivals are different in several respects. While the BSE is owned and run by its broker members, the NSE is owned by state-owned financial institutions such as the State Bank of India and the Industrial Development Bank of India (IDBI), and run by professional managers. Brokers pay fees for using the NSE's services, rather than buying seats on the exchange, as they do at the BSE. And while the BSE still uses brokers and jobbers to quote prices (albeit, since late last year, via an electronic system), the NSE has an electronic order-matching mechanism that marries buy and sell orders automatically.

The BSE has a long but spotty history. It has a reputation for opacity and not strictly enforcing its rules. A 1995 government report referred to "malpractices and abuses with speculative excesses, price rigging, market manipulation, nonreporting of transactions, evasion of margins, and neglect of the interests of small investors."

It was this reputation, reinforced by a scandal in 1992, that led the Indian authorities to encourage the creation of the NSE as an alternative, in the hope that this would force the BSE to clean up its act. The NSE often is compared with NASDAQ, the American electronic stock market that grew rapidly in the 1980s, forcing the country's traditional stock exchanges to revamp themselves. The NSE exercised a similar catalytic effect on its big Indian rival. Today, the BSE seems determined to clean up the Indian bourse's practices. When Reliance Industries, India's biggest company, was accused of issuing duplicate shares to investors, both exchanges quickly imposed a three-day suspension on trading. Their willingness to publicly punish such a powerful firm took many in Mumbai by surprise.

Both companies have expansionist ambitions. The NSE now has over 900 computer links to Indian brokers in forty cities around the country, connected by the exchange's own satellite link. The BSE plans to plug regional exchanges directly into the its trading system.

The two exchanges compete in other areas as well. Both plan depository systems that will shift share settlement gradually from chaotic paper-based systems (source of much of the exchanges' fraud) to electronic book-entry ones. The NSE is also is developing equity futures and options.

The real winners from all of this are India's investors, who now have access to a modern capital market with competing points of entry.

Deregulation's Unintended Consequences

For decades India's public-sector units (PSUs) were the most highly regulated sectors of the economy. The results of reform have turned out to be mixed. In a number of sectors, the anticipated greater efficiencies of deregulated industries were no match for the greater market dominance of public-sector predecessors.

Businessmen swiftly plunged headlong into the newly opened sectors, many of them with foreign partners, project consultants, and management gurus. Five years later, many were licking their wounds. The private sector misjudged two inherent strengths of India's giant state-owned companies. They failed to understand that the actual businesses of the PSUs were in their marketing, not their products per se, and they underestimated the ability of the PSUs to fiercely compete for "their" market once it was threatened.

These twin problems were exacerbated by the government's half-heartedness in completely carrying through its liberalization policies—largely at the behest of vested interests working on the political rather than the economic front.

Major companies that had hoped to break the public-sector's stranglehold on the liquefied petroleum gas (LPG) market found it much more difficult than they realized to put a competitive distribution network in place. In the telecom sector, businesses that successfully bid for licenses to run basic telephone services discovered that their biggest competitor wasn't their private-sector counterparts but the Department of Telecommunications (DOT).

In the steel industry, decontrol brought no dearth of mini-mill upstarts with aspirations of becoming another Tata Steel or a Steel Authority of India. Today, many of their mills work at well under capacity or face extinction, unable to compete with the distribution and marketing arms of the big integrated plants.

In the cement industry, new companies were confronted with overcapacity in some parts of the country, where smaller plants were uncompetitive, and undercapacity in other parts of the country, where importing raw materials was costlier than importing bags of cement.

Many of these examples are related to the fact that, during early deregulation, many business people thought that products embodying new levels of technology and/or marketing strategies were shoo-in successes. However, they quickly discovered that these did not guarantee sales. The DOT, for example, countered by busily wiping out the country's plague of decade-long installation hookup waiting lists. The breezy pace at which the DOT began laying new lines came as a shock to the private sector. In Tamil Nadu, RPG Telecom, which had bid $3.43 billion for a license to run basic services in the state, suddenly faced far fewer subscribers than it had originally expected.

Today, based on the present fifteen-year life cycle of a telecom license, during the first three years the DOT will garner 70 percent of any new telecom market. This ratio will shift to 50:50 between the seventh and tenth years. It is only in the last five years that a private operator's profitability picture has improved. By then, competition will no longer be a matter of increased lines; instead, value addition in services and features will be more important.

Additionally, the biggest benefactor of telecommunications privatization was the government telecom. The license fees bidders quoted in the first round of tenders for basic services—$32 billion—will have to be paid to the DOT over fifteen years. Moreover, the DOT enjoys major cost advantages. Revenues are already flowing in, and it owns its land at historical costs. Private operators will have to pay through their noses for real estate. The net effect of these inbuilt competitive factors neutralizes the DOT's external inefficiencies.

Hence comes the fundamental question many India investors should ask: Where and how can the private sector really take on the state-owned behemoths?

Case Study: Broadcast Media. In the broadcast media, most private Indian broadcasters are hanging on by their fingernails. Some channels have lost their air access because of their inability to pay transponder dues.

At the top of the heap, state-owned Doordarshan (DD) sits serenely basking in the fact that private channels are not allowed to broadcast terrestrially or even uplink from India (some fly their daily tapes to Moscow to uplink there). Here DD has the edge because it alone can telecast live news and sports. In addition, foreign exchange regulations bar nonexporters from advertising on private channels—a monopoly that does not exist in the print medium.

As a flurry of private satellite channels were launched between 1991 and 1993, DD initially stuck its head in the sand hoping that they would go away. When Zee TV ate into DD's revenues substantially, DD did not respond. Programming quality remained poor. In 1993, for instance, the average television rating points (TRPs) of DD's top 10 programs was 15 in a market where 25 is considered just acceptable. Soon some thirty-five private channels were battling it out in the television arena.

Doordarshan reacted quickly once it did react. Innovative programming was introduced, including several current affairs and live programs. News programs were outsourced to cheaper private producers. Programming was marketed more effectively to sponsors. Alliances were struck with ostensible competitors such as MTV, CNN, and the Discovery Channel. DD preempted Zee's pay film channel, Zee Cinema, by introducing a free movie club just days before Zee's launch.

The results were spectacular. The average TRP of DD's shows rose to 40 by the end of 1995. BITV has had its entire equity base erased, DSJ's India TV was aborted before it was even launched, and channels like NEPC, Jain, and Yes struggled for the viewer's eye.

The reason most private channels failed was arithmetic. In India, the software alone to run a twelve-hour channel costs a minimum of Rs 60-crore ($17.1 million) a year. A good-quality program costs approximately Rs 5 lakh ($14,285) an hour. Some channels spent so much on operational software that they could not recover programming costs. If Doordarshan spends Rs 5 crore ($1.4 million) on a program, it should be able to recover approximately Rs 8 crore ($2.3 million) through advertising; private channels cannot easily match this. With so many private channels to choose from but DD boasting the maximum reach, the private channels faced a Herculean task.

Beyond their daily costs, most could not muster the staying-power capital to keep them going for the approximately three or five years it takes to become profitable. Many channels were forced to cut back on costs, which meant shoddier programs. Viewers (like voters, as politicians have ruefully discovered) no longer blindly accept everything doled out to them. Poor programming combined with inadequate distribution proved fatal to the broadcast media sector.

Case Study: The Lubricants Industry. In petroleum products, most private companies' strategies for India hinged on the assumption that the government would eventually deregulate the marketing of diesel and petrol. Most petroleum multinationals, in fact, saw the lubricants free-market sector as a foot in the door to their ultimate business.

In the 1991–1992 high-expectations years of deregulation, the combined market shares of India's three largest state-owned companies—Bharat Petroleum Corp. Ltd (BPCL), Hindustan Petroleum Corp. Ltd (HPCL), and Indo-British Petroleum (IBP)—was 90 percent. Two years later, that figure had fallen to 70 percent, triggering lofty projections in private oil firm boardrooms.

The celebrations were premature. Today, the private-sector's market share continues to hover at around 30 percent despite the arrival of several multinationals. The sense of complacency vanished in the face of some hard marketplace facts.

Although a high-margin business (on average, 3–4 percent of the product mix but contributing more than 30 percent to profits), multinationals were convinced that they could carve out sizable market shares in a short time. Their reasoning was that with the public sector accounting for 95 percent of the market, tackling it by mass marketing methods would be easy.

However, there are crucial differences between Indian and Western markets. To break even, an Indian lube company must sell around 1 million liters a month. Over 90 percent of sales take place at petrol pumps, compared with the West, where lubricants are mainly bought off supermarket shelves. With only the public sector majors having access to the pumps, the multinationals were out on a limb frantically competing for sales via small dealer networks, mechanics, and the bazaar trade. They misunderstood the logistics of operating in India.

The only way to get close to the consumers at petrol stations was to ally with the public companies. Mobil joined hands with IOC, Shell with BPCL, Caltex with IBP, and Exxon with HPCL. Analysts presently feel that, in the long run, only multinationals/public sector tie-ups will survive in the Indian market. Moreover, the tie-ups do not necessarily translate into an easy ride for the multinationals because of brand conflict problems.

Mobil's higher priced product is losing out to IOC's Servo, which is the largest selling Indian brand, largely because Mobil's message of superior quality has not penetrated the shield of Indian feeling of superiority. That feeling is one reason behind the Indian consumers' strong loyalty to their local brand.

Overambition Pays a Price. The lesson from these examples for potential consumer marketers is that overexpectancy can lead to shakeouts even in the most liberalized of sectors. In the lubricants case, with the four PSUs plus long-standing private player Castrol garnering 85 percent of the market, the approximately twenty-three new entrants found themselves battling for tiny shares. Even big global names like Elf and Pennzoil had to be content with only 5 percent. With the electronic media, where cable's total reach is only 30 percent of TV homes and most Indian televisions boast no more than eight channels, many broadcasters are literally out of sight. With DD accounting for 70 percent of the Rs 850 crore ($243 million) ad pie, and Zee TV and Star cornering their own Rs 260 crore ($74.2 million), the remaining players are scrambling for barely Rs 50 crore ($14.2 million). Weaning advertisers away from DD will not be easy—why would anyone leave DD, given DD's reach and the fact that they have been at it for so long? Private broadcasters will have an even longer haul if there is little in terms of content to set them apart. Several channels regularly clone Zee's programming in the hope of repeating a success. However, the risk to this in India's TV market is that the chances of success for blatantly me-too products are weak. Hence a fundamental question that every India investor should ask is: How do we plan to take on the state-owned behemoths?

For all this, there is at least someone who is not complaining: consumers. Suddenly they have what they have been denied for years—choice. The prospect of improved services and higher quality products as a result of competition is certain to inspire a political bottom line that deregulation never anticipated.

These examples show where the private sector fails to compete with the public sector:

- **The public sector is still protected.** Only Indian Airlines is allowed to fly international routes, which means more dollar earnings. Only Doordarshan is allowed to telecast live events.
- **Controls are not fully dismantled.** The petroleum industry wants the whole industry, including petrol and diesel, to be freed, not just LPG or lubricants.

- **The public sector has fought back.** The DOT is aggressively laying new lines and wiping out waiting lists.

- **Misreading the market.** The multinationals in the lubes sector did not contend with the fact that most lubes are sold in India at petrol pumps.

- **Absence of financial staying power.** The entertainment business requires five years to break even. In that period, you need to produce quality programs on a sustained basis, which calls for Rs 5 lakh ($14,285) per hour.

- **Overcapacity.** With DD, Star, and Zee TV accounting for 90 percent of ad revenues, the remaining channels have to fight for about Rs 50 crore ($14.2 million) of the ad pie. The four public sector oil companies along with Castrol control 85 percent of the lube market. Is there room for twenty more companies?

FOREIGN BANK INVESTMENTS IN INDIA

When India began to deregulate its financial sector, the country had few domestic investment banks. Private Indian banks were limited to stock-brokering and advisory work.

Since 1994, foreign financial firms have been busy signing up local partners in India. Merrill Lynch, the American securities house, paid $15 million for a 29.4 percent stake in DSP Financial Consultants, an Indian investment bank. Goldman Sachs paid $35 million for a 28 percent stake in the securities and investment-banking arms of Kotak Mahindra, a Bombay financial-services firm. European firms such as France's Banque Paribas also have set up shop in India.

The foreigners plan on entering several businesses. One is fund management. Foreign joint ventures handle funds for Indian and overseas investors (the latter often via Mauritius for tax reasons. Morgan Stanley leads this trend, with almost $2 billion under management in India. Unit Trust of India, a state-owned fund manager, estimates that the $24 billion now managed by some sixteen different firms could grow by as much as 20–30 percent a year between 1995 and 1998.

The foreign banks also want to trade Indian equities. They have helped Indian firms raise $5 billion abroad since 1992 in the form of Global Depository Receipts (GDRs), which are listed on foreign exchanges and backed by shares held on deposit in India. However, few Indian firms have issued GDRs.

Foreign banks also want to become involved in privatizations; their assumption being that this is inevitable. They are also hoping for more mergers and acquisitions work. Lazard Credit Capital is advising Bombay Dyeing, one of the companies embroiled in India's first hostile takeover battle.

No foreign firm seems to doubt that, sooner or later, it will make money in India. What the newcomers do not agree on is the best way to approach the market. According to official rules for financial joint ventures, foreign stakes of up to 51 percent are approved automatically. Under the present rules (which can change anytime) the stake can rise to 75 percent, providing that the venture has at least $5 million in capital; the balance must be Indian.

As a result, foreign firms have expanded in three ways. Some, such as Jardine Fleming and Morgan Stanley, opt for "sleeping" partners—either friendly overseas Indians or locals who can be helpful with contacts. This means paying for an expatriate and local staff whose salaries are rising rapidly. It also means buying a seat on one of India's stock exchanges ($750,000 on the BSE or Bombay Stock Exchange).

Merrill and Goldman, on the other hand, adopted the strategy of acquiring minority stakes in joint ventures, leaving the management primarily to their local partners.

A third route was taken by James Capel, the investment-banking arm of Britain's HSBC, which bought 51 percent of a small Bombay stockbroking firm, yet put only one of its people in the joint venture as joint chief executive.

Firms that have taken the full-control route can dictate strategy but do not benefit from the expertise of active local partners, which may prove essential in a complex market such as India's. This may explain Goldman and Merrill's joint venture approach, something they have not done elsewhere. Merrill has only a few executives working in its joint venture while Goldman has none. James Capel's attempts to have a partnership of almost equals may be harder to sustain.

Whatever strategy they choose, foreigners may find joint venturing a brand new experience. A linkup between Peregrine, a Hong Kong bank, and ITC, an Indian offshoot of the British conglomerate BAT, collapsed last year, as did a linkup between Britain's Smith New Court (now owned by Merrill Lynch) and a Bombay stockbroking firm, SSKI. Others have foundered during negotiations, sometimes because of a clash of egos or Indian xenophobia. More often they fail because of disagreements over business ethics. It is an open secret that some stockbrokers pay kickbacks to fund managers to win business and shares for their friends.

PRIVATE EQUITY FINANCING

More and more Indian companies are using private equity to finance expansion. Since early 1995, ten new foreign funds have committed more than $500 million to India, of which about one-third has already been invested. India is clearly a hot area for an indefinable time into the future. Indeed, "it is hard to find a fund manager who hasn't got a strategy for India," says John Levack, who is in charge of Asian private equity for JF Electra Ltd., a Hong Kong money manager that in 1996 allocated $30 million for investments in India.

Private equity seems to offer a common solution to entrepreneurs and overseas investors alike. With the global securities markets in the doldrums and commercial borrowing costs that in India average 24 percent, companies see private equity as a source of both quick and long-term capital. Financiers, meanwhile, are investing directly in companies at prices they feel are close to fundamental value and which can offer returns of 30 percent or more. While foreign financial institutions, such as mutual funds, are permitted to hold only up to 24 percent of an Indian company's stock, private equity investors are allowed to hold any stake they want, provided they get approval. Because private equity, unlike portfolio money, cannot flee at the first sign of trouble, government officials tend to approve it more readily.

Private equity funds generally provide expansion capital to seasoned industries such as auto components, textiles, health care, pharmaceuticals, and specialty chemicals. They tend to avoid telecommunications because of overpriced licenses, uncertain government policies, and all-too-visible corruption. Infrastructure also is unpopular because returns generally are capped and most deals have a long gestation period.

In a typical deal, a fund takes at least 25 percent of a mid-size listed or unlisted company, invests $3 million to $5 million for three to seven years, and maintains a seat on the board. To cash out, it either takes the company public or sells its holdings back to the entrepreneur.

The private equity wave is hitting India relatively late. As far back as 15 years ago, Western investors swarmed to China and other emerging markets in the East Asia hoping to capitalize on double-digit economic growth. "The Chinese have been much better at marketing themselves," admits Anil Thadani, chairman of Schroders Capital Partners (Asia) Ltd., a pioneer in Asian private equity. Many investors were hurt when Chinese managers used funds for speculation instead of productive expansion.

Attracted by the market's size and relative transparency, the larger private equity firms set up shop in India during 1995–1996—Schroders; Chase Manhattan; Soros, Hongkong & Shanghai Banking; Donaldson, Lufkin & Jenrette; Goldman Sachs; Warburg Pincus; and JF Electra.

For capital-hungry Indian companies, these developments are a godsend. Many suppliers cannot keep up with demand as manufacturing output skyrockets as a result of liberalization. Until 1995, auto-parts makers only needed to worry about supplying India's three local car companies. Now, they also must satisfy Ford Motors, Daewoo, and others who have flocked to the Indian market. The textile industry is gearing up for a much bigger global presence after the year 2005, when tariff barriers and worldwide quotas on textile imports are scheduled to disappear.

Although investor interest is picking up, demand for capital still considerably exceeds the supply. Indian companies need at least $7 billion to $8 billion in equity every year to keep growing at their current rates. Total portfolio investment in India was only $2 billion in 1995, compared with $20 billion in the United States.

The heavy demand for capital means that private equity investors can often find bargains. India has a large number of well-managed, mid-size companies whose equity can be bought at multiples as low as three to six times the current cash flow, compared with five to ten times in the United States. To sift through potential investments, some funds, such as Pune-based Pathfinders Investment, do their own research—talking to managers, visiting factories, and keeping their eyes open for promising new products. Other companies rely on referrals from investment bankers and accountants, who tip them off to promising businesses in need of capital.

India is hardly low-risk. Many companies are family-owned and do not like having a big-stake equity investor peering over their shoulders. Investments are illiquid for long periods of time. If the business is caught up in a bear cycle, there is nothing an equity partner can do but wait it out.

International financiers believe that in India there exists a growing market with a relatively good degree of safety. Unless India's morose capital markets come spectacularly alive again, private equity is likely to be a growth engine for years to come.

THE SHARES MARKETS

A battle of the bourses is reshaping India's financial scene. When the National Stock Exchange (NSE) introduced computerized trading at its startup in November 1994, the country got its first taste of how a modern market system works. Quickly shedding its traditional open-outcry system, the Bombay Stock Exchange (BSE) followed suit the next year.

Automation improved transparency, which in turn lowered buy-sell spreads and brokerage fees. The rivalry between the NSE and the BSE has focused attention on other inefficiencies in the market. If these are addressed, India could join the world's advanced stock markets in a few more years, attracting billions in foreign capital that India badly needs.

For investors, the new competition has been a boon. The BSE (locally called the "share bazaar") formerly did 90 percent of all of India's stock transactions; the rest was divided among twenty-one regional exchanges. Investors in distant towns who wanted to buy a BSE-listed blue chip sometimes had to pay hefty fees to sub-brokers, who then transacted with authorized BSE members in Bombay. A week later (maybe), the trade would be made at a price fixed by the two brokers—usually higher than the quoted price. Fraud was rampant. Penalties were light. Influential members of the exchange ignored them with impunity. Investors lost out with clockwork frequency but were replaced by newly wealthy hopefuls. The whole affair was a model of privileged myopia.

The NSE has taken direct aim at such practices. Computerized trading has narrowed spreads by 75 percent. Brokerage fees have been halved. Trades are executed within minutes. There are far more stringent listing requirements. The NSE's 940 members trade in the 1,400 stocks that make up 92 percent of India's total market capitalization; the BSE lists those plus 5,000 smaller companies. The NSE exchange saves money for brokers—membership involves a $215,000 refundable deposit. Seats on the BSE that in 1995 sold for more than $1 million were going for one-half of that in 1996.

The good news for investors has its downsides for others. Greater efficiency at the BSE and NSE threaten to make the regional markets obsolete. For years the regional exchanges, with a mostly retail clientele, listed small local stocks that were ignored by the BSE. Now, the NSE has placed some 900 terminals in forty-seven cities. The Chennai (formerly Madras) Stock Exchange, which used to trade $3.5 million worth of shares a day, now does one-half of that volume.

INDIAN EXPECTATIONS IN JOINT VENTURES

A 1996 International Finance Corp study, "International Joint Ventures in Developing Countries," found that in India and five other countries (Argentina, Brazil, Mexico, the Philippines, and Turkey) four basic conditions effected the success of joint ventures between local companies and multinational (MNC) partners:

- The business perspectives of the partners varied more than the partners thought they did. Most often, MNCs had global interests while local partners did not. Disagreements were most common on export rights and tax matters—typically, MNCs did not want the JV to freely export products to markets that the MNC could serve from elsewhere, while to local partners the prospect for exports was a prime motive for expansion. MNCs often wished to minimize their global tax burden; therefore, if taxes were higher in the JV's country, the MNC could raise transfer prices, which had the effect of lowering the JV's profits.

- Differences were most difficult to resolve when dividend and investment policies were not spelled out early by the MNC partners. MNCs with global investment programs tended to transfer funds from one region to another with little concern for what the JV partner thought. MNCs also tended to demand repatriation of profits instead of plowing them back into the JV.

- Relationships come under strain when partners do not agree beforehand to keep the JV's operational management independent, and when the policies of the MNC change after shuffles in its home management.

- Tiffs crop up over product lines, sourcing raw materials and parts, and over the use of technology—the JV may start off producing refrigerators but later may want to make dishwashers as market conditions change, while the MNC wishes to limit the product range.

MNCs that want to open the India market enter into JVs mainly because developing India's markets is risky. Only 58 percent of the companies surveyed listed finance as an important contribution of the local partner. Much more important was that the Indian JV provided a shortcut to understanding local conditions and acquiring access to established distribution channels and brands.

From the Indian firm's side, the desire for MNC finance, management know-how, and, above all, technology is the most important aspect of a partnership. Indian partners think access to export markets is an unwritten benefit in a JV agreement, even though MNCs often have an unwritten agenda to limit exports. A common source of problems is that these expectations are not spelled out from the outset in the JV agreement.

Indeed, the majority of Indian JV partners observe that most problems occur when the JV agreement is not completely structured at the outset. This leads to delays that MNC partners do not anticipate—nearly 85 percent of JV agreements in India take at least six months to negotiate and 20 percent take over eighteen months. The two most important issues dominating JV negotiations are the equity structure of the venture and technology transfer. Four-fifths of Indian JV partners report that the equity structure of the venture was the most difficult aspect.

On the outlook for JV success, 27 percent of those interviewed reckoned that JVs in which they were participants would not continue in their present form, while 33 percent believed that they would.

HOW REFORMS AFFECT DIFFERENT SECTORS

Almost everyone agrees that economic reform has been good for India and that liberalization is here to stay. Yet few studies have been made of the effect of reforms on different sectors of the economy.

Rajesh Chadha and Sanjib Pohit of the National Council of Applied Economic Research (NCAER), working with Robert M. Stem, Alan V. Deardorff, and Drusilla K. Brown of the University of Michigan, have sought to address this need. Their 1996 study for NCAER, "The Impact of Trade and Domestic Policy Reforms in India: A Computable General Equilibrium Modelling Approach," assesses the medium- and long-term impacts of trade and domestic policy reforms on the overall economy and on thirty-four different sectors.

The study highlights the comparative strength of the thirty-four sectors. It estimates the likely changes in the composition and direction of Indian trade. It provides a firmer footing for policies aimed at freer trade and an even more liberalized market regime. Policy makers now have a clearer indication of how different sectors are likely to grow given further liberalization.

One finding is that trade liberalization brought about by reducing tariff and nontariff barriers will stimulate the production of labor-intensive items and bring about a more efficient use of resources. If India specializes in producing goods in which it has a comparative cost advantage, its output growth will allow more sectors to take advantage of large-scale production. Competitive pressures will induce firms to raise production, from which they will achieve more efficient plant sizes and lower per-unit costs.

The impact of the reforms are assessed for two stages: Stage One was the 1991–1992 to 1995–1996 period and Stage Two the 1995–1996 to 1998–1999 period. The survey's main findings are:

- The benefits to the economy in Stage One as reflected in GDP growth increased significantly as India inaugurated fewer import restrictions and a similar reduction in export restrictions. These gains will improve if domestic policy reforms eliminate administered prices and reduce subsidies.

- During Stage One, export growth was almost double that of imports. Of the three resources used in production—land, labor, and capital—increases in the returns on land were higher than the returns on labor and capital, which remained stable. Hence, the terms of trade shifted in favor of agriculture.

- In Stage Two, if reforms continue in the areas of indirect taxes and subsidies, real GDP growth will gain momentum. By the end of Stage Two (1999), export growth will exceed import growth. Returns on land will be higher, and the terms of trade will shift in favor of agriculture.

- Clothing will record the highest growth in production, followed by leather products, footwear, glass products, and nonmetallic mineral products. Mining and quarrying, nonferrous metals, nonelectrical machinery, paper products, fertilizer, and iron and steel will be the biggest losers.

- If reforms are restricted to foreign trade, import growth will be the highest in electrical machinery, transport equipment, and wholesale and retail trade. If there are significant reforms in domestic policy, the sectors that show high import growth will largely remain the same. Some sectors that experience minimum or negative import growth—for example, paper products, fertilizer, iron and steel, and nonferrous metals—can turn into high-growth sectors.

RATING THE STATES' CREDITWORTHINESS

India's states and their subsidiary municipalities are increasingly being assessed by credit-rating agencies. This is largely due to interstate competitiveness over FDI. It is also due to apparent plans to someday issue state-backed bonds, although no one will admit to this.

The ratings loosely follow Moody's parameters and are based on such overall political and economic factors as budget deficit, solvency, and the degree to which the state is encumbered by guarantee commitments made on behalf of municipalities. For example, while rating the bond issue of the Krishna Valley Development Corporation (KVDC) in Maharashtra, the rating agency evaluated the project's costs, income stream, and also KVDC's overall solvency.

The practice began in 1993, when Gujarat's Sardar Sarovar Narmada Nigam Ltd. wanted to market bonds to raise Rs 300 crore ($85.7 million) in 1994. Then the Rajasthan Industrial Development Corporation entered the market. Since then, three other state agencies have done the same.

The Investment Information and Credit Rating Agency (IICRA) completed its research on all states in November 1996. (Their ratings are replicated in Table 1.1.) The Credit Rating Information Service of India Limited (CRISIT) now has rated four states. CRISIT also has been commissioned by the U.S. giants General Electric and J.P. Morgan to assess the creditworthiness of India's states.

The methodology for rating the states is still being defined. Some economists believe that infrastructural and fiscal parameters should be given equal weight, while others give equal weight to political and economic risk factors. Whatever the methodology, with ratings beginning to matter more to investors, the states will have little option but to be more open. With state governments tapping the capital markets more frequently, the need for these ratings is certain to increase in the future.

Table 1.1
Credit Rating of India's States

State	Rating
Assam	BB
Rajasthan	BB
Orissa	BB

Table 1.1 (continued)

Madhya Pradesh	BB
Uttar Pradesh	BB
Bihar	BB
Andra Pradesh	BBB
West Bengal	AA-
Maharashtra	AA
Karnataka	AA
Gujarat	AA
Tami Nadu	AA+
Punjab	AA+
Kerala	AA+
Haryana	AA+
All India	AA-

AAA = Highest safety; AA= High safety; A = Adequate safety; BBB = Moderate safety;
BB = Inadequate safety; B = High risk

PROBLEMS PRIVATIZING THE TELECOMS

Corruption and red tape snarled telecom privatization from the very beginning, when in 1995 it looked like the Indian government had finalized the $45 billion telecom sector privatization. Bell Atlantic, Nippon Telegraph & Telephone, and others had hoped to provide both land lines and cellular phone service to India. Indeed, they were awarded more than $25 billion in licenses.

Then a corruption scandal involving telecom equipment purchases cast a pall on the campaign. The biggest setback was a scandal involving the then-head of the Telecommunications Ministry, Sukh Ram. In 1996, the Criminal Bureau of Investigation raided his various homes and found an unaccountable hoard of more than $1 million in rupees. He was accused of favoring certain telecom equipment manufacturers and service providers over worthier rivals. His method, as one of his lesser ministers primly put it, "was not to do anything wrong; he did only the right things." Reading between the lines, that meant that in consideration for "speed money" he would make sure that certain applications did not sit on desks too long. His indictment prompted the government to review all equipment purchase agreements made in the previous two years. That in turn set back India's much needed telecom overhaul for the next two years.

From the beginning, India's chaotic system of auctioning basic licenses gave telecom players the jitters. Cellular licenses worth more than $2.6 billion were granted on a first-come, first-served basis to joint venture tie-ups including U.S. West, AT&T, Telstra of Australia, and France Telecom. Conventional line licenses, however, were awarded through auctions to the highest bidders. These auctions turned into bidding fever with some Indian companies bidding well beyond their means. The Delhi and Mumbai licenses sold for $4.5 billion and $4 billion, respectively.

Moreover, winners of basic licenses still had to wait for "interconnect" agreements that spell out the rules and technologies to be used to link private networks with the government network. Without interconnect agreements, telecom companies cannot estimate their costs and Indian financial institutions are wary of funding them.

Cellular providers have begun service in Bombay, Delhi, Madras, and Calcutta, but statewide mobile phone services and conventional line suppliers are still waiting.

Today, the telecom sector has systemic problems ranging from the lack of an independent regulatory body to endless delays in signing network-connection agreements. With other emerging markets in Asia liberalizing their telecom sectors, intense competition for capital is building. If investors lose their patience, India will lose its ability to modernize cheaply.

A DRAMATICALLY CHANGING NEWSPAPER SCENE

Indians take great pride in intellectual attainment. Being well informed can carry as much a cachet in business circles than a degree from a good school. Despite the 50 million size of India's TV-owning populace, Indians in the know get their knowledge and facts from the newspapers and weeklies. The quality of content and writing comes as a surprise to first-time visitors, but most quickly adjust to a daily news and commentary fare that is matched in the West only by *The Economist*, *Financial Times*, *Le Monde*, and *Allgemeine Frankfurter*. Moreover, the in-depth coverage and analysis in India's business press far exceds anything emanating from the authorities-dominated press of Southeast and East Asia.

India's newspaper industry is big and rich. While the explosion of satellite and cable TV has received much attention, the print media have undergone a quieter revolution, much of which is related to its growth. Many established players such as *The Times* are far larger and richer than they were a decade ago. Yet it seems that every aspiring tycoon wants a publishing arm. New entrants have flourished, and more are mooted in the business press.

Economic liberalization has brought its changes here, too. India's serious press, in the main, was talking reform long before the politicians were, so it is not surprising that they have made the most of it once it arrived. Competition is much stiffer and is changing the rules of the game.

The most notable change is that the press is becoming more politically independent as it gets more powerful. It is also jettisoning self-imposed restraints that lie at the heart of its dignified, judicious institutional image and is losing, at least in the matter of news, some of its public credibility. In the past, eminent journalists interpreted the thinking of "the Centre" (the cabinet), the "South Block" (the Ministry of External Affairs), and political heavyweights. Editors wrote stuffy analytical pieces that were heavy with academic jargon and references. Lighter articles tended to be anecdotes about government or military service. This is now being seen as passé, even stodgy.

The change of general attitude is part of the larger process of changes in India's media culture all across the board. As the English-language press moves away from its cozy relationship with the political and bureaucratic establishment, its traditional dominance is being challenged by the rise of Indian-language newspapers, notably in northern India's vast Hindi-speaking belt. The total circulation of Hindi-language dailies moved past that of their English-language counterparts in the early 1990s, and appears set to pull much farther ahead.

Most of the big English-language papers were started, or acquired, decades ago by rich *marwaris*—members of the Rajasthani trading community that dominated trade and informal banking early this century. They were respectful of their professional journalists. Journalists enjoyed a high social status, almost akin to that of professors. It often was said that the editor of *The Times* was the most powerful person after the prime minister.

The early newspaper owners were also close to politicians, their links having been forged during the struggle for independence. The late G.D. Birla was a close friend and financial supporter of Mahatma Gandhi. His son, K.K. Birla, is both proprietor of *The Hindustan Times* (New Delhi's biggest selling English daily) and a Congress party member of the Rajya Sabha, parliament's upper house.

Change has come in the last few years. A new generation of proprietors is taking direct control in the three biggest media conglomerates: Samir Jain at Bennett, Coleman & Co., the owners of the Times of India group;

Vivek Goenka at the *Indian Express*; and Shobhana Bhartia (K.K. Birla's daughter) at *The Hindustan Times*.

Samir Jain's distinctive stamp is the most obvious signal of the new era in India's newspaper industry. He shook up rivals by cutting the paper's cover price in New Delhi. After failing to organize a distributors' revolt, his competitors were forced to follow suit. He also closed venerable but unprofitable publications such as the *Illustrated Weekly of India*.

Much more future-forward was Jain's recruitment of marketing executives into senior *Times* editorial slots. Today's editorials in *The Times* and *The Economic Times* are sprinkled with marketing phrases like "brand extension" and "franchise." *The Times'* editor, Gautam Adhikari, has inaugurated other improvements as well. The paper now prints well-researched social exposes, notably a series on child labor. *The Times'* pages now carry more business news and more foreign news from international wire services.

One result is that *The Times* is no longer considered the newspaper to read for the most authoritative reports on government and politics, nor do many people feel that it leads the market in op-ed pieces and book and arts reviews. *The Times'* most successful circulation booster is a weekly color insert called *E-Times*, which is full of gossip about film stars and the coming week's cable TV programs.

Whether this switch to a market-oriented format will show up on the bottom line is debatable. Jain cannot point to a profit surge to justify his approach. In the decade 1984–1994, *The Times'* profits multiplied 110 times over revenues that had grown seven times. Yet the smaller *Hindustan Times*, which dominates English circulation in New Delhi, showed pretax profits of Rs 608 million ($17.4 million) on revenues of Rs 1.82 billion ($52 million) in 1994–without a *Times*-style change of face.

Business readers also have the *Business Standard*, published by the Calcutta publishing house Ananda Bazar Patrika (which publishes a best-selling Bengali newspaper with the same name). Editorial quality is a *Business Standard* highpoint. ABP's owner is Aveek Sarkar, whose English daily, *The Telegraph*, competes with Calcutta's *Statesman*. He has steadily updated all of his papers with high-quality writing and news probity. Sarkar's business editor is T.N. Ninan, who previously built up the *Economic Times*. His tenure at *Business Standard* has seen the putting together of what many overseas businesspeople consider India's sharpest business and economic reporting team.

Circulation growth in the English papers has apparently plateaued somewhat and has become cannibalistic in the process. *The Economic Times* competes with *The Times of India* in New Delhi. Smaller papers include *The Pioneer*, brought to Delhi from its former home base in Lucknow by entrepreneur Lalit Thapar, and the *Business and Political Observer*, which Reliance Industries started in the 1980s. However, both of these have endured that common phenomenon in India, losing money after a promising initial success. *The Telegraph* evenly divides Calcutta's English readers with its rival, *The Statesman*. In most other cities, growth is stagnant or moderate, as with the *Deccan Herald* in Bangalore and *The Tribune* in Chandigarh.

MAGAZINES INCREASINGLY STRATIFY

Magazines were the fastest-growing sector of English publishing in the 1970s and 1980s, notably with Ashok Advanit's *Business India* and Aroon Purie's *India Today*. New magazines are still coming into the market. The highly regarded editor, Vinod Mehta, started a weekly magazine called *Outlook* with backing from Bombay real-estate and cable-TV tycoon Rajan Raheja. South Indian corporate takeover specialist P. Rajarathinam is trying to revive the *Illustrated Weekly* (whose title was bought from Bennett, Coleman).

The fastest growing magazines specialize in the shares (stock) market. This reflects the astonishing amount of conversation one hears on the street on the subject of shares trading. An average ricksha-wallah (*rickshas* are pedicabs, and *wallah* is the slang term for any profession, roughly equivalent to "jockey"—a *computer-wallah* is a computer jockey) will likely converse more authoritatively about the shares market than he will about India's cricket or popstar scenes. A big period of magazine growth in this sector came between the second half of 1993 and the second half of 1994—the Bombay-based *Capital Market*, for example, boosted its audited circulation 48.4 percent, to 82,000 copies.

General-purpose magazines, on the other hand, are under strong pressure from new TV channels and the more interpretive, more imagistic, and less stodgy daily presses. Established giants such as *India Today* and *Business India* have grown through translation into other Indian languages and diversification into video and audio entertainment.

The overall picture is saturation in the English press markets and increases in the regional languages where circulation growth parallels the rise in literacy. The growth in the regional-language presses has been phenomenal. The Gujarati-language *Sandesh* expanded its circulation from 172,000 to 439,000 in ten years. Bombay's Marathi-language *Navakal* was not even audited before 1988, but since then its sales have skyrocketed from 52,000 to 350,000. India's best-selling vernacular newspaper is *Malayala Manorama*, publishing 800,000 copies daily in the Malayalam language from the sleepy town of Kottayam (where local timber yards still use working elephants). (See Table 1.2.)

Supported by advertising from their regional governments, the vernacular papers do very well in their linguistic homelands. By contrast, newspapers in "stateless languages," such as the Urdu used by Muslims in northern India, have languished. The old elite in the north Indian Hindi-speaking belt conducted business and read the news in English, but a large part of the masses who spoke only Hindi were illiterate. Now with the rise in *hindutva* (India's right-wing Hindu nationalism movement) consciousness, Hindi papers have become more popular. It remains to be seen whether they will cut into English-paper ad revenues, especially in products identified in some way with the West, because of *hindutva*'s basic isolationist stance. (See Table 1.3.)

The regional-language papers are far ahead of the English and other metropolitan groups in adopting modern editing and printing technology.

First came computerized typesetting, which shunted aside "hot-metal" typesetting, and now comes fully automatic digital composition. Made-up pages or edited stories are faxed or sent online to remote printing plants, overcoming the sometimes horrendous problems of distributing via bad roads and slow trains. Most of the big vernacular papers print in half-a-dozen regional centers, sending the core pages or stories from a central office to suboffices where editors add local news to the final print run.

Indian-language papers are also less and less beholden to state politicians. State government advertising, once a lifeline that could be withdrawn at a politician's whim, is now a nuisance for the big papers, although

Table 1.2
Circulations of Major English and Vernacular Newspapers

English Dailies	1985	1995	Vernacular Dailies	1985	1995
The Times of India	533,000	715,000	Malayaia Manorama	616,000	782,000
Indian Express	673,000	544,000	Punjab Kesari (Hindi)	395,000	614,000
The Hindu	401,000	499,000	Mathrubhum (Malayalam)	425,000	514,000
Hindustan Times	269,000	410,000	Ananda Bezar Patrika	421,000	486,000
Economic Times	76,000	364,000	Eenadu (Telugu)	375,000	476,000

Table 1.3
Media Ad Revenues

Medium	1993	1994
Press	$664 (million)	$843 (million)
Television	$167	$271
Outdoor	$100	$126
Radio	$25	$39
Cable TV	$27	$34
Cinema	5.4	7.0
TOTAL	$990.72	$1,319.36

it still can make or break many small papers in poorer states. The chief problem is that states want to pay very low "old" rates (sometimes one-third or less of current ones), and then are slow to pay. This has not had a notable effect on editorial policies, though.

The big English groups are able to twist government policy their own way. A public body with the dubious name Friends of Universal Civil Society has stirred up political beehives over the issue of the foreign presses producing special India editions. This organization halted a move originating in former Prime Minister P.V. Narasimha Rao's office to allow *Time* magazine and London's *Financial Times* to set up an Indian edition—an activity that was banned back in 1956.

The most financially powerful English or non-Hindi regional newspaper groups have seen the need to move beyond their core business. In 1995, the *Hindustan Times* established a television-software joint venture with Britain's Pearson Group and Hong Kong's TV5. *Business India* has launched a twenty-four-hour multichannel satellite TV service. The Tamil-language *Eenadu* has booked a satellite transponder and acquired rights to a library of old movies. In a noteworthy example of cross-media thinking for the future, *Eenadu* is setting up a "film city" outside Hyderabad.

Malayala Manorama is extending its empire beyond the confines of Kerala's Malayalam language. Its successful annual review sells 400,000 copies in English, Malayalam, Bengali, and Hindi. The group's English-language *The Week* is now the best-selling weekly magazine in India, with 77,000 copies sold. (Rivals such as *India Today* are fortnightly.) *Manorama* has plans to launch a new magazine aimed at farmers, and its women's magazine, *Vanitha*, will be translated into Hindi. Overall, the strategy of the vernacular press is to attack a market instead of waiting for it to come.

THE "NET" AND THE NEWSPAPERS

> The foreign media's record is not clean. We should not invite more of this mischief by allowing them in.
>
> P.B. Sawant, Chairman of the
> Press Council, 1996

The quote above is not the only illustration that Indian print media magnates tend to see their relation to the Internet (also known as the "Net") or the World Wide Web (or WWW or the Web, for short) as a battleground. They saw electronic versions of popular publications take the West by storm, creating a value-added ad base that no one anticipated. Now the Net's Indian cousins are popping up. Although the print media is perplexed by any new media, it is not so deluded as to think (as some once did of TV) that the new media will not eventually attack the old one's profits.

Hence, publishers do not want to miss the Internet bandwagon, but are unsure of how and when to hop on. (The image is not lost in India, where the same question arises several times a day when trying to catch one of the country's "sardine-express" buses.) Among the first publications to get on the Net were *India Today* and *The Hindu*. While *India Today* chose to offer a limited range of stories, *IndiaWorld*, with a Bombay-based Web site, puts out a weekly updated selection of all of its news items. Taken together, if these three were reviewed on a daily basis, they would be the most valuable way a foreigner considering India could get into business and daily life in India with nearly the immediacy—and certainly much of the verve—of living there.

However, the investment is not cheap. Depending on the service provider and the amount of graphics, someone who wants a Web site in India can plan on spending between Rs 50,000 and Rs 2 lakh ($1,428 and $28,570) to design and host a site. The monthly fee for updates can vary between Rs 10,000 and Rs 1 lakh ($295 to $2,857).

The readiest market for Internet services is Indians abroad who hunger for quick news about home. Many publications slaked that thirst during the 1996 Lok Sabha election campaign, which many Indians abroad viewed as one of the most crucial in recent history. Bennett, Coleman & Co. put up a hurriedly made electoral news site for Indians abroad and decided to create a permanent home on the Net.

The Indian Express has set up a Web site in collaboration with *IndiaWorld*, which in its own right is very popular. *Business Standard, Outlook* also has joined the Net. All-India Radio ran election coverage on the Net. Redif-fusion, a Bombay-based advertising agency, has set up India's first electronic publication, called *Redif on the Net*. The online version of *The Wall Street Journal* has been able to earn money through subscriptions even though rivals offer a similar but not as comprehensive and real-time a service free of charge.

Will there be money in Web publications? Perhaps, but it is doubtful that there will be enough Internet users in India through 1997. Potential advertisers will of necessity have to target Indians abroad. Few foreigners are as yet interested in India, which rules out domestic advertisers.

There are also problems with content. Indian publications on the Web have not yet learned to repackage contents. Stories written for domestic readers are not edited appropriately for readers continents away. Indian media groups have a great disadvantage in not offering audience-specific content.

While publications can recover some costs through subscriptions, most services on the Net are usually offered for free. Profits come only through advertisements. Advertisers are still lukewarm to the idea. Rediffusion hopes to change that by getting India's six largest corporate conglomerates to set up home pages at their Web site. Ambitions like this will be realized only when the base of Internet users grows far greater than its current estimated base of some 50,000.

WHERE IS THE INFORMATION HIGHWAY?

It was only in late 1995 that the Internet was opened in India. The rush to make money was quickly on, even if no one knew where or how to do it. As of October 1996, India had fewer than 50,000 users compared to the U.S.'s more than 20 million. Most of the users were in academic institutions. Commercial connections numbered only 5,200. Yet companies breathlessly offering to create home pages and Web sites were sprouting like ... well, home pages.

One of the grandest plans is being spearheaded by Singapore software tycoon Arvind Agarwalla, formerly from Calcutta. Jointly promoted with the Indian Institute of Technology (IIT), his Rs 5 crore ($1.43 million) "India on Internet" involves a main server in Singapore driving a mirror site (a server that reflects everything in the main server) in India. Several institutions are collaborating to put together a database service that provides information on science, research, technology, government, and business.

Like everyone else, Agarwalla expects no quick returns. Indian companies working on the Internet are really banking on the future, sinking money into technology without any real guarantee of returns—indeed, even without the comforting cushion of market survey numbers, since no reliable ones existed as of late 1996. The rueful standard Internet joke is that the number of customers equals the number of sellers. One is reminded of the complaint made about videotex in the mid-1980s—that it was a product in search of a market—when the fastest modems around were running 4800 baud.

This writer's Web "crawl" in October 1996 turned up 102 Indians firms offering Web site services of a professional, businesslike character. Most were not interactive and provided information and contact fax numbers only. Some, such as personal-effect moving and temporary office facilities in major cities, are exceptionally useful to the arriving business person. Those that were governmental tended to offer the latest updates on tax-incentive regimes and export credits. However, when queried by e-mail and fax, none of them admitted to making any money.

Corporate India tended to offer dumb pages with fairly bland generic information only. They do, however, represent quite a grab-bag, from the Reserve Bank of India to Kotak Mahindra and the National Dairy Development Board. *IndiaWorld* is India's largest and oldest Internet outpost, having been set up in March 1995.

Some companies are specific about who they are targeting: the diaspora of 15 million NRIs (Non-Resident Indians) living abroad. Financial services are doing this particularly well. Interestingly, so is the government of Mauritius, the prime venue of overseas investment into India. In Bombay, ICICI Bank targets its home pages specifically at NRIs who want to invest in India. ICICI's A.G. Prabhu, senior vice president of information technology, confided that inquiries were coming in at the rate of six a day in late 1996. "Frankly, this was much beyond our expectations."

Others are not sure why they are on the Internet, but they are sure that they do not want to be left out in the cold. "This is the future and I want to make sure I'm there," e-mailed Praveen Jain, a furniture manufacturer from Calcutta. Publishing houses are similarly rushing to set up shop. A Yahoo search using the keywords "India and Business" on October 23, 1996, came up with 2,860 entries and an a astonishing array of Indian products one never dreamed existed—herbal cosmetics, Amul Butter, how to invest in Indian real estate. The food descriptions alone were enough to get one on the phone to a travel agent.

Most Indian business people who see the Net in their marketing future believe that the most effective marketing philosophy will be making the computer into the shop, not the sales person. If a surfer is excited at seeing the lush forests and elephant herds of Thokkady, that's fine. But better still if he or she can make travel reservations from the computer screen while the elephants are still on it. That will happen only after electronic transactions are allowed, and India is dragging its bureaucratic heels on this. The RBI says that it is evaluating electronic transactions as India's telecom infrastructure improves, and that demand will be boosted along once private telecom companies take root. That is the end of the RBI statement.

India's "Netters" are also laying the groundwork for *intranets*, the Internet-like subnetworks using browsers that can hop seamlessly from computer to computer. The hope is to provide a service and information-heavy domestic intranet that will connect to the outside-world Internet only when needed—much like CompuServe and America Online in the United States. The firms Folklore and UUNet, for instance, are planning an Rs 80 crore ($22.8 million) thirty-city network of servers called CommerceNet that will service financial companies and banks, among others.

The real key to the spread of the Internet will be when the VSNI, the public-sector controller of electronic gateways out of India, gets competition from private Internet service providers. That involves the contentious issue of licensing—a decision awaiting the telecommunications minister, and telecommunications ministry decisions involving fees have been under a considerable cloud lately. Matters are no less opaque at the VSNI, where chairman Brijendra Syngal has gone on record with the truly bizarre statement, "I love competition. I love killing it even more. Long live competition" (*India Today*, June 30, 1996).

Even given a license, setting up a reliable service is neither cheap nor easy. When the VSNI began Internet access in August 1995, it was widely criticized for inadequate shaky connections and inadequate bandwidth out of India. Stung by sharp criticism of its monopoly, the VSNI is cutting costs and stressing customer care—both unusual ideas among India's public company management theorists.

Hence, while there has been a mushrooming of service providers, the Indian Internet market has yet to define itself. There are three reasons for this: (a) the negligible number of users in India; (b) the high costs of setting up a Web server in the country; and (c) the limited bandwidth out of India.

On the other hand, with a million computers already in the country, real potential exists when Internet access drops to access costs that are not significantly higher than a cable connection. Costs will drop as computer use in India grows and private companies begin to provide Internet services. The new frontiers will become a lot clearer after the number of Web connections rises above, say, 50,000 and electronic commerce arrives.

A SAMPLER OF USEFUL INDIA WEB SITES

The Hindu (daily newspaper): http://www.webpage.com/hindu/

Economic Times (daily news):
http://www.economictimes.com/today/pagehome.html (e-mail: times@giasdl01.vsnl.net.in)

IndiaWorld Business Directory:
http://www.indiaworld.com/open/biz/index.html

India Government Business Directory
http://www.webindia.com/india.html

Software Technology Parks of India:
http://www.stph.net

Gov't of India Business Facts:
http://www.indiaserver.com/biz/dbi/MEA2.0.html

How to Invest: http://www.indiaserver.com/biz/dbi/MEA3.0.html

Doing Business with India:
http://www.indiaserver.com/biz/dbi/dbi.html

Insider News:
http://www.globalindia.com/index.htm

General Info: http://www.indiacomm.com/

Business Services Syndicate consultants:
http://www.indiagate.com/commerce/busi.html

Indian Economy:
http://www.webcom.com/percent7Eprakash/ECONOMY/ECONOMY.HTML

Yahoo Port (search "India and Business")
http://www.yil.com (or) http://www.zdnet.com/yil/

RESTRICTIONS ON FOREIGN INVESTMENTS IN PRINT MEDIA

India's media industry policies were first set in 1955, when the government of Prime Minister Nehru ordered a ban on foreign investment in print media. At that time, the issue was self-reliance and national security for a young democracy. Today, with dozens of satellite-TV channels beaming down on India and foreign publications widely available, the policy has remained the same but its rationale is now protecting India's commercial interests.

At the moment, a foreigner's only route into India is through licensing or syndication deals with Indian media players. Sometimes a foreign magazine sells to an Indian company the right to its name and editorial material, as was done in 1996 by *Cosmopolitan*.

Most publications, however, have decided against this strategy as good for establishing a presence, because it does not make good long-term financial sense. Without equity, foreign publishers cannot benefit from the growth in advertising spending that makes India such an alluring market.

The government's policy is in line for review, although no one knows when that will happen. It is illogical to keep print out of India but let TV in, given that TV is the more influential medium in India. While India technically bars private and foreign television companies from broadcasting in India, it allow them to make equity investments in local companies that produce television programs. Rupert Murdoch's News Corp. effectively owns 50 percent of the popular Hindi satellite channel Zee TV. Pearson and Carlton Communications of Britain have teamed up with Hong Kong's Television Broadcasts and an Indian company owned by a newspaper proprietor for their own channel. Sony has a joint-venture channel. Four international investment banks hold stakes in New Delhi Television, a production company whose programs are aired by state-owned broadcaster Doordarshan. Adding to the anomalies, foreign book publishers also operate in India.

Still, the government has lingering resistance. Even advocates of foreign newspaper investments favor restrictions. The daily *Indian Express* editorialized that three limits must be placed on foreign investment in India's print media: a 49 percent cap on foreign equity, a requirement that Indians serve as editor and publisher, and reciprocal rights for Indian publishers in foreign markets. Foreigners say that this is the Rajiv Gandhi era all over again.

The cabinet set no timetable for the media-policy review. There is considerable support for allowing foreign investment in print, but it will remain a sensitive issue for any government, much less one composed of thirteen parties.

OVERVIEW OF THE TV MARKET

India is a tempting market for broadcasters. It has about 50 million households owning TVs (more than in France and Britain put together), uses English as a "lingua franca," and television-advertising revenues are growing by 30–35 percent a year. It is a crowded medium as well: Some twenty-eight private-sector satellite channels ranging from tiny Dravidian-language channels in southern India to huge internationals like CNN presently jostle for viewers.

Nor is there any shortage of new entrants. Britain's Carlton Media Group announced in 1996 that it was joining the Hindustan Times newspaper group. Britain's Pearson (part-owner of *The Economist*) and Schroders, a British merchant bank, have invested in Home TV, an upmarket Hindi entertainment channel. In an effort to increase its coverage, BBC World, the overseas arm of Britain's public-service broadcasting, switched its current-affairs channel from the Star satellite to PAS-4, a new satellite aimed directly at India. (The BBC's efforts are jokingly known in India as "Bosnia Broadcasting," because it spends so much time on remote subjects.)

These groups are finding that India is a more difficult market than they first thought. Most of the new satellite stations are ad-dependent, but 75 percent of TV ad revenues (in 1995 approximately Rs 90–100 crore ($25.7–28.5 million) go to the government-owned Doordarshan. Another 17 percent were taken by Zee TV, an entertainment channel part-owned by the News Corporation. The other satellite channels scrambled for about $22 million. In contrast, launching a new station costs $36–60 million.

A major problem for would-be broadcasters is that new stations must persuade the 25,000 to 30,000 local *cablewallahs* who wire up somewhere between 9 and 15 million households to take their programs. The number of households that are being served covers such a broad range because so much of it is illegal taps into cable lines. Most *cablewallahs* are small operators serving 150–350 homes from wires strung across lamp posts. Consumers love them for their low fees (Rs 250 or $7 a month buys 15 channels in affluent Delhi) but hate them because the number of channels they offer is so limited and their service makes a visit to the average bureaucracy seem a veritable idyll by compare.

In rural areas, 75 percent of television set sales are black-and-white models that can receive only seven or eight channels.

Another difficulty faced by broadcasters is that the government does not yet allow them to uplink their programs to satellites from inside the country. One example of the kind of problems—and fanciful solutions—this produces is BITV, a Delhi-based operation whose ambition is to be the first pan-Indian current-affairs and entertainment station. BITV's plans to uplink from Nepal became caught up in diplomatic entanglements, so BITV resorted to transmitting its news via telephone lines to Russia, where they were uplinked by a satellite operator there. Lower priority programs were taped and flown by courier to Moscow every week.

TV AND THE *HINDUTVA* MIDDLE CLASS

Hindutva is today's rallying cry for the militant side of Hinduism. The word panders to the regressive, populist, and superstitious side of some of the religion's adherents. Politically, Hindutva is most often identified with the Bharatiya Janata Party, or BJP. The BJP leads the challenge against the first two of Jawaharlal Nehru's Four Pillars of the Indian polity—Secularism, Socialism, Nonalignment, and Democracy. The BJP reflects to some extent India's much larger wave of liberalizers who seek to rectify the Nehruvian and Gandhian legacies that they feel have left India poor and vulnerable.

The BJP's main financial support comes from shopkeepers and owners of small businesses. The latter are often 'twixt-and-'tween in the Hindu caste system, with upper caste names and middle-class incomes.

The BJP's public image is articulated by highly disciplined Hindu revivalists, sometimes called "the saffron brigade." (The adjective "saffron" is a euphemism for Hindu nationalism in the press.) Hindu revivalists appeal to people uprooted by urbanization and swiftly changing life-styles. They couch a strong national identity in chauvinist Hindu terms at the expense of minority rights and non-Hindu viewpoints. They offer status and pride to both upper caste Hindus and those on the rise from lower socioeconomic groups. The BJP identifies itself as the cultural idiom of the majority and projects that identity as what India's national culture should be. Except for the religion, their thinking and behavior closely resemble the religious right in the United States and Europe.

Hindutva's sense of idealized nationalism has been helped by Indian television, especially Doordarshan (DD), the national network, over the last ten years. Watching DD, one would not suspect the existence of any other India than upper caste Hindus in fabulous clothing living out modern versions of dramas that were familiar 2,000 years ago. Ads reflect very little imagery beyond Hindu sensibilities, certainly not the values of other religious groups or the problems being faced by the lower middle classes. Virtually no imagery reflects the conditions or aspirations of the lower castes.

The projection of national culture as elite, urbane, affluent, and prob-lem-free has been a bonanza for advertisers promoting products chiefly geared to satisfying the middle class's cravings for security and ease. Today's debate about the Nehru legacy and "Indian" national culture is largely going on within the Hindu middle class. Those not in the middle class are more than a little resentful about essentially being shut out of the TV medium of Doordarshan. To them, it is unfair that the views and percep-tions of others besides the affluent middle class are exluded from the "India-ness" debate. This is one reason why international TV is so popular and Doordarshan is slipping.

SATELLITE TV AN UNPROVEN MARKET

Cable TV is an amazing niche of insanity in regulation-obsessed India. Rural cable hardly exists. City residents rely on *cablewallahs* who arbitrarily shift channels from one band to another in constant battles with abysmal transmission, competitors sabotaging their hookups, and rain fade during the monsoon season. Their frequently snowy results are interrupted by equally frequent blackouts because their illegally tapped connections have snapped. Switching to another cable operator does not help because *cablewallahs* tend to offer the same terrible service for the same high prices just about everywhere. Much of this is illegal, and all of it is unregulated by the government.

Now satellite broadcasters are preparing to launch direct-to-home (DTH) digital transmission in India. They see a market crying for change. They are right. Will the market get it?

International TV is a much greater force for attitudinal change in India than most people suspect. It has played as great a supporting role in India's embrace of liberalization as disgust with the Congress party and politicians in general. With satellite broadcasters firming up plans to launch DTH transmission, viewers everywhere in the country have the promise of uninterrupted viewing, sharper pictures, stereo sound, and premium international programming—all blissfully free of the unkempt garb and unkempt service of the *cablewallahs*.

Unlike analog transmission, which requires cable (for the same reasons that analog telephones do), satellite channels using DTH eliminate cables altogether. Subscribers can receive hundreds of channels directly from a satellite via a small dish antenna.

The major international satellite TV players that can reach India are Star TV, Zee TV, Modi Entertainment Network, and IN Cablenet; all are shifting to DTH technology. Most channel promoters want the various satellite owners to downlink using KU-band transponders, which are geared to digital transmission.

The problem that all of these face is the limited number of transponders available. Malaysia's Measat has two, which have already been booked by Doordarshan. Thailand's Panamsat-4 has seven. Even India's regional channels want to enter the DTH arena. Madras-based Sun TV is negotiating with Star TV, for example. The Hinduja family enterprises, Star TV, and the southern India channels are aggressively bidding for the Panamsat-4's transponders.

State-owned Doordarshan (DD) stumbled in its efforts to garner transponder space of its own. In January 1996, DD signed a memorandum of understanding with Measat to launch a DTH platform with sixteen channels. The plan was to jointly produce programs and downlink them to the footprint covering all of the Indian subcontinent plus Sri Lanka, Bangladesh, Malaysia, and Singapore—the latter two of which have sizable populations of Indian ancestry. The DD-Measat plan was to develop a pay service and provide other value-added services such as banking, shopping, and even access to the Internet.

Despite these grand plans, DD let the opportunity slip through its fingers. The MOU expired without being moved into a concrete agreement. There were several problems. One was how the new services were to be funded. DD needed at least Rs 300 crore ($85.7 million) for the venture. A commitment like that raised the question of whether the ultrasophistication of DTH was a high priority for DD, which tends to produce some notably unsophisticated programs.

DD's slippage had major implications for the type of TV information India will get over the next decade. Star TV is exploring the possibility of using Asiasat-3, which will be launched in 1997. Zee TV negotiated for transponders aboard Thaicom-3, and was launched by the Thailand-based Shinawatra Satellite Group in late 1996. Other services, such as ESPN, the Discovery Channel, and Sony Entertainment TV, will jump aboard whichever platform is launched. In other words, Indian TV is about to get a lot more interesting, and what will be so interesting will have little relation to India's traditional cultural bonds.

Other satellites with KU-band transponders are also on the way. The Indian Space Research Organization's (ISRO) Insat-2E will be launched in 1997 with two KU-band transponders. The Russian Intersputnik's GALS series satellite Express-6 will have two KU transponders for the Indian subcontinent. The U.S. satellite manufacturer, Loral Space System, and Direct TV, belonging to Hughes Communications, are planning satellites with KU-band transponders with footprints over India. The European satellite firm Eutelsat will launch a satellite called Seasat, with up to 18 KU-band transponders, that can be directed over India if there is sufficient demand.

While they await their foothold on the transmission market, India's would-be hopefuls are first securing their toeholds with marketing plans. Bombay-based Modi Entertainment Network has negotiated the purchase of a DTH subscriber management system. Bombay-based Scat Media Consultancy has tied up with a U.S.-based company to set up a DTH marketing and distribution service called Satellite Management Group (SMG), with Scat having the majority stake in the Rs 175 crore ($50 million) venture. SMG intends to develop infrastructure for DTH services and a dealer network for the hardware required for DTH reception, thus positioning itself as the link between the consumer and the pay channels.

One advantage of DTH technology is the large number of channels it offers. Since DTH uses digital compression technology, each platform can accommodate six to eight channels on each transponder, compared with one in the analog format. In India, this translates into a host of language and niche channels that will expose the country to a wide variety of topics—automobiles, tourism, computers, education, video games, MTV—and taboo subjects like sex and contemporary religions, such as Scientology and new-age beliefs.

But for the cable industry as a whole, the shift from free to pay channels is driven by financial, not social, considerations. Although there has been an explosion of cable channels in the country in the last few years, channel promoters note that advertising revenues are low. They feel that the route to success using DTH lies in the pay market, not the advertising market. Unfortunately for that theory, DTH services are very expensive. Setting up a company for DTH transmission requires an investment of at least $200 million, which includes the cost of leasing a transponder, uplinking, and hardware. The cost of merely leasing the Panamsat transponder is $21 million.

Costs are no less at the subscriber level. Subscribers face costs of approximately Rs 40,000 ($1,145) to install a DTH dish and decoder. The monthly subscription fee is estimated at a breathtaking Rs 150–300 ($4.28–$8.57) *per channel*. It is not going to take the *cablewallahs* very long to see the charms of becoming *satwallahs*.

Foreign analysts wonder if people will invest such large amounts for DTH. *Cablewallahs* complain that they have problems collecting a mere Rs 150 from people (but then their service is so awful that almost everyone wonders why they think they have earned it). However, there is truth to the view that the $600 cost of DTH into one's home has to drop to $100 for real demand to ignite.

Most of the players planning to set up DTH services in India have conducted extensive market research in this area. Scat Media claims that of the 45 million households in India, 12–15 million are already satellite or cable homes. Hence, there are some 30 million households, largely in the rural areas, that receive only Doordarshan. The fact that there is no cable penetration in this huge market is offset by the fact that this is India's poorest TV market, with a heavy preponderance of old black-and-white units and a sizable degree of village rather than private watching.

On the other hand, a study of the Asia-Pacific region conducted by the UK-based Cultures Group shows that there should be a demand for 200,000 satellite decoders in the region by 1998, of which 40 percent will be from India.

Whatever the realities behind these numbers, the success of any DTH venture will depend on its packaging. There have been few studies thus far on the comparative advantages of purchasing, subsidizing, or leasing the receiver decoders to the consumer. Success will lie not just in the channel mix, but also on how well operators work their market.

VSAT COMMUNICATIONS AND THE MEDIA

Indian companies have found VSATs (very small aperture terminals) to be a solution to the problem of data transmission over the country's inadequate, unreliable telephone network. For example, the National Stock Exchange (NSE) has a network of 1,000 VSAT terminals in place and plans to double the number of its affiliated brokers using VSATs for communication purposes, and the Over-the-Counter Exchange of India (OTCEI) has bought 100 VSATs.

Demand for VSATs is increasing rapidly. In 1996, the demand for VSATs rose to 2,500 (which does not include the 1,200 VSATs installed by private network license-holders) and there were seven major players, led by Hughes Escorts Communications Limited (HECI) and HCL Comnet. Several new entrants also had announced their services.

This is a very new market. The first to enter—in February 1995—was HECI. Now the market leader with 430 terminals in place, HECI's clients include Hindustan Lever, Procter & Gamble, and Philips.

Among the new entrants are Telstra V-Comm, Himachal Futuristic Communications Limited, and the public-sector Indian Telephone Industries. Telstra V-Comm is a joint venture between the Telstra Corporation, Videsh Sanchar Nigam Ltd., and Infrastructure Leasing & Financial Services (IL&FS). Its client list includes the Mahindra-Ford auto company and Skyline NEPC Airlines. It planned to set up 200 VSATs by mid-1997 itself and thinks it will achieve a turnover of Rs 140 crore ($40 million).

Another five firms, including the Usha Group and Shyam Microsat Communications, have obtained in-principle approval from the Department of Telecommunications (DOT). The Reliance Group, the Tatas, and the Damodar Valley Corporation also have been given licenses to start their private networks.

The market is expected grow to at least 16,000 VSATs by the year 2000. The industry thinks that it will see its turnover reach Rs 600 crore ($187.5 million) by the year 2000.

A new technology, Demand Assigned Multiple Access (DAMA), also can provide better voice transmission and value-added services, like video-conferencing. Equipment costs for DAMA users are 70 to 80 percent higher than for VSATs; but for the service provider, the costs of setting up the network control center are considerably lower. Private companies are lobbying with the DOT to allow them to hook into the main telephone network, which would enable them to send data to non-VSAT users as well. The DOT is unlikely to block the VSAT industry.

NOTES

1. This book uses Indian numerical conventions throughout. The US$/Rupee conversion rate has been standardized herein at $1 = Rs 35; Rs 1 = $0.0285. One crore of rupees is 10 million, or $285,715. The term "lakh," or 100,000, is also commonly used. In casual business conversations, these terms lose their precise meanings, so someone referring to "crores and crores" of something is using it the

same way a Westerner uses "zillions." Similarly, "lakhs and lakhs" is colloquially equivalent to "a great many."

2. In the popular press, the national government; in the business media, specifically to decisions made and administered by the prime minister and the cabinet.

2

Targeting India's Consumer Market: The Big Picture

The portrait of India's consumer market is vast and complicated. Often, a detailed vignette in an obscure corner can give as good a sense for the whole as a broadly sketched grand scheme. Yet India's broad view is so vast that it begs for a mural rather than a sketch. Hence, we shall take up the next two chapters to discuss India's consumer world in three ever-increasing levels of detail. In this chapter we present a basic overview of the Indian consumer world. In Chapter 3 we link key facets and describe in some detail the complexities of Indian consumerism. Also included in this chapter are a series of sharply focused case studies and data capsules that will convey an accurate picture of the complexities of India's consumer market on the daily level.

IMPLICATIONS OF INDIA'S DEMOGRAPHICS

Consumer marketers gaze out over an Indian market of approximately 300 million with increasingly discretionary income. Of this, the bottom two-thirds has modest to minimal spending power. The main contribution to India's population growth has been the country's sharply declining death rate. Life expectancy has increased by 50 percent, from 41 years in the 1950s to about 59 years in 1996; it is expected to rise slowly but steadily to about age 60–61 by the year 2001.

More of this population lives in towns and cities than ever before. In 1951, only 17.3 percent of the population was urban; in 1991 (the year the last national census was taken), it was 25.7 percent. By the year 2001 an estimated 30 percent of the population will live in cities.

The 1991 population was 51.9 percent male and 48.1 percent female. As with much of Asia, there is a strong Indian preference for male children, especially in the rural areas, since boys are supposed to grow up to be providers for their parents in old age while girls are supposed to have little time for anything but their husbands. This is one reason why the rural market is poor for products for young girls, good for domestic nondurables for housewives, and quite good for products that ease the travails of the day.

For the next few decades the population will increase most among the 15–59 age group, India's prime consumers. This group is expected to grow at an average rate of 2.7 percent per year between 1996 and 2001, at which time it will comprise 57.7 percent of the population. The next largest group, from birth to age 15, is surging because of declining birth rates and greater life expectancies. Its proportion is expected to age upward from 36.8 percent of the population in 1992 to 35.7 percent in 2001. The 60-and-over group will grow about the same rate as the overall population and thus retain its present proportion of 6.2 percent.

The economic condition of the average Indian seems destined to improve no matter which political powers hold office. The origins of what they are able to buy, on the other hand, are vulnerable to the political winds. Per-capita real GDP growth increased to 3.5 percent in the 1980s, which is 2.5 times the 1.4 percent rate of 1951–1980.

Growth of about 6 percent per year is anticipated in quality-of-life aspects of the economy. India's populace is increasingly a younger, more affluent, and more educated one—with the glaring exception of the already poverty-stricken countryside. In general, though, literacy rates increased from 18 percent in 1950–1951 to 52 percent in 1990–1991; there was a sharp drop in the poverty level, from 48.3 percent of the population in 1978 to 28 percent in 1991, and a corresponding increase of affluence in the cities. Per-capita income in the countryside is likely to rise more slowly than in urban areas. Since low literacy is related to population pressure on the school system, low employment will continue to burden rural sectors the most.

These facts translate to a rural consumer market dominated by intense price competitiveness among rapid-turnover nondurables—almost exactly the opposite of the urban picture. Given that India's middle class and its rural sectors have approximately the same aggregate amount of disposable cash, yet with a 100–600 million size differential between them, product marketers are faced with a fundamental choice about which sector they should focus on.

TWO VERY DIFFERENT MARKETS

India's two basic consumer markets are thus the urban and the rural. Each has different needs, social expectations, spending patterns, and distribution problems.

Distribution, for example, is one of the major concerns of businesses importing non-Indian goods or locally producing goods of foreign design and concept. Distribution, in turn, hinges on what is to be distributed. The urban market is the first to embrace prestige-enhancing items, followed by labor-saving and convenience items. Lower income and rural consumers are much more likely to spend their modest cash on necessary but quickly consumed staples such as cooking supplies, cleaning aids, household implements, clothes, shoes, and so on, moving up to labor-saving items only later. In the medium term, the rural market will be more and more attracted to higher end convenience items such bicycles, better cookware, and gas-powered lights and stoves. Luxuries are not likely to be a high priority, except in giftware—most notably for weddings, which are the highpoint of the great majority of Indian lives.

Most consumer spending is concentrated in towns and cities. In 1991, 25.7 percent of the populace was urban; by 2001, more than 30 percent of the population will live there. The greatest concentration of affluence and spending is in India's 25-plus cities of more than a million inhabitants.

India's nationwide market can be somewhat delimited by demographics and history into four major economic regions: the northern Gangetic plain, the West Coastal belt, the Ganges Delta and East Coast, and the Southeast Coastal belt. Each of these has headquarters in a megalopolis of about 10 million—respectively, Delhi, Mumbai, Calcutta, and Chennai.[1]

Each region has its special markets. Delhi has the highest percentage of households (22 percent) in the Rs 70,000–per-year ($2,000) upper middle class income group, as well as the largest number of average households (5.3). Chennai has the fewest high-earners (6 percent) and the smallest number of households (4.6). Delhi is the single largest market for consumer goods, followed by Mumbai, Chennai, and finally Calcutta.

All of these somewhat abstract numbers translate to the quite tangible facts that in 1995 direct advertising costs formed the highest portion of the marketing budgets of companies selling fast-moving, low-priced consumer goods, and these companies were the largest players in India's consumer market.

A Legacy of Anti-Consumerism

Until 1991, consumer-goods imports were permitted only with a special import license or on the basis of proven need. The small quantity of consumer goods imported via smuggling and as baggage by visitors from abroad only lightly effected the overall economy, but created a powerful image among the upper middle to upper classes that foreign goods were exotic, showy, and better than Indian-made products. However, demand from the upper middle class never really took off until both satellite television and import reform hit India in the early 1990s. The Indian government's announcement that import restrictions would be totally removed by 1997 resulted in a rush to import foreign-made products into the country. Multinationals were quick to form liaisons and open distribution channels of their own.

The result was a huge increase in consumer demand (particularly among the young and the newly affluent) and a backlash among groups who saw their power base eroded by a taste for cultural expression over which they had no control. These included Indian manufacturers and social/religious conservatives. Their approach was to try to control social attitudes by controlling access to consumer goods—a hidden agenda of the anti-consumerism planks in various parties during the 1996 election campaign. Their unarticulated fear is a very old one in India: Who should control India's social growth in the future, impersonal outside forces or the forces of tradition?

Hence it is important to take a detailed look at how the Indian business world handled the opening up of imports to the consumer market after trade liberalization in 1991, and the lessons learned thus far about marketing to India.

The 1991–1995 Retail Revolution

Hamstrung for decades by regulations and tariffs that stifled imports, India's opening to foreign investment—and therefore foreign investment in the consumer market—revealed just how much the Indian consumer was a market awaiting the right products.

Before 1991, the conventional wisdom among non-Indian marketers was that Indian product use varied mainly according to:

- religion and caste;

- region;

- income classes within each region.

These strata were the inverse of the market order prevailing almost everywhere else in the developing world. When market analysts and demographic surveyors began to analyze their research after two years of product introductions from foreign producers, a very different picture emerged:

- Income levels dominate the consumer market.

- The basic market arenas are the urban and the rural.

- In urban markets, prestige precedes practicality while price dominates in rural markets.

- Religion and caste imagery are important when advertising Indian products, but "foreignness" is most important when marketing imports.

Effects of Demographics on Positioning and Pricing

In general, India's competitive forces impose a priority of pricing over positioning. Positioning can be a make-or-break consideration, particularly given the cost of advertising and the substantial guesswork involved in how a given market will respond. A good ad campaign can be a waste of money if the item or brand is insensitively positioned. The most common error made by non-Indian companies is trying to sell technical superiority in a market that buys the lowest prices. Following are three examples of how early companies judged the market:

- India's Maharajah appliance-maker based a 1992 dishwasher marketing campaign on the "snob appeal" idea that dishwashers were more reliable than domestic help. The campaign flopped because very few buyers in the market employed domestics. Maharajah quickly revised its message to one which emphasized that dishwashers could clean every item used in cooking, not simply tableware. This was attractive to housewives, who were delighted at the prospect of relief from the fire-blackened pots and pans of India's chattie (open-fire) style of cooking.

- General Foods had to pull its Tang soft-drink powder off the market because Tang could not face competition from its Indian equivalent, Rasna. Tang had been positioned as a pricier superior-taste product when consumers (especially those with children) wanted a lower priced drink.

- On the other hand, a Ray-Ban sunglasses campaign was successful because its ads emphasized its anti-ultraviolet-ray health aspect rather than its European image as a high-class fashion accessory. In actual fact, coating plastic or glass lenses with UV blockers is a simple and inexpensive process any local manufacturer could have quickly introduced, but Ray-Ban got the jump on them in the marketplace.

When researching the price/positioning equation in any particular market niche, a foreign manufacturer must research the following basics:

- overall demographics of the area's consumer community;

- rural and urban market sizes for the product within the area;

- the environment in which the product will be purchased;

- the environment in which the product will be used;

- the pattern of consumption growth for that product category in the defined market area;

- the "image magnet" contribution of nearby metropolises.

By "image magnet" we mean the degree to which regional consumers are likely to be attracted to a certain product because a nearby megalopolis such as Chennai or Mumbai has acquired a taste for it. India's metropolises are the main reason why consumers and retailers alike are becoming more sophisticated. Retailers have begun to understand the need for style on a shelf even though they are conservative when it comes to stock. Eye-level shelf space is invariably given to products the retailer knows will move because of their advertising and marketing support. Quality is a lesser consideration than price in the purchase decision for most products. However, in India's increasingly competitive environment, mediocre products are giving—sometimes grudgingly—way to quality.

Clues to the Significance of Personal Consumption

Given that consumer spending increased an average of 13 percent a year over the 1985–1995 decade, it is not surprising that private consumption in India has soared in the last few decades. The 1996 estimate is Rs 560 crore ($160 billion), up from Rs 340 crore ($97.1 billion) in 1990. In per-capita terms, private consumption grew 2.6 percent per year over the same decade. The proportions shared out to basic necessities (food, clothing and footwear, rent, fuel, and power) declined from 77.2 percent to 72.8 percent while the share allocated to transport, communication, and furnishings increased 60 percent to 12.6 percent of the average spender's budget. Most households still spend the largest portion of their budgets on food, which took almost exactly 50 percent of the budget in 1996.

The average consumer's product mix strongly reflects interest in the outside world. A decade ago, traveling Indians returned bearing instant coffee, razor blades, women's and men's underwear, socks, cosmetics—staples of the ad pages of Asian and European magazines. Today, most of these are produced in India, either by licensing or wholly originating in India. Demand has been stimulated as much by indirect factors such as the progressive reduction of indirect taxes as much as it has by availability, price, attractiveness, and quality.

The growth rates of purchase of consumer durables in the decade 1980–1990 are striking. In this period:

- motorcycle purchases grew by 1,003 percent;
- cars by 480 percent;
- refrigerators by 362 percent;
- wristwatches by 145 percent;
- air conditioners by 65 percent.

On the whole, industrial growth and rising affluence will continue to push up consumer demand, throwing up excellent opportunities for consumer-goods marketers. Consumption will be reinforced by the spread of television advertising, which is also expected to encourage a trend toward uniformity in consumer demand across the country. A new consumerist rural class will develop, leading to growth in industries catering to the rural market.

Disposable incomes also will be enhanced by the rise in the number of working women, especially in the cities, leading to a spurt in demand for convenience products. The population shift to the cities will hike demand in the urban sector for housing. Most rurals own their homes, but rising rural affluence will see a boost in demand by wealthier farmers for more sophisticated fixtures and appliances. The convenience factor weighs heavily in rural buying decisions.

India's savings also are growing. Gross domestic savings as a proportion of the GDP have been rising since 1947; by 1994, they reached almost 25 percent, with the largest contribution from the household sector. In earlier decades, Indians would have found it easier to save, since the choice (and supply) of consumer goods and services was limited. Now, however, with the increased availability of products and services, India's high household savings rate of 19.9 percent can be maintained only if the GDP increases at a good clip.

Rural Versus Urban Markets

By the year 2010, one in three Indians will be living in towns and cities. There will be more people living in urban India than in almost any country in the world except China.

Urban markets show higher penetration for expensive consumer durables, but the rural market is growing in strength. Agricultural incomes are not taxed. The purchasing power of rural India has grown faster than that of urban areas. Between 1984 and 1991, the rural market grew 404 percent, compared to the urban market's 207 percent. In the same period, the rural share of the national market rose from 28 to 39 percent, while the urban share dropped from 72 to 61 percent.

In 1989–1990, there were 9 million rural households with an annual income of more than Rs 25,000 ($715), or about 50 million people; there were about 160 million people in households earning more than Rs 12,000 ($343) per year. This group has long been the target of radio advertising. The spread of television has exposed it to more powerful sales messages, which have affected life-style aspirations. More than one-half of the 190 million viewers of two 1994 blockbusters on Indian television—serializations of the Hindu epics, the *Ramayana* and the *Mahabharata*—were in the rural areas. Each serial was preceded by copious advertising of consumer goods, sparking rural demand.

The rural share of the consumption pie is surprisingly large. Surveys by the quasi-government's National Council of Applied Economic Research (NCAER) show that rural purchases account for more than 50 percent of the total market for many products, ranging from radios, bicycles, motorcycles, and mechanical watches to washing powder, cooking oil, sewing machines, and toilet soaps.

Rural priorities are obviously different, with convenience products featuring lower down the list than they do for urbanites. But the figures for rural market penetration of consumer durables indicate that there is enormous potential in many areas.

The Rural Market. In 1995, rural markets accounted for over 70 percent of the sales of portable radio receivers, mechanical wristwatches, and bicycles; 65 percent of the sales of quartz watches, sewing machines, and table fans; 50 percent of the sales of black-and-white TVs, motorcycles, pressure cookers, ceiling fans, and cassette recorders; and approximately 30 percent of the sales of small color TVs, mixer-grinders, and electric irons. Rural expenditure on packaged goods is growing at 20–25 percent per year.

Indian companies have set rural marketing as a keystone in their overall market strategy. Several companies have used innovative techniques to capture the rural market share. PepsiCo has involved potato and tomato growers in its bid to capture the snack-food market. Unilever's Indian ventures—Hindustan Lever, Lipton, and Brooke Bond—have extremely well-developed distribution networks, particularly in rural areas. Many multinationals have designed products or changed their brand names to give them a rural image.

In addition to television, marketers use other innovative ways of reaching the rural consumer. Apart from regular sales, marketers focus their efforts on the more than 5,000 rural fairs and festivals that are held annually all over the country. These fairs attract about 100 million people—almost the entire rural middle class. This audience and these fairs are a marketer's dream.

Rural consumers are thrifty, not as easily swayed by fashions, and look for bargains without expensive frills. They trust brand-name advertised products, believing that they stand for quality, and remain loyal to them. Marketing investments directed at this class of consumer are more likely to pay off than not. Rural consumers of premium products do exist, but for now demand is too low to make it worth the marketer's while to reach them.

Sales figures reveal that the purchasing priorities of most higher income urbanites follow a set pattern. Entertainment in the form of a color television heads the list. This is followed by conveniences such as food processors, washing machines, vacuum cleaners, microwave ovens, and dishwashers.

The Urban Market. With better quality and increased quantities of goods available, Indians are learning to be consummate consumers. According to government figures, Indians in 1990 bought:

- 1.36 million metric tons of soap and toiletries;
- 5.2 million televisions;
- 7.3 million bicycles;
- 201 million pairs of shoes;
- 1.8 billion meters of cloth;
- more than 5 billion bottles of soft drinks.

It is an important fact of Indian marketing that penetration of consumer goods extends to very low levels of income. (Indian products must have prominent logo symbols and logo colors to help illiterate consumers identify them.) For products ranging from transistor radios to cooking oil and toothpaste, the low and lower middle classes accounted for more than 75 percent of the total purchases in 1994–1995.

Differences in the purchasing power of the rupee in different regions, and in rural and urban areas, is also important. Rs 5,000 ($143) goes much farther in Chennai than in New Delhi—and has even more buying power in a village. Since the government has subsidized farmers through the years, rural purchasing power in general has grown beyond the pockets of affluence created by the "Green" Revolution. Other large, highly subsidized sectors of the work force, such as the military, also have much more discretionary spending power.

Although not a rich country, India does have pockets of affluence—both urban and rural. Defining wealth is tricky, however, because different research groups set different criteria levels. The Marketing and Research Group (MARG) describes an affluent Indian household as one in which the household income exceeds Rs 5,000 a month or Rs 60,000 ($1,714) a year. The National Council of Applied Economic Research (NCAER) identifies high-income households as earning more than Rs 70,000 ($2,000) a year; upper middle income households earn Rs 40,000 ($1,143) to Rs 60,000 ($1,714) a year.

According to MARG, the greatest concentration of wealthy Indians is in the twenty-three metropolitan cities (i.e., those having populations of more than one million). From its research covering twenty-two cities, MARG concluded that there are about 1.2 million affluent households, or about 50 percent of all of the households in the 3,768 incorporated towns and cities of urban India.

Even among these affluent households, ownership levels of most consumer durables (except television sets) are rather low. This is particularly true of household items. Two important reasons for this are availability and high prices due to small production runs. As far as transportation durables are concerned, ownership of two-wheelers is greater in smaller metropolitan cities than in larger ones because of the relatively poor public transportation systems in smaller cities.

The Middle Class

Estimating the actual size of India's middle class is difficult, because there is no consensus on its definition. Most estimates of its size are based on annual household incomes. It has been variously estimated to lie between 150 and 300 million. NCAER which conducts household consumption studies, identified households in its 1985–1986, 1987–1988, and 1989–1990 surveys by five income classes according to their average annual income:

Low (L)	Below Rs 12,500 (357)
Lower middle (LM)	Rs 12,501 to Rs 25,000 ($357–$714)
Middle (M)	Rs 25,001 to Rs 40,000 ($714–$1,143)
Upper middle (UM)	Rs 40,001 to Rs 56,000 ($1,143–$1,600)
High (H)	More than Rs 56,001 ($1,600).

Middle- to High-Income Demographics by Region

Among the states, Maharashtra had the highest percentage share of middle- to high-income all-India households (52 percent), followed by West Bengal (44.77 percent) and Uttar Pradesh (43.27 percent). The smallest percentage was in Himachal Pradesh (1.13 percent), followed by Jammu and Kashmir (3.05 percent) and Kerala (3.63 percent).

In terms of percentage of state population in the middle- to high-income categories, West Bengal scored the highest (25 percent), followed by Maharashtra (24 percent) and Punjab (21 percent). The southern states of Kerala (5 percent) and Tamil Nadu (6 percent), and central Madhya Pradesh and the eastern states of Bihar and Orissa (each at 0.9 percent) ranked at the bottom of the list.

Lower Middle-Income Demographics

Uttar Pradesh had the highest percentage of lower middle-income households (13.68 percent), followed by Maharashtra (11.21 percent) and

Bihar (9.27 percent). The lowest share of lower middle households was in Himachal Pradesh (0.56 percent), followed by Jammu and Kashmir (1.1 percent) and Kerala (1.93 percent)

The northern state of Haryana, which contains the Delhi-Faridabad industrial belt, ranked highest in the percentage of its population (38 percent) in the lower middle-income category. Assam and Punjab were second, with 35 percent each, followed by Maharashtra, Gujarat, and Rajasthan, with 34 percent each.

By contrast, the states that ranked the lowest were Kerala (14 percent), Tamil Nadu (16 percent), and Madhya Pradesh (22 percent).

Low-Income Demographics

Uttar Pradesh, India's most populous state, headed the list of states with the highest percentage share of all-India low-income households (16.53 percent). Tamil Nadu in the south came second with 11.47 percent, and Bihar came third (9.82 percent). The bottom of the list was occupied by Himachal Pradesh (0.55 percent), Jammu and Kashmir (0.99 percent), and Haryana (1.46 percent).

Kerala, despite having the highest literacy rate in the country, had the largest population (81 percent) in the lower income group. Tamil Nadu had 79 percent of its population in this category, followed by Madhya Pradesh with 69 percent. By contrast, Maharashtra, Punjab, and West Bengal had the smallest portions of population in the low-income group (42, 44, and 45 percent, respectively). Interestingly, these three states headed the list of states with the largest percentages of population in the middle- to high-income groups.

Urban Demographics

NCAER surveys have found that cities with populations of more than one million have a relatively low proportion of lower middle-income households, as do the smallest cities—those with populations of less than 20,000. The western zone metros of Mumbai and Pune had the smallest proportions of their population in the low-income category, while the proportions were high in Chennai and the industrial city of Kanpur in Uttar Pradesh state.

In Pune and Delhi, there was a rise in the proportions of the population in the middle- and high-income groups, while in Calcutta there was a decline, although this city still leads in the percentage of its households in

the middle- and higher-income group. Cities with intermediate populations (between 20,000 and one million) tended to have higher proportions
of the lower middle-income group.

The Megacities

Four cities in India have populations exceeding 5 million: Mumbai,
Delhi, Calcutta, and Chennai. Each city is located in one of the country's
four "zones" (west, north, east, and south, respectively) and is quite
different from the others in terms of incomes, languages spoken, types of
economic activity, and so on. Since the Indian government does not gather
data on income distribution within cities, collecting this information is left
to market research agencies.

Delhi has the highest percentage of households (20.5 percent) in the
affluent group, that is, those who earn more than Rs 5,000 ($143) a month;
Chennai has the fewest (6.2 percent of the households). Chennai also has
the highest percentage of households in the lowest income group, that is,
those who earn up to Rs 1,000 ($28.57) a month. It chalked up 48.7 percent,
compared with the lowest in Delhi (14.8 percent). However, Chennai had
the smallest average household size (4.65 persons), compared with Delhi,
which had the largest (5.33 persons).

Mumbai is the largest city in India, displacing as of the 1991 census
Calcutta from the position it held since the turn of the century. Mumbai's
population has more than quadrupled over the past four decades, from 3
million in 1951, to 5.97 million in 1971, to 12.6 million in 1991. Mumbai
is the capital of Maharashtra, and 44 percent of its households are indigenous and use Marathi as their mother tongue. Gujaratis make up the
second-largest community, accounting for 15 percent of Mumbai's population (and almost all its taxi drivers, as visitors soon find out!). The Gujaratis
have established their dominance in trade and commerce—a historical
legacy that goes back at least 1,500 years.

As the commercial center of India, Mumbai is the heart of the business
and corporate worlds and the headquarters of most of the financial institutions in the country. The Bombay Stock Exchange (which still retains
its former name) is the largest in India and accounts for about two-thirds
of all of the national stock market transactions—and, some say without
much exaggeration, 90 percent of India's shares frauds.

Until the first decade of this century, Calcutta was the capital of the
British Raj and, after London, the largest city in the British Empire. Today,

with a population of 10.9 million people, it is the second-largest city in the country.

Compared with the growth of population in Mumbai, Calcutta's has been much slower—from 4.7 million in 1951, to 7.4 million in 1971, to 10.9 million in 1991. It is still the largest city in eastern India and attracts people from the rest of West Bengal and the neighboring states. Despite the influx of outsiders, 72 percent of its inhabitants speak Bengali as their mother tongue.

For most people, Calcutta is a frustrating city in which to live and work. Economic stagnation, an inadequate and decaying infrastructure, and a militant labor force have driven away many enterprises, including multinationals. The state government has made attempts to woo back industrialists to West Bengal, but it has not met with much success.

Delhi is the third-largest city in India and has multiplied nearly six times since independence. Its population has soared from 1.4 million in 1951 to 3.7 million in 1971 and then to 8.4 million in 1991.

Delhi has become a major industrial center. The city itself, along with the surrounding areas of Uttar Pradesh, Haryana, and Rajasthan, have become home to a large number of industrial enterprises.

The bureaus of government continue to flourish in Delhi, so more and more employment is created by and for India's ever-growing bureaucracy. Delhi's considerable political influence has helped to attract industry to the city. In a country where the government plays a major role in the economy, political power often translates into economic clout. All of these factors have contributed toward making Delhi the richest of the four megacities in terms of declared income.

Relative and Real Declines in Poverty

The low-price–high-volume segment is the major market for consumer durables. While the poor may not be getting richer, they continue to buy more and more durables, and comprise the mainstay for most such products. According to a late 1995 All-India survey of 2.8 lakh (280,000) households by the National Council of Applied Economic Research (NCAER), the lowest income group family share of purchasers of consumer durables increased more rapidly in 1995 after two years of erratic buying behavior followed by two years of lightly increasing buying behavior.

While the late 1980s saw a significant decline in the proportion of households in the lowest income segments—those with an annual family income below Rs 20,000—this decline apparently started reversing in

1993–1994. None of the income segments has revisited the dramatic changes of the late 1980s. In the lowest income segment, a sharp rise in consumerism in the 1980s slowed to a more moderate pace in the early 1990s and then picked up again somewhat dramatically starting in 1994.

Some studies have suggested that poverty, after declining in the 1980s from 46.5 percent in 1983 to 35.5 percent in 1990–1991, rose again in the initial years of reforms, and began to decline again after 1994. Consumer-spending data point to the fact that this may not be quite accurate. In fact, poverty actually may have declined all through the period. This view is given credibility by the steady increase in both real wages and procurement prices in the agriculture sector during the reform period.

In 1993–1994, for example, families in the lowest income group owned 47 percent of all bicycles, 17 percent of mopeds, 9 percent of scooters, 11 percent of motorcycles, and 28 percent of quartz wristwatches. The number of new households buying these products in this income category also continued to increase steadily over 1991–1995. Some sections of those who are believed to be below the poverty line are actually buying durables, although in small amounts.

In terms of growth as well as potential, this segment offers the largest scope. While 45 households out of every 1,000 in this income category owned black-and-white televisions in 1989–1990, this number more than doubled to 97 in 1993–1994. For both color televisions and mopeds, the growth was around 50 percent, while the number of households buying motorcycles doubled. The low penetration levels—less than 50 households out of every 1,000 in the country are owners of most other durables—imply a large scope for further purchases.

Not surprisingly, for this income group, hire-purchase (leasing) is not a very popular means of financing. While approximately 3 percent of all wristwatches were purchased through this route in 1993–1994, the maximum reached was in the case of ceiling fans—approximately 9 percent. Gifts and second-hand purchases account for approximately one-tenth of the total ownership for most durables.

The NCAER surveys tend to confirm the increasing importance of rural markets. In 1993–1994, for example, over 70 percent of all bicycles, portable radios, and mechanical watches; between 50 and 60 percent of all black-and-white televisions and quartz watches; and between 40 and 50 percent of all mopeds and motorcycles were sold in rural markets.

For marketers of both consumer durables and nondurables, the extremely low levels of ownership in both urban as well as rural markets can only be good news in the post-1996 election economic picture. However, as the survey illustrates, the market still remains essentially a low-priced one. With the high-income categories still not growing very rapidly, the numbers of very rich are too small to make a substantive consumer base for luxury manufacturers.

The Very Wealthy

The super-rich market is somewhat of a "vapor" market. The NCAER survey findings in the super-rich market segment are not encouraging for the broad range of expensive automobiles and consumer durables being launched in the country. The number of "very rich" is quite low in real numbers—roughly 600,000 households have an annual income of over Rs 10 lakh ($28,570), and of these, only about 74,000 households earn more than Rs 50 lakh ($143,000) annually. (See Table 2.1.)

These numbers must be considered conservative in light of the unquantifiable amount of unrecorded income among the upper middle and high classes. How conservative is an open question. While a large parallel economy is the traditional explanation for the existence of a huge untapped potential for luxury goods, the NCAER survey tries to adjust its figures for the self-evident levels of the black-income economy. Since the poor do not have much hidden income, the NCAER cautions that marketers should add an additional 20 percent to the income of households that earn more than Rs 62,000 ($1,770) annually.

Undeclared income is negligible in rural areas; most is generated in cities. Based on this, it is estimated that approximately 1.4 million families in the country earn more than Rs 5 lakh ($14,285) annually, while approximately 75,000 families have an annual income upwards of Rs 50 lakh. Any upward revision of the share of black income to these income

Table 2.1
The Market of India's Wealthy

Annual Income	No. of Households
More than Rs 500,000 ($14, 285)	14.5 million
More than Rs 1 million ($28, 570)	600,000
More than Rs 20 million ($57,000)	250,000
More than Rs 50 million ($142,000)	75,000

groups will increase the number of rich, but it is unlikely that these numbers will change significantly.

TARGETING THE CONSUMER

The most difficult task for manufacturers and product distributors is to determine the best way to reach all of these customers. Companies have to consider the following variables:

- finding the right market;
- marketing to that market;
- distribution;
- retailing and merchandising;
- competition;
- pricing;
- taxes;
- parallel imports and smuggling;
- protection of intellectual property rights;
- human resources.

Everyone agrees that India's middle class is a potential marketing bonanza. But where exactly is it?

The magic number that consumer-products marketers use is 200 million. This is the approximate size of India's population with enough spending power to be worth courting. Visa International uses this number to estimate that there are approximately 20 million Indians who have the PPP (purchasing power parity) equivalent of a $40,000–per-year European-American standard of living. *Forbes* magazine puts the PPP number at 40 million.

This is the target market for the inside-front-cover and back-cover ads featuring the Rs 25,000 ($715) Italian suits and Rs 7,000 ($200) Swiss shirts, Rolexes, Opel Astras, and all-inclusive health insurance plans that one sees in *India Today*, *Business Today*, and their upscale colleagues. The data for these campaigns are, in turn, derived from product surveys taken at the shops most likely to sell them—the Khazana Shops at Taj Hotels, Vama at Mumbai, Heritage and Jainsons in Delhi, and so on.

The Luxury Market as a Niche Market

Indian and international marketers have discovered pockets of affluence that were not perceived as such at the beginning of this decade. Overseas luxury goods' manufacturers have invested a considerable amount of money and prestige in the belief that India has untold numbers of affluent people who prefer goods priced dozens to a hundred times higher than their local equivalents, all because their brand name is more important than their price tag.

Is this a significant purchasing class? A stroll through the midmarket shopping districts on the outskirts of cities reveals few Rolexes but many Titans and few Levis 501s but many Newports from Arvand Mills. Benetton has struggled since 1987 to achieve its sales of Rs 40 crore ($11.4 million) in a country with 20 million "emerging European-American" consumers. There are more Baskin Robbins ice-cream parlors in Singapore than in India. The Giorgio Armani brand name sells poorly while Mr. Armani's second-line label, Emporio, does well.

Overseas investors who intend to penetrate the consumer market must seriously grill the market survey providers from whom they get their information. It has become common for marketing firms to tell their clients to target the highest end of the market. Clients have to remember that this is the market that is most likely to result in high ad billings and agency markups. An MBWA (marketing by walking around) visit to the bins of superstores anywhere in India reveals India's middle class buying much more heavily in the shops where well-made shirts are priced Rs 300 ($8.57), a pair of jeans at Rs 500 ($14.20), and a color TV at Rs 15,000 ($428).

Value-for-money and money-for-value thinking works in India pretty much as it does anywhere. Yuppieism has affected India in much the same the way it has the West, but there is a sizable difference in the real numbers. More important to look for are signs of the downpurchasing trend that now is operating among comfortably affluent buyers in the United States and Europe.

The Massive Retail Market

India's total number of retail outlets is estimated at one million in urban areas and 2.54 million in rural areas. Of these, grocers and *kirana* (corner-store) merchants constitute 44.5 percent, followed by general department stores at 15 percent, cigarette shops at 7.8 percent, chemists at 6 percent, and bakeries and confectionery stores at 4 percent.

Manufacturer-owned and retail-chain stores are springing up in major urban centers to market consumer goods to the middle class in very much the same style as malls all over the world. The number of these outlets is growing at an average rate of 8.5 percent annually. In towns with populations of between 100,000 and one million, the growth rate is 4.5 percent.

Chemists (pharmacists) are following the example of their counterparts in the West, turning themselves into major outlets for a mixed range of premium toiletries, cosmetics, and snack foods.

While these new types of outlets are catching on, supermarket retailing has never quite taken off. The small number of entrepreneurs who have set up supermarkets have not managed to make the kind of profits that would suggest the next step up into warehouse bulk-sales outlets. The Delhi-based D'Mart supermarket, run by the Dolphin group, is finding profits elusive— its Mumbai-based Garware outlet closed in 1995.

Others are doing tolerably well. The Escorts group recently opened two shops in Delhi in association with Nanz of Germany as part of a plan for a chain of forty stores. Nilgiris and Readymoney operate supermarket chains in the south.

In supermarket retailing, the real winners have been the downmarket government-run chains—Superbazar and Kendriya Bhandar in Delhi, and Sahakari Bhandar in Mumbai. Turnover at Superbazar's 150 shops, which stock 40,000 products, was Rs 1.05 billion ($30 million) in 1995. Sahakari Bhandar notched up Rs 390 million ($11.1 million) in sales.

Product Positioning

Indian consumers lean toward brands that they trust and are familiar with. A "branded" product is associated with quality and value. Correct positioning is vital. To take an example, India's Nirma is the largest-selling detergent in the world. Its success in the Indian mass market is based on:

- no expensive softeners or perfumes;
- unelaborate packaging;
- modern advertising and marketing.

Nirma came into existence because a large segment of consumers could not afford the expensive brands but wanted something that cleaned just as well. Nirma stormed that segment of the market without cutting into the share of the higher end detergents. For the right product, it is easier to build a mass market base and then go on to build premium niches. Consumer-products giant Procter & Gamble entered the Indian market in a tie-up with a local company, Godrej, at the premium end (a relationship that ended in early 1996). Procter & Gamble now has a host of products that cover all of the segments of the consumer pyramid. A buyer of a Procter & Gamble product who aspires for more premium goods will probably reach out for another item within the Procter & Gamble range.[2] Indeed, one of the toughest problems for foreign consumer-goods manufacturers is understanding how to scale a product to the targeted Indian consumer.

The Growing Number of Brand Flops

Statistics on brand mortality in India are hard to come by; there has been no comprehensive research done on the subject. Anecdotes, however, abound—most of them floridly embellished by the gossip mill. Some observers claim that eight out of every ten brands launched between 1992–1996 bombed. Others feel that the figure is more like one-half, but they concede that a goodly number are limping their way into oblivion.

Liberalization has brought more brand failures largely because there are more being launched. Today, most brands fail for two reasons: (a) because there are more brands than a few years ago, and (b) customers have become choosier and are quick to reject brands that do not match expectations or promise. The most consistent cause is too high a price in the quality equation.

Toilet soap launches end in fewer than one in ten brands surviving. In tetrapak drinks, more than forty brands have been launched since the mid-1980s, when the technology first came into India. Apart from Frooti, a mango-based juice that has carved out a successful market for itself, only one or two are still around. In the cigarettes sector, only one out of every five brands launched will succeed. Both of these are mature-market categories, which implies that would-be marketers really need to do their homework on the world of launching in India.

While flops abound, there are relatively few total disasters that take companies down with them. There appear to be two reasons for this. First, companies have become cannier. Knowing that the marketplace has become far more competitive, they are doing better homework. Hard data from market research are replacing gut feelings. According to Research International (India), a body that tracks the market research industry, the commercial market research business (excluding social research) was Rs 65 crore ($18.6 million) in 1994–1995. This is a sharp increase from Rs 45 crore ($12.9 million) in 1993–1994 and Rs 39 crore ($11 million) in 1992–1993.

Several companies do their own research. They take their cue from Hindustan Lever, which has had an in-house team for nearly forty years. The Lever market research group conducts product testing, advertising, pretesting, simulated test marketing, and pricing-and-habit studies.

Other companies that do significant in-house market research include Procter & Gamble and Colgate. Among Indian companies, Parle Agro launched its Retail Barometer (covering 342 towns on a monthly basis) in the early 1990s to keep a finger on the pulse of the marketplace.

The second reason is that it now has become possible to do phased roll-outs. When Doordarshan was the only television option, it made little sense to launch the product in one city while advertising it nationally. Today, several regional channels have sizable viewerships. Cable operators' channels also can be used effectively for a localized launch.

The acumen of market research is often wasted by companies in too much of a hurry. Advertising agencies complain that today's new generation of international business people are more inclined to gamble everything on a major splash than settle in for the long haul. Consumer products are especially vulnerable to this type of thinking. Often they are brainchildren of organizations whose core competencies are in unrelated activities— real estate, for instance.

This has been worsened by the tendency of Indian companies to get into businesses that have no synergy with their existing activities. Editor's Choice tea from the Times of India publishing group lasted barely one season.

Denial plays a strong part in Indian thinking, and this is no less the case with market research. Despite the increasing use of research, it is not generally seen as a way to prevent problems before they occur. Many Indians complain that market research can tell you whether an existing product is a success or a failure, but it cannot tell you *if* it will be a success or a failure. Those same people are likely to be the ones to come up with fascinating explanations for their product's failure that do not mention words like price, positioning, product, and promotion.

With product life cycles getting shorter, the arrival of more brands is inevitable. As companies try to imitate a big success's advantage, there is every likelihood of even less homework being done on them. The future for great goofs is quite bright.

The Fillip of Consumer Financing

India's widespread sales and distribution network is supported by an equally extensive banking network. The State Bank of India has 8,763 branches. In all, there are about 61,235 branches of banks in the country, some 55 percent of these in rural areas. These link even remote rural areas with large cities. Banking services in the country have been strengthened with the entry of several multinational banks that have launched several schemes to facilitate monetary transactions across the country.

Consumer financing is the normal form of consumer-goods marketing in India. The presence of several nonbanking financial companies that derive their income predominantly from leasing and hire-purchase activities has substantially boosted consumer-goods sales. The recent entry of GE Capital, in alliance with the leading finance company HDFC, has fueled expectations of a boom in consumer financing.

Credit card usage has seen tremendous growth in recent years, indicating the increasing affluence of the Indian consumer. The number of card holders has doubled in the last two and one-half years to over one million. The products of several international companies like Diners Club, Visa International, and American Express Bank have a presence in the country along with the cards offered by about fifteen domestic banks.

COMPETITION ISSUES

For the first time, India's big business houses are facing increasing competition in key market segments from foreign firms. They are not thrilled. Yet they largely agree that the influence of fresh and keener competition has forced many Indian companies to rethink corporate strategies, with significant consequences for foreign entrants. More and more, local firms are:

- forging strategic alliances with foreign multinationals;
- selling off peripheral businesses to concentrate on core areas;
- relinquishing control of joint-venture firms to foreign partners;
- becoming production bases for large multinationals;
- launching new products and brands.

In a bid to protect their turf, several Indian market leaders, in sectors ranging from consumer products to drugs to telecommunications, have entered into joint ventures with foreign firms. This is particularly the case in sectors and products where technology is key and competition is intense. For foreign firms, joint ventures are the easiest access point to Indian markets.

If they find that they are unable to compete with established foreign brands, Indian companies tend to become production bases for multinationals. This widens the scope for foreign companies looking to enter the country. However, Indian firms are finding that they have considerable more innovative capacity than they thought they had. Some devised marketing strategies based on their knowledge of ethnic values, pricing psychology, and their inbuilt mastery of India's withering distribution system. Ethnic-specific brands, for example, have been used successfully for hair-care products, toothpaste, health tonics, and baby-care items.

Other companies hope to preempt competition from new entrants into the market by creating new products and models. Hero Cycles launched three different bicycle models—one for the city, one for cross-country, and one for children. Godrej Soaps introduced a premium-quality soap called Evita. However, budgets to launch products are still not particularly generous by overseas product-launch standards. There is a shift away from lavish advertisements to plug a product. More manufacturers now rely on direct marketing or trade promotions to get their message across.

Monopolies

Monopolies and market dominance are not illegal in India—only unfair trading practices are. Trading practices that are considered illegal include:

- maintaining prices at unreasonably high levels;
- inhibiting competition in the production and distribution of goods;
- promulgating false information about products.

Most restrictions on a company's freedom to sell are found in the MRTP Act, which defines a restrictive trade practice as "any action that obstructs or distorts competition in any manner, manipulates prices or affects market supplies of goods in order to impose unjustifiable costs or restrictions on consumers." Arrangements relating to such practices must be recorded with the Registrar of Restrictive Trade Agreements. The government generally regards the following sales practices as objectionable:

- insistence on resale price maintenance;
- prohibition of sale of competitors' products;
- making supplies of one product contingent on sales of another;
- any restriction on the class of persons to whom goods may be supplied;
- imposition of territorial restrictions and allocation of markets;
- provision of rebates, discounts, and commissions;
- establishment of an exclusive dealership;
- awarding of incentive bonuses.

The MRTPC may investigate any trade practice:

- on receiving a complaint from a consumer or a voluntary consumer organization;
- at the request of the central or state government;
- on receiving an application from the Registrar of Restrictive Trade Agreements.

Predatory Pricing

Manufacturers are prohibited from demanding minimum resale prices. Most types of packaged goods must carry tags that state the maximum price allowed, including local taxes. All packaged goods must show price, quantity, date of packaging, and expiration date.

Dual-pricing systems are also prohibited. These apply mainly to staple goods. A network of government-run shops sells wheat, rice, sugar, kerosene, and other staples at subsidized rates to ration-card holders. In the open market, supply and demand determine prices.

Companies must label products with a "maximum retail price inclusive of all taxes." This means that companies have to calculate the taxes that retailers in every single town must pay and then equalize the price of the product so that all retailers get the same margins. If sales taxes are higher in one city, a retailer has to sell the goods at a lower margin compared with a retailer from a town where taxes are lower. Whatever the local taxes, customers across the country are not obliged to pay more than the marked price. Retailers "blaggard" (vilify) this system with a florid vocabulary that begs for description but unfortunately cannot be printed here.

Competition from Black Markets and Smuggling

Consumer-goods marketers should not underestimate India's thriving market for parallel imports and smuggled goods. It is quite easy, given the right introductions, to place an order for a specific product and brand and take delivery in two weeks. Whether it is a Dior perfume or a refrigerator seems to make little difference.

While the lowering of duties on imported consumer goods and durables has eased the problem somewhat, the sale of select smuggled consumer items is still brisk. The strongest competition that Kelvinator faces for sales of microwave ovens is not from its four legal rivals, but from smugglers. On the other hand, there is no smugglers' market for Kelvinator's major product, refrigerators, because locally made brands are affordable and of reasonably good quality. The same is not true of microwave ovens.

Most of the smuggling was and continues to be from the Gulf states, which are home to a large Indian expatriate community. Smugglers view India as a market that, as a result of high import duties and significant purchasing power, offers considerable potential. Among the items smuggled in vast quantities into India are gold, toiletries and cosmetics, cigarettes, electronic goods (mainly entertainment), and white goods.

Smuggled items come in through two routes. Large items come via boats or sail-powered dhows that land their cargo along the vast Indian coastline. Some of these boats sport four high-powered outboards that can hit 120 kilometers/hour (75 miles per hour) and can outrun any customs vessel. The second route is people returning from abroad. Smuggler syndicates send couriers to the Gulf and Southeast Asia to bring back durables and other consumer goods. With a larger number of affluent Indians traveling overseas, even more foreign goods are finding their way back. It is a pity that more of these people are not in the bureaucracies, where this kind of efficiency is needed.

Knock-Offs, Piracy, and Indian Patent Law

The inflow of foreign goods also has brought about the availability of "knock-offs" and copies (locally made products sold in original foreign packaging). Most of the Scotch whisky consumed in India is not genuine, although it may have a whiff of the lochs somewhere in it. One can purchase a Seiko or Citizen watch for less than $10 in India; most who do say you get a working lifetime of about one minute per dollar.

Although the country's courts do indeed punish violators of intellectual property rights, foreign companies should be alert to piracy. Prosecutors may win an injunction, damages, or an account of profits in lieu of damages, as well as delivery or destruction of all infringing articles in the defendant's possession. Protection is available for three forms of intellectual property:

- patents;
- trademarks;
- copyrights.

Basic Patent Facts. Under the Patents Act of 1970, a patent is granted for any "invention," which is defined as "any new and useful process, method, or manner of manufacture; machinery, apparatus, or other article; substance produced by manufacture; or act, including any new improvement of any of these."

It is very important to be aware that, in foods, drugs, and chemicals, only the *process*, not the product, is protected. This has resulted in many patented foreign drugs being "replicated" in India using different processes. Companies that do this rationalize the practice by citing nineteenth-century German Patent Law, which was similar to India's current law and which they aver is necessary to the early stages of a country's industrial development. They also like to point out that there are several countries, such as Austria, Brazil, The Netherlands, and Norway, with similar laws. All of this conveniently neglects the vast body of world practice that frowns on India's policies.

It normally takes about two years from the date of filing to get a patent. Between April 1992 and March 1993, the patent office granted 318 Indian and 1,112 foreign patents. Also registered were 67 foreign and 679 Indian designs.

The law allows the government to use any patent noncommercially without paying royalties, although it provides reasonable compensation for the use of patents that existed when the law took effect in 1970. The government may also import patented drugs or medicines for its own purposes.

The American government has taken exception to the Indian position that only processes can be patented, and in April 1992 it suspended duty-free treatment of pharmaceutical imports from India. For its part, the Indian government maintains that if product patents are permitted, the costs of many products, mainly pharmaceuticals, would shoot up, and this would be against the interests of the Indian populace. However, the government is not wholeheartedly supported by India's own industries. Many domestic food, pharmaceutical, and chemical companies also consider India's patent protection to be inadequate. They have three major complaints: the five- to seven-year duration of patents, compared with fourteen years for patents in other areas; the restriction of patent availability to manufacturing processes; and the ability of the government to issue compulsory licenses if a patent is not worked in India, not "worked sufficiently," or "abused."

Trademarks. Trademarks are protected in India through the Indian Trade and Merchandise Marks Act of 1958. Once registered, the mark is valid for seven years and can be renewed for further periods of seven years. Applicants are required at the time of registration to have a genuine intention to use the mark, and such use must be made within five years of registration, failing which the mark could be canceled. Misuse of a mark can be remedied through civil and penal action.

Under the act, unregistered marks are also protected if it can be demonstrated that the mark, whose use is sought to be restrained, enjoys goodwill in India. Goodwill also can be used by a foreigner who owns a mark abroad that is not registered in India.

Under a United Nations development program, trademark registries in India are being modernized and computerized. The government plans to revise the Trade and Merchandise Marks Act to shore up protection for trademarks and extend recognition to service marks.

Copyrights. Copyright protection is provided through the Copyright Act of 1957. Under it, a copyright subsists in all original literary, dramatic, musical, and artistic works, cinematographic films, and records. India is a member of the Universal Convention as well as the Berne Convention. A person who enjoys a copyright in any of the convention countries automatically enjoys copyright protection in India. The act now also covers computer programs.

In theory, the laws for copyright infringements are tough—punishable by imprisonment ranging from three months to six years and by fines of as much as Rs 200,000 ($7,000). In practice, the rate of conviction is poor. The piracy of videotapes and computer software is a particular problem. The American companies Lotus and Microsoft have both tried various ways to curb violations, including raids on dealers of pirated software. The government now permits legal duplication of imported software. On approval from the Reserve Bank of India, Indian software reproducers now may conclude agreements with overseas copyright holders to reproduce software on payment of a royalty (up to 30 percent of the published price is allowed).

Co-Marketing Patent-Sensitive Products

Patents do not last forever, and in India sometimes they do not last at all. Until quite recently, Indian companies did not honor product patents. It was easier for them to copy a molecule rather than to R&D it; so, to save effort on both sides, they developed co-marketing arrangements. These were mostly confined to the R&D-sensitive products of multinationals.

For example, in 1995, UCB Belgium faced the problem of marketing their new drugs in India. The company's Indian affiliate had only forty-five marketing representatives, far short of the number needed to popularize a new drug before its molecule was copied by Indian companies. Cipla and Dr. Reddys—two big local companies—could have cloned and registered a tiny variant of new molecule a few weeks after it showed up on the market. This could occur because Indian businesses often did not recognize patents (although India is fiercely protective of its software innovations).

The easiest solution was to co-market through local manufacturer-distributors. It was a way for Indian companies to create public awareness of themselves and a new product without spending money on research. It worked especially well when awareness had to be created quickly. It was also often the only way to launch some other company's product when its patent could not be circumvented. Multinational pharmaceutical companies tended to protect their market niche by differentiating the product molecule via an innovative value augmentation, such as its delivery system.

Indians still tend to structure co-marketing efforts like franchise arrangements. Most often, the original company is remunerated by becoming the sole source, less often via royalty payments. However, distributing companies often promptly develop their own competing brands. These are remarkably close to, and are packaged and marketed similarly to, the parent product. Sometimes the service offered by sales reps acts as the only point of differentiation.

The Indian distributor's attitude towards pricing is that different brands have to be priced the same to inhibit them from getting into a price war. In addition, if two to three companies market at the same price, it creates a barrier to new entrants. Indians do not regard these practices as carteling, since brand ownership is spelled out clearly at the agreement stage and single-tier pricing maintains brand competitiveness. However, once a distribution company creates a successful brand, it is likely to switch to a cheaper source for the bulk drug. One prime problem in co-marketing arrangements is the original producer-supplier's ambiguity about from whom the distributor is really sourcing.

Moreover, Indian distributors worry about losing control over promotions people, who are wont to cut private deals on their own. For pharmaceutical companies using local manufacturer-distributors, this means the Indian partner selling the same molecule under its own label at a higher discount.

This said, there remain certain advantages to co-marketing. Rather than doing everything oneself in an unfamiliar market, they keep a work force low. As international pressure moves Indian companies toward honoring patents, the utility factor of co-marketing is increasing over its necessity factor. Its best application will continue to be, as in the case of drug companies, instances that combine a complex distribution structure with short windows of opportunity.

ADVERTISING

Advertising billings swelled 150 percent between 1988 and 1992, then increased yet another 50 percent from 1992 through the end of 1995. Advertisers in India reach about 75 percent of the population through television, and almost the entire population through radio. Certain televised programs enjoy a viewership of more than 100 million. Advertising expenditure grew at nearly 15 percent per annum in the 1980s to reach Rs 17 billion ($486 million) in 1995. Hong Kong's Star TV, with a 1995 Indian viewership of 4.9 million households, has given a boost to advertising and exposed Indian audiences to foreign products and services.

The potential for advertising has attracted the best international agencies to India. Arriving businesses have a good choice of professional, experienced companies. Of the top twelve advertising agencies in India, ten have international affiliations and six have foreign partners. Young & Rubicam, Lintas, BBDO, J. W. Thompson, McCann Ericsson, Leo Burnett, Bozell, and Publicis are among the majors that have meaningful presences in the Indian market. Many companies have their own in-house advertising agencies.

Despite higher expenditures, increasing literacy, and the spread of television, the reach of media is still fairly limited in rural areas. Compared with the urban areas, where there is 91 percent penetration of at least one medium, in rural districts it is only 66 percent. Radio has the highest reach in the villages (42 percent); the press has the lowest (20 percent). In the urban areas, television has the highest reach (77 percent), and the cinema the lowest (49 percent).

Advertising Regulations

Relatively few advertising controls apply to the Indian media, except for the government-controlled stations for television (Doordarshan) and radio (Akashwani), which live with quite elaborate regulations.

The rules of the Code for Commercial Advertising on TV are:

- Advertising shall not offend the morality, decency, and religious susceptibilities of the people.
- No advertisement shall be permitted which derides any caste, creed, race, nationality; incites violence or disorder; adversely affects relations with foreign states; and exploits the national emblem, the constitution, or a national leader.
- No advertisement of a religious or political nature is permitted.
- No advertisements for cigarettes or tobacco products are permitted.
- Advertisers must be prepared to produce evidence to substantiate any claims.
- No disparaging reference to another product or service is permitted.

The Advertising Standards Council of India (ASCI) was set up in 1985. Its membership comprises advertisers, ad agencies, media, and market research companies. It provides the following codes for self-regulation in advertising and lays down the code of advertising practice:

- Do not bring advertising into contempt or disrepute.
- Be truthful and do not mislead the public.
- Do not make any claims that are so exaggerated that they are bound to lead to disappointment.
- Do not create advertising that creates confusion in the mind of the consumer (e.g., imitation of a brand name).
- Do not be indecent, vulgar, suggestive, or offensive.

The ASCI invites persons to write to its Consumer Complaints Council if they find an advertisement offensive. Moreover, it provides a forum for adjudicating interagency and interclient disputes on advertising.

The Media's Reach

Media penetration into urban India has grown dramatically, with television—an almost nonexistent medium as recently as the mid-1980s—increasing the most. Television today has a much wider reach than the press, largely because of India's low literacy levels. In rural areas, the press is very weak; radio is currently the dominant medium. It is only a matter of time before television takes over the top spot from radio.

Urban India. While the media's reach has lengthened significantly in the past decade, penetration—even in the megacities—is still relatively low compared with that of the big cities in Southeast and East Asia and China. There are major differences even among India's four megacities.

Upmarket Metropolitan. Although exposure to the media is relatively low in smaller towns and in less-affluent segments of the cities, the scenario is different in upmarket metropolitan India. According to the 1992 Second Upmarket Media Survey conducted by MARG, exposure to the press and television is noticeably higher within these affluent sections. The survey studied the media habits of adults in upmarket households from twenty-five large cities and had a sample size exceeding 11,000. Upmarket households were those earning more than Rs 4,000 ($114) a month. Radio is widely spread across all segments. Regular listenership among upmarket metropolitan adults is not higher than among all urban adults. On the other hand, the advent of the VCR and cable TV has made visiting a cinema comparatively infrequent among affluent metropolitan Indians.

The Press

India has more than 27,000 publications in several dozen languages. Nationally distributed publications are in Hindi or English, which account for about one-half of the total circulation of all publications. Most other languages sell predominantly in their home states, and their average circulation is fairly small but sharply specific. The last few years have also seen the growth of specialist publications that do not have large circulations but offer good coverage of the target group. Advertisers rarely include more than 100 publications in a media plan; in many cases, the list is confined to about twenty.

Although English and Hindi publications have a wider reach, many regional ones have much higher circulations, particularly in states with relatively high literacy levels. For instance, Kerala accounts for less than 4 percent of the population of India, but because its literacy level exceeds 75 percent (versus an all-India average of 43 percent) it is home to some of the largest-circulating publications in the country.

Six categories account for about 63 percent of the total advertising expenditure on press and television. The data on advertising expenditure for these categories show that fast-moving consumer-goods (FMCG) companies are moving away from heavy spending on television toward advertising in the press. In the case of semi-durables and durables, television's share of the total advertising pie is increasing.

Television

There are an estimated 33 million television sets in India. The largest number are in the west and the smallest in the south. Most television advertising in India continues to be on state-owned Doordarshan, which reaches viewers across the country. More than 3 million sets are linked to cable or satellite and are exposed to pan-Asian advertising on Star TV, Zee TV, and a host of new arrivals.

A rising amount of advertising focuses on cable and satellite viewers, who are considered to be a more sophisticated, high-income group. Exposure to foreign products is high among wealthy urban Indians, usually through friends or relatives living abroad.

Doordarshan estimates that its signals cover 63 percent of India and 82 percent of the population. The state-owned system has three major segments:

- The national network is beamed all over the country and broadcasts mostly in Hindi and English.

- The regional networks broadcast in the regional languages; these networks exist in most major states outside the north Indian Hindi-speaking belt.

- Recently launched Metro channels broadcast in the four megacities—Mumbai, Calcutta, Delhi, and Chennai.

Doordarshan—India's National Network. The national channel has a massive reach and is a cost-effective method of reaching the target group for products that are widely used. While the CPT (cost per thousand) is low, many advertisers on the national network find the absolute sum too high for frequent use, although this has not deterred the large FMCG companies.

Most leading firms also use the regional networks for greater reach, particularly in states such as Maharashtra and Tamil Nadu where the regional networks are strong. Such networks are used to advertise products that have a regional bias. SmithKline Beecham Consumer Brands, the manufacturer of the health beverage Horlicks, and Cadbury, which manufactures Bournvita, advertise on the national network but concentrate on Tamil Nadu's network because the state is a solid market for their products.

Zee TV's rates depend upon whether the buyer wants the commercial to appear in the broad band of an hour (say, from 8–9 P.M.) or at a fixed time (in the capsule at the end of a specific program) or at any time during the day. The rates therefore do not vary by programs or by time slots. It is believed that Zee TV offers packages to advertisers where it may allow an advertiser who buys, say, a "run of the schedule" time on Zee TV to upgrade to "a fixed hour" at no extra cost.

Women's Exposure to the Media

The Indian housewife—known as "Srimati India"—decides which consumer durables to buy and when to buy them. Media planners must ponder the psychographic profiles of the various manifestations and aspects of this updated deity.

The most comprehensive reference is the *National Family Health Survey*,[3] based on research conducted in 1992–1993. Its sample was 89,777 married women aged 13 and 49 years (see Table 2.2).

A major finding reflects the rural nature of Indian society: Nearly one-half of the respondents were not exposed to any kind of mass media (television, radio, or the cinema). Radio scored highest, with 44 percent of women reporting that they listened to the radio at least once a week. Television lured 32 percent weekly. Only 15 percent of the women went to watch a movie at the local cinema at least once a month.

What matters, apparently, is not so much how old they are as where they live, how educated they are, and which religion or caste they belong to. Those who watched television ranged from 31 to 35 percent all across the age spectrum. Women under the age of 20 are much less likely to watch television because women who come from the less educated and poorer groups almost always marry young and have little time for television.

More women listen to the radio than watch television—between 34 and 45 percent. After age 24, women listen less often to the radio. Younger women are more likely to go to the cinema at least once a month.

Table 2.2
Indian Women's Exposure to the Media, by Province (%)

	Watches TV once a week	Listens to radio once a week	Attends cinema once a month	Not regularly exposed to any media
ALL INDIA	31.0	43.5	15.0	47.3
NORTH				
Delhi urban	82.8	63.6	5.7	13.3
Haryana	49.0	42.2	2.0	39.9
Himachal Prad.	47.1	54.6	2.9	33.2
Jammu	50.1	64.2	2.5	27.8
Punjab	57.3	42.0	2.3	34.5
Rajasthan	17.2	27.2	5.2	69.9
CENTRAL				
M. Pradesh	26.7	32.7	10.0	59.0
Uttar Pradesh	19.0	29.7	4.1	64.5
EAST				
Bihar	12.7	25.9	5.2	70.5
Orissa	16.1	34.9	7.4	60.5
West Bengal	33.3	48.3	16.1	38.7
NORTHEAST				
Arunachal Prad.	28.7	40.7	14.4	53.4
Assam	18.0	32.8	4.2	60.9
Manipur	38.2	63.1	16.5	32.2
Meghalaya	23.8	37.6	5.4	53.6
Mizoram	25.3	55.1	0.6	38.7
Nagaland	22.5	42.4	1.5	55.4
Tripura	34.3	56.7	6.7	34.5
WEST				
Goa	70.6	69.3	3.9	14.8
Gujarat	39.4	47.0	9.5	44.6
Maharashtra	46.4	52.3	14.9	37.2
SOUTH				
Andhra Pradesh	39.1	69.4	48.8	24.8
Karnataka	39.5	62.9	30.3	29.9
Tamil Nadu	50.4	59.7	42.6	22.0

Media exposure is far greater in urban than in rural areas. In towns, 81 percent of women are regularly exposed to some form of the mass media, compared to just 43 percent in villages.

The more educated the woman the greater her likelihood of being attracted by the media. Only 36 percent of illiterate women are exposed to any form of the media, while those who have at least passed high school make up 94 percent.

Significant differences exist between India's states. Women from Delhi, Goa, Kerala, Tamil Nadu, and Andhra Pradesh account for over three-fourths of those who are regularly exposed to the media, compared with Rajasthan, Bihar, Uttar Pradesh, Assam, and Orissa, where fewer than 40 percent of women are regularly exposed.

In the latter group of states, women's exposure to television is less than 20 percent at least once a week, while over 70 percent watch television regularly in Delhi and Goa. The figures are over 50 percent of women in Punjab, Tamil Nadu, and Jammu.

It is in the South where more women buy tickets for films—these states have the highest percentage of women who visit a cinema or movie theater at least once a month

Using the *National Family Health Survey* statistics to focus on the potential buying habits of target consumer groups is not easy. Using the *Survey's* statistics on family planning messages on radio and television, the electronic media reach only 42 percent of the sample. This is mainly because only 21 percent of Indian households own television sets and only 39 percent own radios. About one in four women reported hearing a family planning message on both the radio and television in the month preceding the survey. The urban-rural divide is clearly evident: Urban women reported hearing more messages, almost equally divided between television and radio; but for rural women, the radio was by far the most important medium.

INTRODUCING NEW PRODUCTS

Attitudes Toward Foreign Goods

Foreign multinationals have been operating in India for several decades; some were in the country before its independence in 1947. Companies such as Unilever, Glaxo, SmithKline Beecham, BAT, and ICI, for example, have been around for more than half a century. Over the years, many of these firms have developed products especially for sale in India. Many of these are downmarket.

In many cases, when international brands are on offer (e.g., Lux soap from Unilever), the quality has been poorer in quality to the global product. This has happened for three reasons:

- Some companies have suffered capacity constraints. Increase in capacity requires permission from the government, which is often not forthcoming. Since the multinationals could not benefit from economies of scale, they debased the product to meet bottom-line needs.

- In many industries, the government operates formal or informal price controls. Many companies therefore are unwilling to invest because returns are unsatisfactory—yet another reason to debase the product when input costs rise sharply.

- At times, the government forces industries to either use or not use certain raw materials that affect the quality of the final product. The use of tallow in hydrogenated fats is banned, and lard cannot be used in biscuits. Soap companies are also asked to use oils that are not primarily used as edible oils to manufacture their products.

Indian consumers thus have been buying multinational brands that were made in India but were usually only marginally superior to products made by local companies. There were two reactions: (a) products manufactured abroad were better than Indian-made ones; and (b) if a multinational manufactures in India, its products are of lower quality than the same product made in the home country.

This attitude still prevails for nondurable consumer products, but is changing for durables. Until about the early 1990s, upper income households preferred to buy imported televisions and washing machines. In recent years, however, many foreign companies have tied up with Indian companies. In the case of entertainment electronics and white goods, many leading Indian brands are imported in either CKD (completely knocked down) or SKD (semi-knocked down) conditions and assembled in India. Their quality is therefore good. This has meant that Indian customers are willing to buy such durables; consequently, purchases of such smuggled products have declined. The results are:

- Smuggled foreign brands are much higher priced than good-quality Indian-made brands.

- Service and spares are also not usually available in India for foreign brands; local companies, on the other hand, can provide both for their products.

- Durables are not changed frequently in India—built-in obsolescence does not work in this market.

- It is often difficult to get spares in India.

Market Research Firms

Until the mid-1980s, multinationals spent the most money on India's market research. Today, Indian companies conduct their own quite sophisticated and reliable market intelligence, retail audits, consumer panels, television rating services, national readership surveys, and so on.

Although the market research industry is not audited and most firms are either private limited companies or divisions of advertising agencies and proprietorships that do not have to report detailed financial figures, the size of its commercial billings is estimated at between $25 and 40 million. Since the price of research is much lower in India than in Europe or Asian countries, the actual research volume is much higher than their known billings suggest.

The Indian market research industry compares favorably in technical ability with similar firms in Southeast Asia. Some of the better-known resources are:

- **National Council for Applied Economic Research** (NCAER), the leading survey-based economic research institution on consumer demographics in the country. NCAER conducts surveys of around half a million people on a regular basis to provide marketing statistics to Indian industry.

- **Marketing and Research Group** (MARG) and **Indian Market Research Bureau** (IMRB) provide high-quality primary market research services.

- **Operations Research Group** (ORG) conducts detailed retail audits of India's retail outlets.

- **Francis Kanoi Marketing Research** performs industry-specific, syndicated market studies.

- Management consultancy is also well developed, and players like **Arthur Andersen, McKinsey**, and **KPMG** provide market feasibility studies and country entry strategies.

- **Consumer Pulse**

- **Feedback Marketing Services**

- **Hamsa Research Group**

- **Marketing and Business Associates**

- **MODE Research**

- **MRAS—Burke**

- Pathfinders India
- Quantum Market Research
- Research International

NOTES

1. "Chennai" is the new name for Madras (the change occurred only in mid-1996), whereas "Mumbai" has been slowly replacing Bombay for several years. Since these ancestral names will probably come to replace their more familiar but long-disliked colonial-era names, they are used throughout this book—with an occasional reminder for readers who may be dipping into chapters at random.

2. In India, a product "line" is called a "range."

3. International Institute for Population Studies, Bombay, 1995, based on research in 1993 by the Ministry of Health and Family Welfare.

3

Some Complexities of Indian Consumerism

COMPARISON WITH ASIA'S OTHER CONSUMER MARKETS

Although events in Asia's other large consumer markets have little direct impact on India—India is indeed another Asia altogether—it is useful to compare them briefly.

Japan's consumer market is still characterized by a web of high tariff barriers and duties. Although consumer spending in the country is still the highest in Asia, consumers have become more prudent. The caution can be blamed on the banking crisis and a sluggish economy that has curbed wages and cast gloom over employment prospects. Japan's half-decade bout with political change and high-level economic catastrophes give many Japanese consumers doubts about the financial securities they once took for granted. This has not been helped by a volatile North Korea and an aggressive China. The absence of job security and high consumer prices, especially for durables, have driven much money into the investment sector that once went to consumption. This is likely to continue as long as the perception remains that business and government leadership is not as competent as it was once thought to be.

Hong Kong's consumer future is uncertain as China's volatile political moves send strong retrogressive signals to business owners. China's economic signals are that Hong Kong's role is a high-level investment and banking conduit, not an entry point for consumer ideas and goods. Hong Kong's role as home to Asia's happiest consumers is likely to erode seriously.

No one can predict what retailing and distribution barriers loom on its horizon.

South Korea's consumer markets center on Seoul, which accounts for 65 percent of the country's total. Residents of Seoul save twice as much as their counterparts in other South Korean cities. Although aspirations are climbing in tandem with incomes, and consumers want better quality and a greater variety of durable and nondurable goods, South Korea is likely to be East Asia's smallest importer of consumer goods for quite some time, with the notable exception of designer fashions.

Taiwan's consumption expenditure is mainly among its free-spending youth, who buy consumer goods at fashionable shopping malls both in and outside the country. International brand-name marketers seem willing to absorb the high costs of setting up in the prohibitively priced shopping districts in Taiwan just to advertise their labels. The shadow of China looms large over Taiwan, prompting the blasé attitude that no matter which way the political wind blows, now is the time to buy all you can.

The Philippines' consumer market is small. It is concentrated in Greater Manila, which accounts for 70 percent of the country's consumer spending. Because of the country's historical links with the United States, American brands and American-style products perform better than do items made by other Western and Asian countries. Manila's department stores and shopping centers are well stocked with the latest consumer goods and are likely to remain so, but there is only a small market that has the big money.

Singapore's market is small but affluent and likely to remain acquisitive for a long time. Private consumption growth is forecast to continue to decelerate to about 4–5 percent in the 1990s, having been an average of 5.9 percent throughout the 1980s. The reasons include a wavering economy, slowing population growth, wage freezes among salaried employees, and, as of late 1996, anxiety over having placed too many eggs in the semiconductor manufacturing sector. Consumers are becoming increasingly particular about prices. Retailers overextended themselves in the mid-1990s and now face restructuring and downpricing. The Chinese have a cultural mistrust of discounting ("If it's cheap, it has to be bad"), so it seems likely that retail woes will continue even if demand rises.

Thailand is showing growth mainly in its key consumer market, Bangkok. Like their counterparts in South Korea and the Philippines, consumers in Thailand spend their money showily and lavishly. New department stores and supermarkets are mushrooming in Bangkok. Adventurous retailers are investing in less-known markets such as Hat Yai, Chiang Mai, and Nakhon Ratchasima.

Malaysia has a broad consumer base spread pretty much evenly in all of its large cities. Kuala Lumpur has broadened itself into a long affluent axis from the city itself down the Klang Valley to the sea. This is now spreading southward in the face of plans for a huge new airport, a new capital called Putrajaya, and a Multimedia Corridor joining this axis to Kuala Lumpur. Although incomes are low compared with Singapore, Malaysia has a larger population base and a seemingly endless upward economy. Only the popular belief that a large-scale economic recession will strike after the 1998 Commonwealth Games hinders Malaysia's economic prospects over the next decade. With its combination of high growth and low inflation fueled largely by foreign investments, Malaysia has the potential for becoming Southeast Asia's largest and most enduring consumer market after Singapore. It also has consumers who demand more and more quality as their incomes increase to pay for it.

COMPETITION STRATEGIES

As competition for the market place heats up, many Indian consumer-products firms realize that the only way to survive is to restrain prices and offer better value. Competition, domestic as well as foreign, is forcing both the old monoliths and new entrants to undertake price wars, launch new products, improve the quality of their existing range, and improve after-sales service, even if it means compromising on profitability.

To take one study period as an example, a Centre for Monitoring Indian Economy (CMIE) January–June 1995 sampling of forty-nine companies showed a trend in which sales increased by 31 percent while operating profits rose by only 20 percent, compared with the same period in 1994's sales increases of 37 percent and operating profits rise of 47 percent. To take another of the January–June 1995 indicators, corporate expenditures rose by 34 percent but sales grew by only 31 percent. Together, these indicate a trend of decreasing profitability.

Some companies admit that they have consciously decided to beat the competition by lowering profit margins to concentrate on volumes. The Rs 369 crore ($105 million) Pertech Computers decided in 1994 to reduce its operating margins from 17 percent to 12–13 percent, even though the industry average is 25 percent. Pertech's general manager, W. S. Mukund, believes that "Competition is forcing companies to look at the total value customers want—better product specifications, superior quality, add-ons. Only companies which fulfill these criteria will succeed." Pertech is increasing its dealer network from 300 to 500 to improve its reach and ease of after-sales service. Pertech's rival, HCL Frontline, countered by offering 24 hours of training spread over four weeks for customers of their home Beanstalk model of computer.

Other sectors evidence a similar decline in real prices. A 1.5 ton air conditioner that cost Rs 27,000 ($771) in January 1996 cost Rs 32,000 ($914) in January 1993 (60 percent of the reduction, however, can be attributed to the government's reduction in excise duties).

In the lubricants business, prices in the diesel automotive segment (the maximum volume segment) have been stable for the past 18 months, as opposed to annual 8–10 percent increases in the pre-1991 period.

The perennial Coca Cola and Pepsi rivalry manifested itself in the form of no price increases for two years and several value-addition moves such as visicoolers in dispensing machines that ensured drink availability at the right temperature, four- and six-bottle take-away packs, screw-on caps, plastic crates, and 1–liter bottles. Consumers were happily finding themselves being offered a 300-milliliter bottle for the same price as a 200-milliliter one.

The value for money market-share theory is not new to Indian markets, having first shown up in the early 1980s at the inspiration (critics say instigation) of foreign consumer-products makers. The effect was felt strongest in detergent wars, where companies used quality to gain an edge on other companies that sought higher margins by compromising it. Since the mid-1990s it has taken a quite different direction. Today, nearly everyone perceives that this tactic increases sales only for a while, and erodes a product's brand equity. J.D. Singh of the Delhi-based International Management Institute observes, "What is cheap will not make a difference. What's economical will. That means giving more for less—in fact, a lot more for a lot less."

The banking sector now has begun to demonstrate the same state of mind. In June 1996, the Reserve Bank of India deregulated interest rates on deposits of over 2 years. Private banks such as Global Trust Bank increased interest rates from 12 to 14 percent, but many public-sector banks like Canara Bank increased it to only 12.5 percent. Here, competition pushes interest rates higher as banks vie for deposits

This approach naturally is strongest in the credit card segment. Multinational card issuers turned active in 1992–1993 when the government became more liberal. Since then, cash advance limits as a percentage of the credit limit increased, service rates declined from 4 to 1.5 percent, banks began offering insurance cover, and even credit points in which a certain amount is credited every time the card is used. Farhad Irani, country

head of Standard Charter's Bankcard Division, believes that these phenomenon indicate a trend: "As spending volumes increase, artificial revenue generators like annual fees will decline."

Airlines are another competition-driven sector. Better service for customers and a series of innovative gift and frequent-flier schemes have
helped private airlines attract nearly one-third of the domestic aviation
business away from public-sector Indian Airlines. Airlines are also going
in for more extravagant gifts. East West Airlines offers luxury gifts worth
Rs 30 lakh ($85,700) to passengers on its Delhi-Bangalore run. However,
in their attempts to woo customers, private airlines have to be careful to
keep up their value/profit ratio in order to maintain the volumes that can
safely sustain lower margins.

Some Examples of Competitive Strategies

Bank Cards
CitiBank
Income eligibility (Classic card): Rs 50,000 ($1430)/year
Entrance fee: Rs 950 ($27.15)
Annual fee: Rs 750 ($21.40)
Credit limit: Rs 12,000–Rs 40,000 ($343–$1143)
Cash advance: 60 percent of credit limit
Cash advance fee: 1.5 percent plus 2.75 percent interest

Standard Chartered
Income eligibility for the classic: Rs 60,000 ($1714)/year
Entrance fee: Rs 200 ($5.71)
Annual charges: Rs 600 ($17.14)
Cash advance: 40 percent of credit limit
Cash advance fee: 1.75 percent and interest of 2.75 percent

Computers
HCL Frontline
Rs 65,000 to Rs 1 lakh ($1,857–$2,857)
Free 4–week training
Tele-support services free in first year
Fax/modem card
Access to bulletin board services
25 CD-ROM titles

Pertech Computers
Rs 50,000 to Rs 1 lakh ($1,428–$2,857)
120 educational packages
21 CD-ROM titles
Enhanced dealer network support services

Cellular Phones

BPL Mobile
Dropped advance booking fee of Rs 2,000 ($57.14)
Free air time for 1 month
Bills customers in 1–second units
Discounts for high-use accounts

Max Hutchinson
No advance fee
Initially gave unlimited air time for Rs 5000 ($142.86) per month
Plans to give shares market updates
Accident insurance coverage

DESIGNING FOR LOCAL CONDITIONS

A common error is importing household equipment designed for use in Europe or America, forgetting that it will be subjected to very different uses in India. The mixer-blender that in Europe purees soft fruits or in America whips boiled potatoes will in India be asked to grind lentils, rice, and spices together, sometimes *before* cooking. The vacuum cleaner that in the country of its design is expected to see its bag emptied after a few uses will wait weeks in India until the illiterate, low-caste *dhobi* figures out how to do it (few people will demonstrate anything to someone low-caste). The washer accustomed to jeans and tee shirts will be faced with 6–yard sarees and 3–yard sarongs that clench around the gyrator like a snake around a mouse.

After having paid their dues learning the Indian marketplace, brands like Braun and Moulinex know to put heavier-duty motors into their mixers, and temperature-sensitive automatic shutoffs in their appliances. Sumeet's washer motors weigh 40 pounds—the entire weight of many rival models—because their machines have to handle long, twining sarees and sarongs up to the water line. Sumeet's wet-and-dry vacuum cleaner is built to suck up the water volumes of wet-mopping rather than the thin film of wet-and-dry because Indian housecleaning women flood the floors with water by the bucket from the well rather than a genteel film from a mop and a pail.

India is one place where a little reverse engineering—taking apart the competitor's product down to the last screw—can yield valuable lessons before entering the market with products from one's homeland.

CONSUMER CREDIT AND CO-BRANDED CARDS

Indian retailers rely on credit to customers to a greater extent than in Southeast Asia or the West. For example, neighborhood grocers compete with one another at service levels when they cannot at price levels. They commonly offer home delivery to be paid conveniently at the end of the month. Many consumer durable outlets provide installment payments. Credit is very critical in rural markets, where fertilizer, seed, and pesticide retailers must offer credit to farmers who cannot pay until after the harvest. Wholesalers or stockists offer similar credit terms to retailers.

Most Indian consumer credit is informal and on short terms—the examples of month- or harvest-end being typical. Retailers have a limited capital base and hence can offer only limited credit. In most cases, the customer already has an established relationship with the business, so the retailer is assured of repayment. In many such cases, the credit is "free" in the sense that there are no extra fees to the customer.

Much less utilized is credit to unknown customers designed to stimulate sales, introduce new and somewhat expensive products, or establish market share. In India this is known as "marketer-managed" or "organized credit."

These two types of credit are still underdocumented as marketing tools. Ease of credit has not yet made it an attractive tool. For one, rates are likely to be higher, although easier to get, than credit from banks. In many high-end product categories like automobiles, consumer durables, and furnishings, marketers see credit as a key new element in their competitiveness. Automobiles are typically financed at levels of 70 to 80 percent of the sales price. In India this is termed "owing on credit," in contrast to the Western term "buying on credit"; the phrasing hints at the stigma generally associated with debt of any kind.

The international practice of bundling products with credit runs up against its own "terminology trap" similar to the above. Distributors see credit as a promise of payment in the future in exchange for an acquisition in the present. They do not see the offer of credit as additional value to the customer. Above all, they are rarely clear on the four requisites to credit as a distribution mechanism:

- Acquisition of adequate capital to finance the receivable.
- Setting up the credit mechanisms of appraisal, setting credit limits, deciding repayment options, and pricing the credit.
- Setting a mechanism for recovering their receivables.
- Establishing a distribution channel for credit.

Since consumer credit is so relatively new, there has been little systematization of these four key elements—in fact, one of the initial roadblocks is explaining these piecemeal in such a way that the entire package is not intimidating.

Of those distributors already familiar with its ramifications, most at the stockist or retailer manage this entire process on an informal "know-thy-neighbor" basis. In the automobile industry, independent finance companies perform the role. Following the major global auto manufacturers, Maruti, Bajaj, Kinetic, and Telco all have set up subsidiary finance credit companies. In the case of higher end hard-to-introduce durables like washers, specialized companies like Countrywide Finance have been set up to finance consumer credit. New companies entering India can tie up with these companies to offer credit without the arduous and pitfall-filled problems of daily credit operations. Credit card companies usually demand too high an interest rate to finance most consumer products. Banks offer credit on better terms, but their cumbersome procedures have not made this avenue very popular.

Into the above somewhat predictable mix has now arrived the co-branded credit card. These got off the ground in 1994 but did not really take off until 1995, when Philips launched a co-branded card with CitiBank, targeting the hard-to-crack high-end durables market. Their collaboration relied on outsourcing many of the credit management processes—rating agencies to appraise applications, collection agencies working on percentage of the balance (ranging from 15 to 40 percent) to retrieve from errant customers, and so on. There are no countrywide rating agencies of the TRW type, largely due to communications problems.

However, marketing credit is still in its infancy. Companies are in the position of having to innovate credit offerings to customers due to the unfamiliar terrain of formalized credit in a society that long has relied on moneylenders. The moneylender, rapacious though he may be, is still a local. The relationship can be likened to a rocky but steady marriage. The lesson for foreign firms is that any credit offering in India should be seamlessly married with the product and offered as a one-stop shop.

Beyond social inertia, there are other problems. The first is establishing the most acceptable local credit price. States like Kerala and West Bengal, with their strong heritage of Communist political influence, are much more interest-sensitive than entrepreneurial Gujarat and Maharashtra.

Recently, the Singer Company expanded its installment-plan approach downward from its legendary sewing machine line. Singer's installment system thrived in its mature sewing machines category, in which it married acquisition of its product to payment in installments; purchase and payments occur in the same shop, local with local, just as in a marriage. Singer's system worked so well because it has so many of its own retail shops. Now Singer has extended its installment plan system to its mixers, toasters, cooking grills, irons, and so on.

Singer's downscale shift signaled a new territory in consumer credit purchasing. Emulators were not long to follow. Lotus Book House, a Mumbai-based book shop, now sells encyclopedias on installment.

In India the prerequisite to any credit service offer is simplicity—simple for the customer to understand, simple in procedure, simple in payment. The marketer needs to be most discreet with proving one's ability to pay—too cumbersome or inquisitive a process will inhibit not only customers, but also the dealers who must push it. In consumer credit simplicity is the key to the marketplace.

ISLAMIC BANKING

Some 150 million Indians are Muslim. Interest is forbidden in Islam, so Islamic banks and consumer financial institutions have come up with a variety of methods that obey the letter of Islamic *shariyah* law and yet still enable banking and consumer finance operations to be done.

In a conventional bank the depositor and the bank normally share a contractual relationship in which the bank charges and pays interest. Islamic banks call this profit sharing and charge a fee on expenses. The bank's administrative costs have to be met and are not fixed. The Koran only lays down strictures against interest itself. Profit sharing (*mudrabaha*), leasing (*ijara*), and sale of goods at a specified margin (*murabaha*) are not included.

The Islamic bank's route for mobilizing working funds is by means of *mudarabahs*—agreements in which one or more partners provides finance while the others contribute management. The profits are shared in an agreed proportion while losses are borne by the financiers alone in proportion to their share capital. None of these funds, except *amanah* (current deposits), give any guarantee of either repayment of the principal or assurance of a rate of return. The rate of return is variable and linked to the return earned from the deployment of the funds. The bank also gets a share of the profits (losses are not shared) or a fixed fee for managing funds.

These funds are also allowed to be invested jointly by the bank, usually in real estate, construction projects, equity, or other productive assets, and are not subject to taxation as a composite entity.

Even though the handful of those involved in Islamic finance is growing fast, there have been compromises along the way. The Indian Islamic bank Bait-un-Nas'r was set up to mobilize deposits on a no-profit-no-loss basis. It has 100 percent current deposits and no assured rate of return apart from repaying the principal. Deployment of funds are generally in interest-free secured loans. Since the organization was not allowed to profit from this activity, it has devised a method of working out its administrative costs on a quarterly basis and charging these to its borrowers as a service charge. This service charge, which is in the range of 12 percent per year and similar to that charged by other banks, is a cause for some embarrassment to proponents of interest-free finance. Similar service charges are recovered from borrowers by most credit-cooperative societies and are in the range of 5 to 12 percent.

Leasing and hire-purchase companies have fewer structural problems.

Some banks have worked out innovative interest-free deposit schemes linked with interest-free loans, for example, *Iqra* (education) deposit, *Aqad* (marriage), and *Haj Umra* savings programs. Savings under these schemes entitle savers to an interest-free loan of up to 25 percent of matured deposits.

The Islamic banking format allows much freedom to experiment, since reserve requirements are lighter and the rate of interest or rate of return can be variable. Even if it is linked to profits, it allows interest-free organizations the freedom to tailor their deposit mobilization and deployment in a manner suited to their individual needs.

Key Islamic Banking Terms

- *Riba*: the practice of interest, which is category-disallowed; avoiding the payment of interest is the cornerstone of Islamic banking.
- *Kard-i-hasa*: an interest-free loan.

- *Sahib-al-maal:* the financier as distinct from the *mudarib*, or individual or institution, that provides the entrepreneurship and management.

- *Shirkah:* a partnership in which two or more people share the financing and management of a venture.

- *Ijara:* refers to leasing activity and recognizes the legitimacy of rental income since the lessor is partaking of the full loss of the business activity.

- *Mudarabah:* one of the most favored Islamic formats, this refers to an agreement in which one or more of the partners provides finance while the others contribute management. Profits are shared in an agreed-upon proportion and losses are borne by the financiers alone in proportion to their share of total capital.

- *Murabaha:* the sale of goods at a specified profit margin. The term is used for describing a sale agreement where the seller buys the goods for the buyer and sells them at a fixed price that includes a markup. The payment has to be settled within an agreed-upon period, either in installments or as a lump sum.

A DETAILED LOOK AT SIX MARKETS

Color Televisions

India's Rs 3,000 crore ($857 million) color television sets (CTVS) market is a convenient benchmark point from which to consider the consumer electronics market in general. How is India likely to cope economically and politically with the multinational onslaught of information and entertainment exposure undreamed of a few years ago?

India's consumer electronics business has not been the same since the multinationals arrived *en masse* in 1994. Until the early 1980s, the market for CTVS was virtually nonexistent. A perceptible change in consumer preferences began to emerge in 1982, prompted by the Asian Games in Delhi. The upswing in demand continued until 1988, when sales of CTVS peaked at 1.3 million sets. The upper middle-class market became saturated and sales stagnated at 1.2 million sets in 1989 and 1990 before declining sharply through 1991 and 1992. Although the drop was precipitated by a steep hike in CTVS prices resulting from rising import duties and the depreciation of the rupee, lack of channel choice did not help.

Liberalization brought the first major satellite channels—CNN in February 1992 and Star TV in October 1992—which immediately boosted CTVS sales. The same year brought the first fruits of lowered import duties on CTVS and their major component, picture tubes. CTVS finally came within the reach of middle-class buyers, and sales showed the power of the middle-class market: Between 1993 and 1996, CTVS sales zoomed at an annual growth of 17 percent.

Liberalization also brought the multinational CTVS makers into the Indian market through joint ventures and fully-owned subsidiaries. With them came newer brands and more choices for consumers, pushing CTVS demand to even greater heights. By 1997, the Deve Gowda Administration had confirmed the forward momentum of reform, inviting Sony, Panasonic, Samsung, Akai, Thomson, Grundig, and LG Electronics (formerly Lucky GoldStar) to take long-term positions in the market.

What lures the foreign players is not so much that India is such a large market but its long-term growth potential. Per-capita television ownership is low and the growth in the size of the middle class is high compared with the other Asian countries. The multinationals expect India in 1997–2005 to perform very much the same as the Chinese economy in the 1980s.

Surprisingly, after two years of intense effort to establish themselves in the market, the seven multinational brands were still being outperformed by the big Indian brands—the "Big 7" garnered an anemic 7.4 percent of the market in 1995–1996, although this shot up to 14 percent in the first three months of 1996. The foreign majors who have been able to increase their market shares are Akai (3.3 percent), Sony (3.1 percent), and Samsung (3.0 percent). These compare with India's Videocon International (26.6 percent), BPL India (21.7 percent), Onida (12.7 percent), and Philips India (12.0 percent).

The locals claim that the multinationals entered the CTVS market too late. Maybe, but they are hardly sitting on their labels. Most are actively forging technical collaborations—Videocon with Toshiba, BPL with Sanyo, and Onida with JVC. These will offer the same latest technologies as the multinationals, but also the much more important built-in retail network all across the country. The co-brands' reach and service network is likely to keep them ahead of stand-alone competitors for some time.

Indian manufacturers also have a leg up with their strong market R&D and manufacturing bases. These enable them to design products that are more sharply focused on the sensibilities of the local market. Their plants were amortized long ago—new players will find plant costs disproportionately high. Most important, Indian CTVS brands have a built-in home-team image. The multinationals will be much less adept at serving the ad-appeal tastes of different parts of the country's multicultural society. For example, Samsung got good response in the north with a high-profile ad strategy but the opposite response in the south.

The multinationals also experience the curious phenomenon of being too multinational. Although India's CTVS market is growing, it still accounts for only 1 percent of the global market. Product designers in, say, Pusan or Kyoto are not keen on incorporating features mainly of interest to Indian consumers. Adaptation to local needs has emerged as the key strength of the Indian brands. The hard-earned wisdom of the Indian TV market is that buyers buy value for money, not brand.

The crucial factors to CTVS brand survival are generally agreed to be the following.

Retailing. Dealers play the most crucial role in CTVS marketing. If a particular brand is not available with a dealer, a consumer usually chooses another brand rather than another dealer. Dealer margins reflect their own awareness of their role: 5 percent in early 1995, steadily increasing to 10 percent by late 1996.

The dealer's new-found power may be short-lived, though. CTVS companies are setting up their own showrooms that enable the consumer to comparison view their product with others (which may be fiddled with). More important, it gives the company's sales reps a (briefly) captive consumer to explain their product's features better than most dealers.

Price. The low demand for CTVS is largely due to low disposable incomes. Although a CTVS' average life is ten years, an Indian consumer will not even consider replacing a set before it is seven years old. Sales tactics based on price-cutting, discounting based on trade-ins, or gifts like pagers are strategies adopted only by the new players. In the long run, the ability to sustain low prices will be the key to success.

Financing. Consumer financing is becoming the key to CTVS sales. The availability of financing at reasonable rates and comfortable repayment terms is crucial. Financing is provided by dealers with links to consumer finance companies. Philips has become the first company to strike a direct pact with Countrywide Finance, a venture between GE Capital and the Housing Development Finance Corporation, for customer financing.

Program Quality. The improvement in the quality of programming, especially Doordarshan's, has had a strong positive impact on CTVS sales. The many new channels and cable networks have boosted the demand for multichannel CTVS sets, and the impact of satellite TV, when it breaks through the middle-class price ceiling, will probably be as great as all of these together.

Product Features. Consumers expect a product with auto-tuning, personalized preference, and auto-search. Sets without remote controls are out of fashion, although plenty still are sold. The Japanese companies are designing slimmer sets with better clarity, but at a price the Indian consumer finds hard to sustain. High-definition television (HDTV) sets are very expensive; their producers are sure to have an edge over their Indian rivals, but they may have an edge over a market that barely exists.

Replacement Market. This accounts for a significant part of CTVS sales. It can be classified into three segments:

- People shifting from black-and-white television sets to CTVS form 40 percent of the replacement market. Most consumers go for 20–inch models at the lower end of the model range, where prices range between Rs 16,000 and 20,000 ($457 and $571).

- People replacing a CTVS purchased seven or more years ago. This group comprises about 30 percent of the market and normally opts for premium models in the 20–inch category costing more than Rs 20,000.

- Demographic replacements occur when joint families separate into nuclear families, or when young couples get married and live in the same home of spousal parents but with their own television (often part of the dowry); these comprise about 30 percent of the replacement market.

The premium segment of the 20–inch category is almost the entire replacement market. The 14–inch portable television has been positioned to tap the second-set market and comprise 80 percent of it. The second-set market has enjoyed a 1996 growth rate of 16 to 18 percent in the various metro markets.

Seasonality. The demand for any consumer product is higher in the second half of the fiscal year, after the harvest season, when the income of the agricultural community is more liquid. "Monsoon fade" tends to boost sales during July through September, although it is not receiver technology but bandwidth that causes it.

Outlook for Color Televisions. The short-term outlook (through 1997) is that only the top three or four Indian companies will survive because of their early entry into the market, strong distribution network, and brand equity. Smaller CTVS players are likely to be wiped out.

It is expected that high-quality manufacturers like Sony are likely to target mainly the top-end niche segment. Their market share is unlikely to be more than 5 percent. Samsung and Akai may be able to garner between 7 and 9 percent each over 1997–1998.

However, as the multinationals popularize themselves, their competition is expected to heat up. The local majors like BPL and Videocon International have countered by extending their brand names into the white goods business, where they can utilize the non-television distribution network and dealer experience. They are sufficiently uneasy about foreign competition that they are trying to diversify into quite unrelated areas like power, telecommunications, and real estate to protect themselves against competitive erosion in the consumer durables business.

Apart from diversifications, joint ventures, mergers, and acquisitions are also survival strategies. However, these strategies are hard to distinguish between competitive strategy and simply joining the general business potpourri that is India these days.

Not all multinationals are keen on acquiring in-country competitors. Most are more keen on setting up their own greenfield plants. Samsung and LG Electronics are two examples of multinationals who are already looking beyond India's home market to the export markets of the Middle East and Africa.

The Electronics Market

Although their 1996 combined market share was still very healthy, the consumer electronics majors are witnessing a drop in margins.

When some of the world's largest consumer electronics companies prepared to invade the Indian market a year ago, industry experts quickly agreed that the going would get tough for India's "Big 4": Videocon, Philips, BPL, and Onida. Although nobody can ignore them, until now the Sonys, Akais, and Goldstars have not managed to make a major dent in the market. In color televisions, four out of every five sets are sold by the "Big 4." Yet the majors are feeling pinched. Although their combined market share is still very healthy, the threat of competition is straining profits. It is also putting to the test ideas about globalization that sound good on paper but turn out to be not so good when they arrive in your own marketplace.

The first indication came when Philips India announced its financial performance for 1995. Although its sales went up by 31 percent, net profits fell by a substantial 48 percent. Operating profit margins at the company fell from 9.9 percent in 1994 to 5.2 percent in 1995. Videocon International's results for 1995–1996 told a similar story. A 41 percent rise in income was accompanied by a modest 3.5 percent increase in net profits. At Mirc Electronics, which makes the Onida TV range, income went up by 31.7 percent while net profits rose by 22.4 percent.

Declines in profit margins resulted in a conscious strategy by the majors to protect their territories from the new competition. Their goal for some time was to increase volumes and market shares even if it meant lower profits. All four companies have stated in the press their readiness to sacrifice profits to stay at the top.

Although the consumer electronics market did not grow at the 25 percent or so many initially expected it to, it saw growth of between 10 and 15 percent in volumes. The earnings-per-share (EPS) of these companies have not been affected by the fall in profit margins largely because of the offsetting growth in sales volumes. With economic growth and poor current penetration levels, most expect the market to continue to grow briskly beyond the year 2000.

Making a mark in this growing market is expected to become more difficult. The market is getting more competitive—the main reason for the fall in profit margins in the industry.

The current strategy among consumer electronics companies is still to increase market shares. With the exception of Philips, none of the companies has access to multinational financial backing. Most foreign companies have already made it clear that their parents are ready to bankroll losses for as much as a decade to help their Indian subsidiaries establish a foothold. Videocon and BPL divert a part of their cash flows away from their main business into infrastructure projects such as power generation and telecom services. Many analysts consider these diversifications to be defensive moves: If things get bad in consumer electronics, some other source of profits will be needed.

Although they do not have the cash to match the MNCs, the Indian companies have a dominant market presence, which is a major competitive plus. The MNCs appreciated the point. Most recent takeovers in the consumer-goods industries seem expensive when valued solely in terms of cash flow. The main strength of the dominant four is their market share in each segment of the business. The natural result is an attempt to increase sales volumes while protecting market shares. This has translated to lower prices and higher marketing costs.

Most Indian analysts of this market expect that prices will be highly competitive. This will lead to further price erosion. The main consideration presently is price. The industry as a whole has not increased prices in real terms for the past few years. Effective prices have come down in three ways: (a) outright price cuts; (b) many brands have been technologically upgraded but sold at their old prices; and (c) TVs, radios, and the like are sold with more freebies thrown in. All of these eat into company revenues.

Companies compromise on revenues in other ways as well. Over the past year, dealer discounts have been increased by as much as 30 percent. Trade credit of up to 80 days is now available. This hits hard an industry that requires sizable amounts of working capital. All types of selling costs have gone up sharply. With increased competition, costs in terms of publicity and promotions have increased.

Companies see higher volumes as the key to recovering these costs. At Philips India, ad spending jumped 52 percent in 1995, reaching Rs 55 crore ($15.7 million). Onida's ad spending and marketing costs have shot up from Rs 27 crore in 1993–1994 to Rs 40 crore in 1994–1995 to Rs 58 crore in 1995–1996 ($11.4 to $16.6 million). This increase came partly because of the escalation in advertising rates, but also because of the segmentation of the media—with so many television channels and newspaper supplements, a company has to spend a lot more than it did a few years ago.

The marketing bills for the major consumer electronics companies is already around Rs 100 crore ($28.5 million), between 10–15 percent of their revenues. A truism in India is that a company cannot devote more than 5–6 percent of its turnover to selling expenses. If these are at Rs 100 crore, the company or companies need a minimum turnover of Rs 2,000 crore ($571 million)—and this to merely maintain market share. In tougher times, they will have to generate even greater sales volumes. The same argument holds for R&D: Companies can spend on it effectively to develop new models and technologies only if the costs are spread over large volumes.

The present stress on the profits of the consumer electronics companies is unlikely to be a temporary aberration brought about by the post-1996 phase of liberalization. Each factor points the way to thinner margins in the future. Before the current round of competition set in, profit margins on an average were at 10–11 percent. Globally, industry margins are closer to 6 percent. Downward adjustment to global levels has already started in India. That they have shown a readiness to let profits rather than market share slip is enough proof that the "Big 4" see the giant Catch-22 that lies in their future.

The High-End White Goods Market

"Trolling the bootlegger's den" or, more simply, "fishing the den" is Mumbai slang for finding a good smuggler. For today's "high net worths" the choices in the "white goods" market—consumer durables that used to be painted white—are mind-boggling. But instead of the smuggler, although still a reliable source for cigarettes and whiskey, one goes to "the post-lib" (liberalization) shops where there is no shortage of international products at international prices. This is termed "the pull-in trade," and its growth is referred to in the business press as "pull-in demand."

Demand in the high-end white goods market has been stimulated largely for external reasons: The government cut the import duty on washing machines with washloads above 5.5 kilograms (12 pounds) and refrigerators above 300 liters from 200 to 80 percent between 1993 and 1996, and it is likely to decline further. One result was that a market once dominated by Kelvinator, Electrolux, Hoover, Whirlpool, and Carrier has now attracted Korea's Daewoo, Samsung, and Goldstar (LG Electronics).

Presently, this is a rarified market with a minuscule number of buyers. However, almost everyone in it is betting that this market will grow between 20 and 25 percent for mid-ticket items such as Rs 30,000 ($875) refrigerators up to top-of-the-line double-door models with water and ice dispensers, door-ajar alarms, and deodorizing systems costing 1.2 lakh ($3,425).

Kelvinator-acquired Whirlpool started the upscaling trend in 1995 with its 305–liter double-door refrigerator and its front-load fully automatic washing machine (priced at Rs 30,000). Nine months later, Daewoo Electronics introduced five of its twenty-seven-model refrigerator line into India, all in the then 300–600-liter range and priced between Rs 30,000 and Rs 1 lakh ($2,860).

According to a 1996 internal survey by LS Electronics, by the year 2005, one-half of all refrigerator sales in India will be in the double-door segment. Currently, 85 percent of refrigerator sales are single-door 165–liter models and only 20 percent are fully automatic. In the washing machine market, 80 percent will be fully automatic, compared to only 20 percent now.

Multinationals are the vanguard in the premium-price white goods segment. Opinions are divided whether to come on-shore for production. Sweden's AB Electrolux was the first to manufacture overseas-designed brands in the country via its majority stake in Maharaja International. Its first introduction in late 1995 was a 6.5-kilogram front-loading washing machine with a rinse-hold option to keep delicates from creasing—a feature which indicates that Electrolux anticipated even then today's demand for increasingly sophisticated luxury fabrics. So far, the company has introduced only two versions, an 85 percent dry model at Rs 30,000 and a 100 percent dry model at Rs 45,000 ($1,285). Electrolux is convinced that the sticker shock will be more than offset by the draw of practical—not to mention "statusy"—features and performance extras.

The few models and prices mentioned above are a very small fragment of the whole picture. Most of the majors in the white goods market have introduced similar models with similar features at similar prices. Such across-the-board confidence implies that much thought is being given to the "ground realities" of on-shore manufacturing, distribution, and after-sales infrastructure. Few if any companies in the white goods market will long content themselves with simply shipping their products in complete form. Modi Hoover (a joint venture between Maytag and the S.K. Birla Group) plans to work into the upscale market by first importing in KDK or knocked-down-kit form—for which there are both tariff and freightage advantages—until it achieves reasonable volumes, and then manufacture at a facility planned for Pune.

Others do not want to take that risk, perhaps because they have no local partners. Daewoo plans only to import fully manufactured refrigerators and washing machines direct from South Korea. Indeed, all three Korean companies seem to feel that it has not been demonstrated that the trade-off between the cost of installing an in-country plant will be significantly offset by the larger share to be gained, compared with direct importing and a lower market share.

Still others are even less sanguine. Voltas, which offers a 360–liter frost-free refrigerator from Japanese giant Hitachi priced at Rs 31,000, feels that the volume of this market is so small that it does not make sense to manufacture top-end models on-shore. They are content with the arithmetic of high margins and low volume.

Available figures indicate that the market is far from the critical mass stage that would trigger large-volume on-shore manufacturing. Modi Hoover sold 450 units of its 664–liter refrigerators and 500 units of its top-loading 10-kilogram washing machines between November 1995 and June 1996. Delhi-based Weston Elecroniks sold only 200 of its 330- to 736-liter White Westinghouse refrigerators in six months—perhaps because they were priced from Rs 39,000 ($1,115) to 1.26 lakh ($3,600). Figures of this magnitude support the belief that "high-tag" products from less-known manufacturers are there mainly to build brand awareness while awaiting further clarity of the market's across-the-board potential.

This theory is somewhat substantiated in the case of air conditioners. All of the high-end attention is focused on split models. Amtrex's Quadra model, a split system, fits in the center of a room to circulate in all directions so that there are no hot pockets. This may be advanced beyond belief to the legions of office workers whose previous experience with "air conditioning" has been a wheezy fan and plenty of hankies. The price tag is Rs 50,000 ($1,430) for a 1.5-ton model. Carrier's 1.5-ton cordless split high-wall mounted unit is Rs 55,000 ($1,570). SEL's split 2–ton high-wall model is also Rs 55,000. The obvious neglect of window models in these offerings comes from the fact that windows are smaller in India than they are in America or Europe, and people do not want to block what little light and view they have.

After-sales service is quite different in this market. Modi Hoover does not allow its regular dealers to handle its high-end refrigerators. It sends its own staff directly to the customer's house to deliver and install. Samsung equips their service staff with pagers and mobile vans.

Given the small nature of their markets, the high-ticket white goods majors use little mass advertising, except as a brand-building exercise on satellite television and a few advertisements in the prestigious magazines and major dailies.

Despite the youth of this market, its strategy is generally clear: build brand equity as a prelude to a larger presence, exploiting as much as possible the image value of premium brands. This strategy so resembles the chess tactic of creating a highly visible diversion in one corner to mask the real attack across the table that chess-adoring Indians are sure to appreciate it. The question is, will it sell well enough in the post-lib market to create demand in the mass market?

The Home PC Market

In India there is as yet only a minuscule home personal computer (PC) market as it is understood in the West. The home PC market as it is understood in India is interlinked with the small office/home office (SOHO) market. Most PCs for use at home are bought by professionals and small business people rather than parents for their children. The percentage of parents buying their children top-of-the-line PCs (with multimedia, interactive capability, speech recognition, etc.) is presently minimal.

That may change as PCs begin to look and act more like televisions. The view at long-standing home-market player Apple—and now also being articulated at Wipro-Acer and Tata Information Systems Ltd.—is that the home PC market will take off at the end of 1996 because manufacturers are bundling multimedia so effectively.

However, the players differ in their opinions about the size of this market. There are no official figures. The most common "guesstimate" is in the region of 50,000 PCs, with growth expectations of 50 to 60 percent a year. Other estimates are much cooler, averaging between 20,000 and 25,000 units in 1996, with growth expectations of about 25 percent per year.

In India's PC world, market share and price are more closely related than market share and features. In 1995, Apple bet on features, introducing its Performa range of home PCs in September with a price tag of Rs 1.4 lakh ($4,000) for the Performa 6200. Prices quickly dropped due to low response. The 6200 now costs Rs 90,000 ($2,570). This price plummet was reflected all across Apple's product range.

But Aptiva and Aspire computers also are priced at around Rs 1.4 lakh, and they were not dropped. The main reason appears to have been product bundling. Parents are more apt to go for the best multimedia PC if it has the best multimedia educational and entertainment software. Still, it is a tiny market: only some 3,000 and 5,000 multimedia PCs in the Rs 1 lakh-plus range ($2,860) were sold in 1995.

The verdict on catchy design is iffier. Wipro-Acer bills their Aspire as the first truly "Home PC," designed and colored to look like a home consumer electronic item. It is marketed as though it were a television and a video player rolled into one. Aspire also claims ease of use, with a special user interface on top of Windows '95 to make it simple for first-time users.

Ease of use is the other factor besides bundling that seems to tilt a buy decision. Apple traditionally has had a clear run in the ease-of-use category. Indians feel that Windows 3.1 and Windows '95 are still a long way from being as friendly as Mac OS. PC distributors have not grasped this well, for, except for Aspire, they still bundle Windows 3.1. Most analysts feel that Aspire's ease-of-use approach will eat into Apple's reputation as it outmaneuvers the other PCs. Speech recognition and messaging features are given low priority by purchasers; they are seen as gimmicks embodying still-crude technology.

Since the home market is still in its infancy, there are no clear indicators beyond the above as to what most motivates a buy. Price will remain a major deciding factor, especially in the under-Rs 1 lakh ($2,850) region. Apple's reversion to a sub-Rs 1 lakh pricing strategy helped boost its sagging Performa sales.

The unanimous sentiment from consumers is for more brands. To them, wider choice means a better negotiating position and therefore lower prices.

Auto Parts and Supplies

The revolution in India's auto industry has spawned a similar one in the components industry. The relationship between domestic auto manufactures and their component companies has been redefined largely by the example of Chrysler Motors in the United States.

India's auto components industry is huge: 7,000 crore ($2 billion). Prompted by expectations of a major competitive shake-up as a dozen or more foreign auto majors prepare to set up in India over the next few years, the industry has cut its production costs largely by cutting its parts costs. The main tactics are compressing its vendor base, using subassemblies instead of components, and enforcing stricter quality controls to weed out poor performers.

One objective is cutting costs by forcing vendors to cut theirs. Auto makers want to eliminate expenditures on inspection of vendors' facilities, testing of product quality, and communications. They have found that this is easier via long-term relationships with fewer but more trustworthy suppliers. For example, Maruti Udyog, India's largest auto maker, used to pride itself on the size of its vendor base. In 1994, it was the first to cut back on its suppliers by sourcing subassemblies. In the case of mufflers, the company previously bought from thirty-two separate companies and assembled them at its factory at Gurgaon in Haryana. By mid-1996, Maruti was outsourcing all of its muffler systems preassembled from Delhi-based Jay Bharat Maruti.

Maruti claims that 5,400 square feet of shop floor space were freed for other use and 4,800 man-days in labor costs were saved. In October 1996, Maruti started sourcing the entire engine compartment—parts for which it hitherto procured from seven different vendors. The floor space for this no longer needed function was turned into a new production area.

Much of the domestic components industry has rapidly adjusted to these changes. They have been encouraged to do so by their trade group, the Automotive Component Manufacturers' Association. The ACMA estimates that total component industry turnover will triple to Rs 20,000 crore ($5.7 billion) by the year 2000. Setting an example for them is international auto systems supplier Delphi Automotive. Its Rs 2,650 crore ($757 million) India venture will supply six different systems—steering, engine management, chassis, heating/air conditioning, interior lighting, and electric—to local auto companies. They will not sell individual components—and in fact will not even make the components required for these systems. Delphi will buy them from domestic suppliers.

Sona Steering Systems, a major vendor for companies like Maruti, has decided to develop and market fully assembled steering systems and axle assemblies. Sona Mahindra will manufacture complete clutch systems and drive shafts. The Anand group—which includes companies like Gabriel India, Purolator, and Perfect Circle—has its sights trained on brake, air conditioning, and exhaust systems.

However, a 1995 study by the Association of Indian Automobile Manufacturers showing that the industry's shift to subassemblies would require investments of close to Rs 10,000 crore ($2.85 billion), not many vendors will be able to make the transition. The result is a hierarchy among component manufacturers.

Tier One vendors supply complete subassemblies and systems directly to auto manufacturers. Tier Two vendors are smaller companies selling components to Tier One vendors. Tier Three vendors supply minor items like forgings to suppliers in the tiers above them. This reorganization of the component industry is not likely to result in a reduction in the overall number of suppliers, and hence the restructure has not caused serious pain to the smaller players—a major psychological plus in worker-conscious India.

However, it has caused a great deal of attention to focus on the quality factor of value addition. Two concepts are just catching on (and getting much attention in the trade press): (a) switching to a just-in-time supply system, and (b) shifting quality control from the auto manufacturer level to the vendor level.

Into this situation the entrance of foreign makes has brought considerable problems. There is a wide technology gap between domestic component manufacturers and their overseas counterparts. Virtually no Indian auto manufacturer has developed its own vehicle. All of the vehicles one sees on the streets today, from the antique Ambassador to the more-or-less modern Maruti, were models that were phased out in their home countries. Indian manufacturers simply bought the drawings and since then have had little incentive to innovate or upgrade.

Another reason why Indian vendors lag in technology is the auto makers' policy (until recently) of relying on many vendors as backups to each other, which kept the vendors from producing on a large enough scale to generate the revenues to support research and development.

All of this has motivated a very real fear that foreign auto companies will bring their own vendors into India, snatching business away from Indian vendors. The foreign makers are not blind to the consequences of such an event. Several have formed joint ventures with Indian counterparts. The Anand group, for instance, has signed no less than five joint venture agreements, with Echlin of the United States to manufacture hydraulic and air brake systems; with Behr of Germany to manufacture air-conditioning systems and aluminum radiators; with Dana Corp. of the United States to make drive shafts, universal joints, axles, and clutches; with Chang Yun of Korea for synchronizer rings; and with Arvin of the United States for exhaust systems.

Similarly, Delhi-based Rico has tied up with Daewoo Precision Industries of Korea to manufacture castings. Their Rs 90 crore ($25.7 million) project will be implemented in two phases: the first a dedicated line for DCM Daewoo; the second for other buyers and export manufactures.

Another strategy is to join hands with more than one overseas company to make the same product. Pune-based Kalyani Brakes, which already had a joint venture with AlliedSignal of the United States for brake systems, last year took on as a partner the Japanese brake manufacturer, Nabco. Now, each of the three partners has a 28 percent stake in the company. Gasket material manufacturer Reinz Talbros has added to his earlier collaboration with Reinz of Germany a 50:50 joint venture with the Ishikawa Gasket Co. of Japan to make asbestos-free gasket material. In both cases, the strategy is to leverage European and American car companies in India to acquire Japanese and Korean collaborators, even though European auto components and subassembly design are totally different from East Asian design.

Having vested interests in component manufacturers translates into higher degrees of technology transfer. DCM Daewoo, whose Cielo model was introduced in India in 1995, has ambitious expansion plans for India. These include collaborations between six of Daewoo's Indian suppliers for mufflers, seats, rear axles, lighting, forgings, and castings. DCM Daewoo even has taken equity participation in five of these.

Despite all of this promise, achieving ISO 9000 levels of quality is still over the horizon for most of the component industry. While overseas vendors talk of rejection rates in terms of pieces per million, in India they still talk of pieces per thousand. Quality is one of the most serious problems that India's parts industry has to contend with, but there are more subtle problems as well. Vendors supplying complete subassemblies have to pay sales tax on the components used to make them. Unless the tax laws are changed, developing subassembly systems carry a cost burden that makes it harder for them to compete.

As the country's automobile industry prepares for the 1996–2000 revolution, the component industry has a number of hurdles to leap if it wants to catch up with the rest of Asia.

Opening Up the Insurance Sector

The Indian insurance sector remained tightly shut as of late 1996, even though two years earlier a reform-investigating body known as the Malhotra Committee recommended that the industry be thrown open to private enterprise. Still, there is a long list of aspiring entrants, both domestic and international. The government's decision to include deregulation of the insurance sector has continued to encourage the number of hopefuls queuing up outside the insurance sector's door.

Forever hopeful that deregulation will arrive any day now, some of India's leading business houses have signed MOUs (memoranda of understanding) with some of the world's insurance majors. Examples include the Tata family's agreement with U.S.-based AIG Insurance; ITC's tie-up with BAT Industries' associate, Eagle Star Insurance; the Housing Development Finance Corp. (HDFC) with Standard Life of the United Kingdom; Bombay Dyeing's collaboration with the U.K.'s General Accident; and the Peerless Group's proposed partnership with Guardian Royal of the United Kingdom.

According to most estimates, if India's public insurance sector were thrown open today, some Rs 50,000 crore ($14.2 billion) could materialize in premiums over the following three years. Compared to the rest of the world, India is still a grossly underinsured market. Insurance premiums in India contribute just 1.6 percent to the GDP, compared with 8.5 percent in Japan and 3.3 percent in Malaysia. While every Indian spends an average of only Rs 182 ($5.20) a year on insurance, the Japanese spend $2,575 and Malaysians $105. The business yet to be developed is enormous.

However, few Indian companies want to venture into the field alone. Even firms as well established as the Tatas (their New India Assurance was nationalized in 1972) are wary of learning the hard way about the intricacies of today's global market. One important reason is the length of the hiatus. It has been almost 25 years since an Indian private firm ran an insurance company, and most company leaders know they are more than just a bit rusty. The risks and complexity of insurance mushroomed during those years.

Hence, India's domestic aspirants are willing to settle for minority holdings in insurance-sector joint ventures. Minority status also helps lower the entry barrier for Indian firms. Even though the Malhotra Committee stipulated that a paid-up capital of Rs 100 crore (28.5 million) be required of all new entrants, it also stated that the promoters equity should not be more than 40 percent of the paid-up capital ($11.4 million). Hence, as minority partners, Indian companies would have to cough up less than Rs 20 crore ($5.7 million) as their equity contribution.

Domestic companies interested in the insurance sector fall into three broad categories. The first includes groups like the Tatas, ITC, and Peerless, which have vast distribution networks throughout the country. Peerless, for example, has a network of 4.6 million agents who can be turned into insurance sales reps.

In the second category are financial-sector giants such as the Industrial Credit & Investment Corporation of India (ICICI), the State Bank of India (SBI), and the Shipping Credit Investment Corporation of India (SCICI), for whom having a presence in insurance would give them a complete range of financial services. This group also includes a large number of smaller finance companies. Among these are the Chennai-based First Leasing, Anagram Finance, and Sundaram Finance. All three have set up asset management companies (AMCs)—widely considered to be the first step toward getting into the insurance business—in collaboration with British partners. Companies such as these also have a wide distribution network, a sound track record, and good credibility.

The third category comprises companies such as the HDFC and Fortis Financial Services. These see synergistic advantages in insurance for themselves. For example, since life insurance has always been sold successfully in conjunction with housing finance, the HDFC sees its foray into insurance as a logical extension of its existing mortgage business. Similarly, since Fortis's parent company, Ranbaxy, has a core business in pharmaceuticals, medical insurance is a likely diversification.

There are two obstacles to privatizing the insurance sector: (a) leftist opposition in the government, which sees insurance as yet another capitalist plot to rob from the poor; and (b) since the public-sector Life Insurance Corp. (LIC) is required to invest 70 percent of its premium accruals in government securities, public-sector insurance is a cheap source of funds for the Centre. If the LIC's monopoly were broken by privatization, the government's cost of borrowing would rise automatically.

CASE STUDIES

Analyzing the Television Market[1]

The head of marketing at the country's largest television company was a worried man. As a marketing manager, Jitendra Vikram had been involved in Joy Visual Products' (JVP) triumphant run in the marketplace with its Companion brand of black-and-white and color television sets. Now Vikram was faced with a market crammed with competitors imitating every innovation that his company had demonstrated. Worse, the findings of a market survey suggested that buyers of Companion televisions were developing a negative image about the product. Observations about buying behavior did not augur well for the brand either. For instance, the majority of buyers upgrading from black-and-white to color sets preferred a new brand, which meant that Companion's vast market share in the black-and-white segment was acting against it. What marketing strategies should Vikram deploy? Can a pioneer beat its old image to win new customers?

JVP was a front-ranker in the Rs 4,200 crore ($1.2 billion) Indian television industry with a turnover of Rs 650 crore ($186 million) in 1995–1996. Set up in 1979 and based in an electronics zone on the outskirts of Bangalore, the company had been manufacturing and marketing both black-and-white and color television (CTV) sets since. After launching and consolidating its products in south India, JVP had within five years extended its reach to western India, the largest market for home appliances in the country. By 1989, its flagship brand, Companion, had gone national, cornering 40 percent of the all-India market. The success of Companion was largely attributed to two factors: smart positioning and product-line development.

Vikram had suggested the brand-positioning themes that had worked so well for Companion in the past. The simple, straightforward positioning platform had attracted customers with its direct appeal. As an increasing number of entrepreneurs established television-manufacturing facilities to cash in on the burgeoning market, positioning soon became a routine competitive activity. As a result, JVP was compelled to find innovative ways to stay ahead of the competition. Vikram was the first to moot the idea of using market research to probe television consumer behavior. JVP used market feedback to develop new models of Companion catering to various price segments. These models—the first to be focused on customer needs—became popular.

Vikram also organized a nationwide logistics network—a critical factor in the success of any home appliance in India. Having established an infrastructure that could ensure continuing market leadership for Companion, Vikram turned his attentions to training and developing JVP's field sales force. Competitors regularly adopted strategies that JVP had pioneered in positioning, pricing, segmenting, and technological improvements. It was in this context that Vikram had commissioned the study by CRI.

In the early 1980s, when the television market had not yet been developed fully, there were only three brands that could be truly called national. Another two brands were doing well but were confined to regional markets. Companion's early positioning was based on the generic nature of the product itself. Vikram realized that the product features emphasized by other brands were not doing well with consumers who were unable to see any benefits amid the technical jargon. He suggested that Companion position itself as the product that offers "life-like pictures." This simple approach made a tremendous impact on consumers. As the market and the number of competing brands grew, JVP shifted its position focus to a broad range of products. The positioning for these later models was on the "new experiences" they offered. As soon as competitors copy-catted with their own models, JVP's market shares would again decline.

At the time that Vikram commissioned the CRI study of the organized sector, JVP's black-and-white televisions had market shares of 40 percent in the metros and 60 percent in the rest of the market, while the corresponding market shares for its CTVs were 64 and 36 percent, respectively. The company sold five black-and-white models and eleven color models through some 1,800 dealer outlets, twelve of which were exclusive showrooms in large cities. Virtually every leading brand was now equally placed in terms of positioning, range of models, price, and after-sales service. Securing a differentiation in the marketplace was becoming a bigger challenge every year.

Vikram's brief to CRI was, "Why not investigate a new area, on how consumers felt after buying a brand—any brand—not just in terms of performance but also in terms of the satisfaction which results from selecting the brand?"

He felt that CRI's findings could provide clues to ways of achieving product differentiation in a highly cluttered market. While briefing Narasimhan, Vikram observed, "We need to work out a new marketing strategy. There seems to be no differentiation among competing brands today. We would like you to look at two things: the process of buying, and post-purchase behavior, examining associations with specific brands wherever possible." CRI decided to conduct two distinct studies. One would investigate the buying process with regard to black-and-white and CTVs without focusing on any particular brand. The other would probe the post-purchase feelings of consumers who had specifically chosen Companion products.

Vikram added the stipulation that the survey cover semi-urban areas as well. His objective was to differentiate between the urban and the semi-urban consumer—assuming that there was such a difference. While most companies, including JVP, had been concentrating on the consumer's pre-purchase behavior, Vikram thought there would be several advantages in understanding what the consumer felt after he had selected a brand.

The finished study covered three major metros and 300 other towns, in two phases. The first phase examined the buying behavior of consumers in both metros and semi-urban areas. The second focused on the post-purchase responses. The targets in both cases were two groups of consumers: the first earning between Rs 2,000 and Rs 6,000 ($57 and $171) a month, and the second between Rs 6,000 and Rs 15,000 ($171 and $428) a month. A crucial criterion for identifying respondents had been previous ownership of a refrigerator or a two-wheeler, since first-time buyers of a consumer durables often exhibit a typical behavior. The findings were as follows.

Phase One: Buying Behavior of Television Customers

Black-and-White Television Buyers in Metros:

- Most respondents had visited at least five showrooms to evaluate all available brands.

- They had spent more time on brands with high ad visibility, including Companion.

- Price had a significant impact.

- Consumers inquired at length about the after-sales service provided by a company.

- Most respondents chose a brand within 30 days of their initial visit to the showrooms.

- Nearly 90 percent of the respondents had not visited exclusive showrooms.

Black-and-White Television Buyers in Small Cities and Towns:

- Cities with metro-like life-styles—such as Pune and Coimbatore— exhibited metro-like buying behavior.

- Advertised brands were considered too expensive by buyers in other cities and towns.

- Lesser known brands were considered cheaper and adequate for the purpose.

- Consumers purchased assembled products from the unorganized sector at low prices.

- Buyers were unaware of formal after-sales services, relying on their dealers for repairs.

- Dealers' recommendations were crucial to brand selection, whether national or local.

- Some 70 percent bought their televisions from the dealers who had sold them their first durable.

- Some 75 percent bought their television from dealers who offered installment schemes.

CTV Buyers in Metros:

- Most buyers based their selection on word-of-mouth publicity from friends and relatives.

- About 65 percent had upgraded to CTV after a period of between two and five years.

- About 70 percent bought CTVs from the dealers who had sold them their black-and-white sets.

- About 45 percent of the consumers had availed themselves of installment schemes for their purchases.

- Only 10 percent had retained their black-and-white sets after buying their color sets.

- Only 25 percent had bought the same brand of CTV as their black-and-white set.

Television Buyers in Small Cities and Towns:

- Cities with metro-like life-styles—such as Pune and Coimbatore— exhibited metro-like buying behavior.

- About 35 percent of the buyers had upgraded to CTVs from black-and-white sets.

- Higher incomes were the primary motivation for 80 percent of the upgraders to switch to CTVs.

- About 80 percent of the consumers had availed themselves of installment schemes to buy their television sets.

- Dealers' recommendations and assurances were crucial in brand selection.

- Recommendations of color-television–owning neighbors also influenced brand selection.

- Nearly 70 percent had exchanged their black-and-white sets for color sets after paying the price differences.

- Some 40 percent of those who had traded in for CTVs had offered black-and-white sets from the unorganized sector.

Phase Two: Post-Purchase Behavior of Companion's Buyers

- About 35 percent of the consumers felt that their dealer had talked them into buying a model that they did not need. However, most of them agreed on the quality of performance.

- Between 60 and 65 percent of the consumers felt that the special system did not match the expectations generated by the advertisements.

- About 40 percent of the buyers felt that they should have chosen a different brand. However, they were unable to give specific and concrete reasons for this feeling.

- Only 15 percent of the buyers of the Companion television sets reported complete satisfaction with their choice of brand.

- About 25 percent of the buyers had experienced problems with the product and had developed a negative opinion about Companion in the process.

The post-purchase responses clearly did not augur well for Companion. Uniform across metros and smaller cities and towns, they revealed the brand's falling stock, which meant that the word-of-mouth publicity—so crucial to buying decisions—was no longer working to Companion's advantage. Vikram decided that he would have to address two specific issues: (a) formulating a strategy to capitalize on the buying behavior of television consumers, and (b) enhancing the brand image of Companion among those who had already bought the product.

Questions the overseas marketer might well want to compare with his or her own experience are:

- Was Vikram on the right track?

- Could JVP formulate an innovative marketing strategy in light of the findings of the report?

- Did the changing nature of the television market necessitate a completely different approach?

- How could JVP retain its cutting edge in a market that, although competitive, did not lend itself easily to product differentiation?

Strategies During Times of Slow Growth[2]

Someshwar Roy had not moved from his desk at the company's headquarters in Mumbai for the past three hours. He was engrossed in the reports submitted by each of the sixty ghost shoppers, an army of market researchers, let loose by Tarang a fortnight ago into textile showrooms in the southern city of Bangalore. Their brief: monitor the ready-made shirts counter, track whoever walks up to the counter, observe shopper behavior, and record everything of significance.

Operation Ghost Shopper was one of the exercises that Roy had deployed as part of an attempt to understand the dynamics of the ready-mades market. The exercise, which was confined to retail showrooms dealing exclusively with men's apparel—including shirts—had a major stimulus— Roy had been exploring the profitability of a new business segment: men's ready-mades. He had wanted to identify the potential customer, and find out his needs before examining related issues like investments, funding, and technology

Tarang Textiles, a strong player in the midprice segment of the shirtings and suitings fabrics market, was trying to strategize its way out of slow growth. With the fabrics market growing by only between 3 and 5 percent per year, Someshwar Roy, Tarang's sales and marketing director, was debating the merits of forward integration into branded shirts, where the growth rate was an inviting 25 percent per annum.

Tarang had been manufacturing and marketing fabrics for suitings and shirtings for over two decades, and had built up a reputation among dealers and consumers for its product quality. It had a share of 18 percent in the fabrics market for shirtings and suitings, recording a turnover of Rs 225 crore ($64.3 million) in 1995–1996: 63 percent of it from shirtings and 37 percent from suitings. The single largest contribution to sales—amounting to 20 percent—was from the institutional segment, comprising school and corporate uniforms. Tarang had maintained a middle-of-the-road approach in terms of market segmentation, with four brands each in suitings and shirtings slotted into different price bands.

Tarang also had a few subbrands, which were introduced four years ago under both of its product lines. However, these brands were used primarily for segregating and monitoring in-house operations like loading, packaging, and despatching rather than for marketing purposes. In fact, customers were not even aware of their existence since Tarang never advertised them. In any case, the general awareness of Tarang's different brands was far lower than for the company name: most customers simply asked for a Tarang fabric in a particular price range rather than asking for specific brands.

As the textiles market became more and more competitive in the early 1990s, Tarang had found it necessary—as part of its survival strategy—to restructure its business operations. The exercise, which began in mid-1991, had changed the sales and marketing functions in three ways: by inducing professionals at various levels, by forming brand management teams with cross-functional inputs, and by commissioning market research studies to gauge consumer preferences. In fact, one of Roy's first tasks on joining Tarang four years ago had been to appoint the market research agency, Profile, to provide support to the company's marketing activities. As the first few reports from the focus groups organized by Profile started coming in, Roy had begun to examine the various options for expansion and diversification.

It was within six months of his arrival at Tarang that Roy had mooted the idea, at one of the executive committee meetings, that the branded ready-made shirts market deserved a critical look. "There are two reasons why we should examine it seriously," he had said. "First, this market is valued at Rs 800 crore ($228 million) today, and even a marginal share of 5 percent will boost our turnover by about 20 percent every year. Second, it has considerable potential. The ready-mades segment has been growing at the rate of 25 percent per annum for the last three years versus the rate of between 3 and 5 percent in the case of fabrics. Surely, it will be worthwhile entering this segment."

The idea had appealed to vice-chairman and managing director Suresh Sampath, who enthusiastically agreed that it was a growth area. But he was also somewhat skeptical: "The men's apparel market is very strongly brand-driven worldwide, and I'm not sure if it is any different here," he had said. "While we could certainly check out the option, I think we should also be looking at ways of developing Tarang as a brand and giving it a brand personality. Once we do that, it would make our entry into ready-mades much easier."

That was the cue for Profile to conduct a series of studies over the next year throughout the country, aimed at arriving at a profile of the existing customer for Tarang's fabrics. Two distinctive segments became evident: the "climbers" and the "settlers."

The "climbers" segment consisted of people between 25 and 35 years old, earning about Rs 5,000 ($142.85) per month, with an average family size of five. Typically, they were executives in small- and medium-scale companies, who had put in between 4 and 12 years in nonexecutive positions, usually in the same company. Most of them had bought durables like two-wheelers and television sets only in the last four years. Their hobbies included reading magazines—mostly regional—and watching films on television. This class of consumers was concentrated in cities and towns in south and west India—where Tarang had a strong presence, contributing about 40 and 23 percent, respectively, to its turnover.

About 40 percent of this segment were regular buyers of Tarang suitings and shirtings, while another 22 percent had bought the brand at least twice. Both categories had ranked Tarang highly in terms of durability, price, and crease-resistance, in that order. They felt that their search effort in the showroom was minimized because they were able to find a brand of their choice which satisfied them on the attributes that they were looking for in a fabric.

A life-style analysis of the segment obtained through a different questionnaire indicated that they were ambitious and aspirational by nature. Hard work, perseverance, and a drive toward materialism were the significant values associated with them. Paradoxically, symbolism—identification with brands that had an aura of prestige—ranked low, although they were by no means too old for the current consumer boom. This was an unusual finding in a situation where brands in virtually every product category—especially textiles—were using life-style appeals to create differentiation.

The "settlers" segment had consumers in the age group between 33 and 45 years—there was a slight overlap with the "climbers" in terms of age—and earning between Rs 4,000 and Rs 8,000 per month ($114–$228). The average size of families in the segment was the same as for "climbers" (five), and they were employed generally in mid-range companies in both the manufacturing and the services sectors, with 60 percent working for banks or public-sector companies. Children's education and savings for a retired life were found to be the priority areas in their mindset. Shopping with the family was the only activity identified as a hobby.

An interesting finding was that there was a strong base of respondents who bought Tarang suitings, but had only occasionally tried Tarang shirtings. Most of them switched shirting brands regularly. A majority of these respondents were found in cities and towns in south India. Tarang was ranked high in this segment on price, durability, and easy availability in terms of proximity to homes. When probed about their loyalty to Tarang's suitings brands, buyers in the segment cited nonavailability of other brands as the reason for choosing Tarang. These consumers were also apprehensive about buying from retail shops that dealt with a spectrum of unknown brands.

Could these buyers be the core target for Tarang's ready-made shirts? To find out, Roy followed up the Profile studies by mapping the branded shirts market. As he discovered, pricing appeared to start from the Rs 250 ($7.14) level for casual-wear, going beyond Rs 1,000 ($28.57) for formal shirts from brands with global reputations. The three premium brands were from the same company and accounted for a 40 percent share of the market, while none of those lower down the line had a market share of over 10 percent each. In addition, the market was marked by the presence of boutique brands priced in the middle of the market range.

Almost all of the middle and premium brands used life-style and imagery approaches to create niches in the minds of consumers. All of them operated through exclusive retail outlets, which ranged between twelve and twenty-five in number for each of the brands in about seven cities. In contrast, the popular end of the ready-made shirts market had just two major brands: Prize, a national brand, and Rans, a regional brand well entrenched in southern cities.

Both brands were positioned on the economy price platform, making considerable impact on middle-class consumers. Research showed that these brands—like Tarang—lacked a distinctive personality. Prize did not have a single exclusive showroom and was distributed through the retail chain of a large textiles company active in the fabrics market. Although it was a national brand, its retail outlets were dense in north and west India, where 65 percent of its turnover came from. Rans, on the other hand, had exclusive showrooms in only four major cities in south India, and was clearly a regional brand.

Roy's thought turned to his company's strong points. If Tarang did decide to enter the branded shirts market, what were the strengths that it could leverage? Its forte was the retail distribution chain it had built over a long period of time. Tarang had 530 exclusive retail outlets across 248 towns, with south and west India accounting for about 65 percent of them. Apart from exclusive outlets—some of which were franchised—there were other outlets in these regions that retailed Tarang's brands along with other brands. Although the turnover from them was not very significant, awareness of Tarang had been enhanced because of their presence.

Roy recalled an earlier study by Profile which had revealed that the price segment between Rs 225 and Rs 475 offered immense potential in terms of volumes of about 10 million shirts per annum. Roy knew that if he could somehow get the middle-class consumers to connect with the emotional overtones of his brand, history could be created. Roy wondered if a brand personality could be created for Tarang in ready-mades that would take into consideration the target segments and the company's image.

Roy was also struck by the commonalty underlying some of the statements in the reports from the ghost shoppers. A typical comment in each report: "A consumer in his late 20s apparently, upwardly mobile, approached the counter for ready-made shirts. He seemed confident and self-assured. He spent over 15 minutes looking through the collection, analyzing the texture, observing the fall, and concentrating on several shades of grey." Roy was not sure if there were hidden clues somewhere in these reports, and whether any of them would lead him to solutions to the crucial questions: Should Tarang enter men's ready-mades? If so, what should be the platform on which it should be launched? Should Tarang stick to the downmarket segment with which it was familiar, where its fabrics already enjoyed some kind of equity, even at the risk of cannibalizing its fabrics sales? Or should it take a crack at the upmarket segment, in which it had little experience and where it would have to face competition head-on? What personality would suit Tarang's brands? Was Tarang really ready for ready-mades?

High-Tech Entrepreneurialism

Shiv Nadar's success in making HCL India's leading manufacturer of computers and office equipment is an archetype of opportunity being turned into reality in India. Revenues in the privately held company have gone from just $500,000 in 1975, when the company was founded, to $500 million in the fiscal year that ended March 31, 1996.

Nadar, 50, is a good example of today's high-tech entrepreneurialism that adapts deftly to India's changing economic and technological climates. He moved to Delhi from his native Tamil Nadu in 1968 to work as an electrical engineer for conglomerate DCM Ltd. He really wanted to run his own business, so he persuaded six DCM colleagues to join him in launching a company that makes office products such as copiers.

He also wanted to make computers. At the time, imports of computer hardware were restricted except for certain components. Domestic demand was growing, but supply was limited. Supply tightened further in 1978, when Indira Gandhi forced IBM out of India using an equity law. HCL stepped into the vacuum. It took another four years to develop the technology, but by 1982 HCL had its first computer. Today, some 77 percent of HCL Corp.'s revenues are from computers and software. Office automation accounts for just 14 percent, and the rest comes from the National Institute of Information Technology, HCL's nationwide chain of 150 computer training centers.

HCL developed quickly when the domestic computer industry was protected. When the government began deregulating the economy, Nadar's response was to team up with the competition. He formed a joint venture with Hewlett-Packard. Within a year, HCL-HP was listed in Mumbai. Today, it is the largest maker of information technology products in India.

 While concentrating on growth at home, HCL also has been spreading its reach overseas. Its Singapore subsidiary, Far East Computers, recently achieved a breakthrough in imaging technology, which, among other applications, enables computers to read handwritten tax returns. Singapore's Internal Revenue Service now uses Far East's software.

In the United States, a software subsidiary, HCL America, has reaped rich benefits by taking advantage of global time zones. Every morning, the company's Chennai office receives software assignments from the United States, just after work stops there for the night. A team of Indian engineers, with salaries much lower than those of their American counterparts, complete the jobs and modem them back in the evening. Far East and HCL America account for almost 20 percent of HCL's annual revenues.

The availability of inexpensive software specialists in India is one reason why Nadar wants to concentrate more on software than hardware. HCL is moving quickly into licensing databases, making money off royalties so that profitability rises despite low investment. HCL also avoids going head-to-head with other strong Indian hardware manufacturers such as Wipro, which has links with Apple.

In March 1996, HCL tied up with General Instruments in the United States to devise products for India's burgeoning cable television sector. There is a very large potential market in products that link computer software to cable television—more Indians have access to cable televisions than to telephones.

The concept is to use technology to create a demand where none exists. "Whenever we speak of new ideas, we are looking at what we think is a gap," says Nadar. Once he makes up his mind about a project, he picks a team and then leaves it alone to get on with the job. To motivate managers, he offers a financial stake in the venture. "It is good for people to convert blueprints into results," he says. "This is the freedom my company gives." His attitude is to sustain internally the entrepreneurship that has carried HCL so far so fast.

Technology and the Traditional Sari

India's sari market is about the last place one would expect innovative technology to alter earning power, market trends, and taste. The sari has long been among the most lush, time-consuming, and tradition-bound garments in the world. Now the bastions of India's most traditional garments have been bitten by the designer bug.

Being hand-loomed, however, limited the number that could be produced. All that is being changed by the power loom, the prime innovator in India's shift toward mass fashion based on traditional garments.

Aside from its technical improvements, the chief impact of the power loom has been that it can double turnover. Where the hand-loom weaver earns a meager Rs 150 to Rs 600 ($4.28–$17.63) a week, a weaver working on the latest power loom can reach between Rs 1,000 and Rs 1,500 ($28.57–$42.85). Where an intricate hand-loomed wedding sari can take a month, a Mysore crepe replica can be done in a day.

The roots of this technology began in the early part of the century, when the first Mysore crepe rustled out of the power looms of Mysore state. The looming technique originated nearly two centuries ago in France, when a weaving technician named Jacquard invented a way to program power looms so that they would weave nongeometric designs into fabric. The result was the addition of an exotic palette of florals, images, and fantasy shapes into cloth that then could be cut and tailored like any other cloth.

In the decades since this method was translated in Mysore crepe, Indian women have been dazzled by saris made of this light fabric. Now the past five years have seen the evolution of the power loom, which boosts the speed without detracting from the quality (although some disagree vehemently with this). Boosted by the 1995 reduction in import duty from 85 to 40 percent, the Karnataka government encouraged smaller units with investment and regulatory perks. Today, a Karnatakan who owns fewer than eight looms is exempted from all of the conditions laid down in the Factories Act. Weavers lost little time translating their looms' speed into the freedom to innovate.

The Karnataka State Industries Corporation (KSIC) stuck to typical Mysore crepe until 1995, when it relented and brought out its "Hoysala" range of sari designs inspired by the temples at Hoysala. The response was tremendous. The Hoysala range became KSIC's most sought-after products. KSIC's sales zoomed to Rs 27 crore ($7.7 million) in 1995–1996, a 25 percent increase over the year before.

Design innovations aside, the core revolution in power-loom technology is price. The original Mysore crepe used pure silk. By switching to tested silk (blends of silk with other fibers), prices dropped by 30 percent. The simplest Mysore crepe using real silk now sells for Rs 3,000 ($85); a much more elaborate designer version with tested-silk motifs sells for the same amount. At the lower end, a good-quality sari is Rs 2,000 ($57), and the maximum price rarely exceeds Rs 6,000 ($171).

The biggest change resulting from power-loom technology is social: The designer sari is no longer the preserve of the elite. The new power-loom sari also introduced a number of value additions—crease-resistant finish, water-resistant surface, perfect drape. The result is a garment that can be worn all day long without compromising on elegance or convenience. This is a sari ideal for today's much more active urban women just as those women are becoming more active.

Alayn Soap Bars: How India's Ad Market Works [3]

After riding the crest of the premium-category non-soapy detergent (NSD) bar market for a year, sales of Zenter India's Alayn brand were beginning to slump. This surprised Rudra Vasisht, account planning director at Lee Gram, Zenter's ad agency.

Alayn had a very good chance in the Indian wash-products market, cluttered though it was with NSD bars that claimed to clean whiter, be gentler on the hands, or remove even the most stubborn stains. Alayn's ad focus was that it was good for every kind of wash. Positioned as a premium bar and offering value for money, it straddled both the premium NSD bar and popular laundry soap segments.

In India, the use of detergent bars is the consumer's first step up from laundry soaps to detergent powders. The shake-out during the shift from bars to powders in the market revealed that the main demand for detergents was in low-priced powders. However, when wash results were not up to the mark compared with higher priced formulations, conversion slowed. Zenter's counter-tactic was to take the consumer a brief step backward to the scrub wash with a better NSD bar that provided a quality wash.

Premium NSD bars in general melt in water. *Dhobis* [the washerwomen caste] were not allowed to use them, since dhobis tend to leave the bar in water when not scrubbing. However, Alayn was formulated to last longer. Moreover, it could be used for all kinds of fabrics, from highly soiled linen to delicate synthetics. Alayn's advertising focused on this versatility.

So why did Alayn's sales plateau? It had been a proven success for 20 years in Indonesia, where washing habits are much the same as in India, and now dominated the market there. Alayn's Indonesian marketing and advertising mix had remained virtually unchanged for 20 years. When the brand was extended into other markets, Zenter Worldwide had insisted that the marketing and advertising mix remain unchanged, reasoning that it was the reason behind the brand's success. Every new market Zenter Worldwide entered—Nepal, Pakistan, Bangladesh, and Sri Lanka—tended to reinforce their assumption.

Alayn was launched in India with a test market in the tough Western Region consumer market. Sales were so encouraging that Zenter India soon went national. Within a year, it had seized a big chunk of the market.

Lee Gram had dutifully replicated their client's proven formula, "Alayn, the long-lasting detergent bar for all kinds of clothes." The idea was to show Alayn as a diverse wash product that was fit for every use.

In retrospect, the industry attributed Alayn's swift success to the high trial rate of new products in the premium category. Since trial risk in this category is low ("it's only a soap bar, so why not?"), industry wisdom had it that Alayn's initial volumes were deceptive. A more insightful argument was that, amid the evolution and growth of the wash-products market, consumers were beginning to choose different wash products for different washing needs. Hence, Alayn as an "all-purpose bar" was bound to plateau.

Rudra Vasisht, Lee Gram's account planning director, dismissed these as standard theories used to explain any brand's slipping performance. He felt that there was a clear niche for Alayn in the Indian market. There was little doubt from past history in the market that initial trial rates would be deceptively high, but he felt that Zenter was not myopic in its overall market forecasts.

Vasisht wondered if the problem could be Alayn's advertising, especially the message on the artpulls pinned on his brand chart—*The quality bar that does not melt.* "Is this copy communicating?" he asked himself. "Is the consumer hearing what the copy is trying to convey?"

He decided that the ad was not motivating enough. For one, it did not hint at any value addition. The television ads were based on a maid washing under a tap on the floor and a housewife washing clothes in the sink. Many scrubs later, the Brand X wash quality was far from good and the bar had turned soggy. Then an Alayn bar was thrown in, which the skeptical maid and housewife at first used with suspicion ... and presto! The clothes were washed clean, their hands were soft, and the bar was as firm as new.

Nice, thought Vasisht, but what's new about that? Consumers probably reacted with, "You have said this before." The fatigue factor in a commercial like that was likely to be high, he felt. It was one thing to portray a scenario that the consumer identified with, but how many people would actually enjoy seeing the maid, the housewife, and their soggy bar every day—and on every channel? Besides, replace the Alayn bar with any other and the ads would be any other detergent bar commercial. Hence, what was Alayn saying that others had not said?

Vasisht knew that it would not be possible to review the brand's ad strategy. Like his counterparts elsewhere in Alayn's ad agencies, he was bound to the documented success of Zenter Worldwide's emphatic dictum that the international strategy for the brand should be replicated in every market.

Zenter Worldwide's contention was that, since the advertising had helped position the brand successfully for 20 years in Third World countries, why should it not work in other developing markets? If everything else in the mix worked, why not the advertising?

"It's possible that the proposition works for some countries but not for others," commented Tara Durrani, Lee Gram's associate director. Vasisht could not fault her observation, but he also realized that when it came to international recipes, local agencies did not usually question them.

Vasisht wanted to know what Zenter's assessment of the bar's performance was. "Alayn is chugging along," said the company's marketing manager, "but it is not measuring up to the norms that Zenter would put down for a successful brand." This meant that Alayn's performance had become disappointing. Zenter had also felt that India was a price-sensitive market. Alayn was generating high trial rates that, when discounted, were selling in high volumes. When a Rs 2 discount (13.3 percent) was offered, volume went up. "Clearly there is a pricing issue," the marketing manager said.

Not long after that, Vasisht received a call from Ernest Wood, the regional head of Lee Gram in Singapore. "We have been watching the

Alayn brand closely, and its performance in the central Asian countries has been causing us concern. Is this happening in India?" he said. "Have you tested the efficacy of your advertising?"

Lee Gram India had created the advertising based entirely on the Indonesian prescription. Vasisht replied, "The advertising is communicating, but I am not sure whether it is persuading. The Indian people comprehend the message, but they are not being convinced."

Part of Alayn's problem, he felt, was India's household products consumer dynamics. A premium bar at Rs 15 (43 cents), even if twice the size of an ordinary bar, was likely to be bought only by housewives whose household budgets were flexible or who could buy in discount stores or at discount volume. But in India's myriad of small metros and towns, housewives usually purchase bars as the need arises. That pattern did not allow for a full-price Rs 15 bar. Such a housewife needed more than the rational appeal of quality. She needed an emotional entreaty.

Shortly thereafter, Vasisht was pleasantly surprised to receive a fax from Zenter Worldwide's regional coordinator: "We have examined the issues surrounding Alayn's performance in India. I feel it is necessary to review the advertising. The only point of caution is, please ensure that we do not get away from the core brand value that has been defined for Alayn."

Vasisht called in the client servicing team working on the Alayn account. "The housewife-maid scenario can be set aside," he said. "We have more maneuvering room with the 'quality bar that does not melt'. However, expressing it must be motivating to the consumer. Therefore, peel the brand layer by layer and look at its elements. We will then rebuild element by element a brand called Alayn whose name and core value are all that are given."

Hence, what was unique about Alayn? It was a detergent bar that did not easily melt in water. It lay in water during the entire washing yet did not become soggy. It was a quality bar, tender on the hands and kind on the clothes, but tough on stains and grime. Plus, it lathered well. In short, it was a great detergent bar for a consumer who, in the haste to convert from strenuous scrubbing to powdered detergents, had overlooked the quality of the wash.

Having peeled the brand, the Lee Gram team examined its architecture to see what drove the brand. "We know and understand the core value," said Vasisht. "We need to now try and articulate the relationship of that core value with the expectation of the customer. That's what brands are built on: relationships between customer and brand. They relate to the core value of the brand. It's all in the subconscious," said Vasisht. "For instance, if you asked somebody, 'why do you like Philips?', he might not be able to answer that offhand. But in his subconscious he associates Philips with integrity. In the same way, articulate Alayn's core idea and you will be able to churn out 50 commercials based on that core value."

"Emotional layering is what makes a brand," Vasisht told the ad team. "Therefore, articulate the brand relationship and discriminate it from the rational reasons for the brand's preference. People do like Alayn: that's real. No amount of advertising can sell a bad product. It can trigger trials, but it can not ensure repeat purchases."

At this point, Vasisht felt that a dip-stick study of consumers could assess the feelings that the brand evoked. "Go only to people who are brand loyalists," he advised his team. "The loyalists are the ones who give you the right answers. We do not need research; we need an audit of the feelings the brand evokes."

The research team also needed to check audience response to the ads. Did they evoke curiosity, did they bore, or did they leave the viewer indifferent? "Check the intended communication," Vasisht ordered. "What does the brand 'seem' to say to them? Is that what they want to hear about it? Is this ad saying things that are important, relevant to them? If so, how credible are these statements?"

The consumer audit revealed responses like, "Yes, it is a nice bar," "It does not dissolve easily", "It is good value for the money," "Good bar, lathers well, smells good", "so convenient." These indicated consumers were responding most favorably to the values of quality and convenience.

Vasisht reasoned, "Now that we have peeled the brand, let us take the symbolisms out, the housewife and the maid, the soggy bar. Let's go into the washing culture."

Vasisht is of the view that brands must remain contemporary. To ensure that the expression of the core value was in line with changing times and role models, the brand had to be re-engineered from time to time. "The core value does not change, but the manifestation of that value should change," he believes. "Change the manifestation, change the expression and the articulation of the core value. Do you want to express the core value through clichéed symbols of soggy soaps and chapped hands? We need to give it a more modern face. Therefore, let's get into the washing culture. For instance, what is on a maid's mind when she is washing? What makes her forget the bar in water? Or the housewife. What are her preoccupations?"

"So where is the bar in all this?" asked another team person.

"Under the tap, probably melting away," replied another.

"Alayn does not melt away like any other bar. It lasts longer!" Vasisht concluded. "There's your visual expression."

Once the brand audit was done, Vasisht took the team through the next stage. "What are the things about the brand that you want to carry forward; what are the things that you want to drop—things that are dragging the brand down? Surround the brand with modern symbols and rituals, and perhaps more modern and contemporary situations. What new situations can we position so that there is a clear expression of Alayn's long-lasting quality. We need to create a culture model that can unravel Alayn's external manifestations, to get across its core value."

Hence the problem boiled down to how to personify "long-lasting quality." A bar that did not melt or get soggy was too simplistic. There were plenty of advertisements that showed a forefinger scraping undissolved detergent from a bar's surface. Every sketch the team showed Vasisht evoked the same question—"Where is the emotional layer? We know our bar does not melt in water. We know it washes well. We know it is versatile. We know it lasts longer. Indians are more likely to buy a brand if they like its advertisements, but mere likability is not enough. The consumer must be able to relate to it," he recalled.

The story boards produced by the creative team captured the idea. One shows a housewife washing a party dress in a wash basin when the telephone rings. She quickly wipes her hands dry and rushes to the call. A few minutes later, the line disconnects and she returns to the wash basin. At first glance, the bar lying under the running water alarms her. Then she checks the surface of the soap for sogginess, but turns over a clean finger to the camera. The voice-over says, "Thank God, some things last!"

The second shows a housemaid humming a tune as she scrubs and hammers the clothes (beating clothes is common in Asia) while the water flows freely. Then she hears the signature tune of her favorite soap serial wafting from the drawing room. She leaps up, wipes her hands dry on her sari (i.e., the maid at a middle-class home) and rushes to the television, forgetting the bar in the water. The power fails and she returns to her chore looking disappointed while the voice-over in the lady of the house's voice admonishes, *Leelabai, sabun!'* (*sabun* is a generic word for "soap bar" over much of Asia). The maid (Leelabai) smiles as she checks the bar for sogginess. Turning over a clean finger, she says, "Thank God, some things last!"

Vasisht had thus crafted a format that identified and built brand value based on his particular brand's generic composition. No more should his brand communication be distanced from the advertiser's strategic tools. His brand-specific format for Alayn also included Zenter's integrated marketing, "what I call relationship marketing," he observes. "This method of extracting core value from a brand will help us forge consumer-brand links."

His second commercial aired and was rated highest in a consumer viewership poll; it later went on to win a Best Creative award. Zenter International so liked it that they modified it slightly by replacing the maid with the housewife's mother; they then used it for their international market. "For a communication to be effective, it must reach into the brand's architecture. We went into the essential architecture of the brand, examined its personality, and articulated a communication that expressed likability. Likability is the best predictor of sales effectiveness."

NOTES

1. The following was edited from a study published in *Business Today*, 1996. It was prepared by S. Ramesh Kumar, assistant professor of marketing, Indian Institute of Management, Bangalore, and is reprinted with the kind permission of *Business Today*.

2. This case study was written by S. Ramesh Kumar, professor of marketing, Indian Institute of Management, Bangalore, and appeared in *Business Today* 9/22–10/6, 1996, pp. 138–140.

3. Condensation of a case analysis that appeared in *Business World*, 29 May–11 June, 1996.

4

Marketing and Advertising

MEET YOUR NEW MARKET

Raj and Mati are in their early thirties. Both have careers. His is in software design and medium technology manufacturing. Hers is in advertising, client services, and marketing. When they got married, there were no marriage brokers, no astrologers, no dowry. They were simply two young, energetic Indians making their own kind of Indian life. Today they do not think of themselves as unusual, although the life they lead runs very much counter to the world's idea of "Indian."

They live with their child in a modest apartment. There are no relatives in residence, no live-in servants, and no *puja* shrine packed top to bottom with a myriad of deities and reeking of incense and moldy oranges. Like the majority of middle-class Indians, they live comfortably on under $500 a month (a good salary in India). They are not rich, and they do not really want to be. Many Americans, Europeans, and East Asians would feel quite at home with them.

Raj and Mati entertain friends and business contacts at home—very different from the older tradition of dramatically separating family from the world. A nice dinner with a good bottle of wine (or beer, if it is a wine-killing curry) and an evening of worldly aware conversation that touches on business subjects, films, the latest in-things to buy, cricket, soccer, and casual wear from California.

"We furnished our house from the bare walls," Raj will tell you. "We chose our own furniture, beds, the dining room table, the fridge. We started with a second-hand black and white TV, then we got a color TV. Now we have a VCR. We save to get what we want. Our first car was an old Fiat. We got the Maruti in 1989."

Raj and Mati are in professions where there is a need for their talent. At the top of their careers they can get a salary of about $20,000 a year. "In rupees that's a lot," Mati adds. "We and our friends don't want the average extended Indian family. We love what's fashionable and most people our parents' age don't."

What is fashionable includes American (and some French) slang, voting, makeup, jewelry, sexy movies, higher education, imported ice cream, women managing their own incomes, smoking, drinking, and wild colors. They are worldly, practical, neither idealistic nor cynical, and ready for anything. Mati wears a sari only when she has to meet clients or when one of their mothers is coming. The rest of the time she "goes Western."

Raj and Mati are charter members of a new class in India. They are a true class—greater than a caste but not quite a *varna*. Nearly all of India's 3,000–odd traditional castes are tied to occupation and birth status, and Raj and Mati are almost defiantly beholden to neither. *Varnas*, or paleo-castes, are the most ancient social hierarchy in the subcontinent, introduced some 3,500 years ago to classify humanity into the hierarchy of priest-teacher, warrior-aristocrat, provisioner, and laborer.

Raj and Mati's peers are software entrepreneurs in Bangalore, the architect in Calcutta working with urban rehabilitation, the public relations executive in Mumbai whose wardrobe is 90 percent Western, the stock analyst with a nonstop social life, the lecturer in Madras who takes the bus to save for a foreign vacation. Few of them identify with the politics of New Delhi. Instead, their role models are who and what they see on satellite television, all 500 channels of it, none of them carrying the syrupy Hindi movies that Doordarshan—India's network television—airs.

Raj and Mati live in Bangalore, Pune, or Goa, in suburban townhouses and condos popping up in clusters around India's urban cores like architectural mushrooms around a moldering stump. Cities are, by Raj and Mati's understanding, India's future. Cities have become, like Los Angeles in the 1970s, the fountainhead of a mix of new attitudes and subcultures, drawing people from all over to work in new-wave industrial research or anything to do with "marketing." These suburbs have the most modern shops, thriving cafes, a pub culture, satellite dishes, hoardings (billboards) proclaiming financial opportunity, and high interest rates.

Raj and Mati are real people. They are also ad identities—demographic profiles used to designate the new-generation middle class with a penchant for pioneer purchasing. "Raj" is short for "Raja" or "King," which is the word the lovestruck girls sing so often in the Hindi love songs. "Mati" is short for "Srimati India," India's ad-world generic name for a housewife. Raj and Mati are among fifteen to twenty demographic profiles that define the presently very fluid vocabulary of Indian marketing terms.

Middle class too, but in a very different way, is the Karnataka, Orissa, or Uttar Pradesh farmer who sleeps on his *charpoi* bed of woven twine but has a new tractor parked under the tin roof that used to house his goats. The goats, accommodatingly enough, find that sleeping under the tractor is no worse than sleeping under the roof.

This is the unseen, rural middle class, slowly growing affluence-conscious behind the veil of dust and sun that shimmer over the vastness of India's rural plains. The Maruti is only a dream, but the wife has a "mixie" or electric blender, and here—right here in this ad—Kelvinator and Electrolux have brought their refrigerators down to almost the same prices as washers and, what's more, offer interest-free credit payments (interest-free, that is, until you add up the total number you have to make).

This is the "Mixie Class," part of an Indian phenomenon of gigantic size and gigantic change. There are said to be 100 million Maruti Class Indians who qualify as upper middle class, plus another 200 million in the Mixie Class who qualify as low-budget yuppies if the definition of "middle class" is expanded to include the ability to buy an electric fan, a bicycle, or a small television set. In India, these two classes are a mere quarter of the population. But to international marketers they are a two-tier buying bloc that is twice the size of Japan's entire population and nearly that of the United States.

Dazzling but Delusory

Multinationals are dazzled by India's middle classes. Politicians and religious leaders court them. Old-time Indian nationalists deplore them. Marketers are scratching their heads trying to figure out how to define demographics out of them. Foreign companies and investors want to tap the market they are.

The Maruti and Mixie Class are cheerfully material and Western in their material outlooks, but not necessarily in their social outlooks. The rumpled Gandhian asceticism and crisply ironed white *dhoti* are for the pretentious politicians and British film makers. They love domesticities—hair dryers, pressure cookers, microwaves. They also give their treasured possessions cutesy nicknames like the ones dowagers give pampered pets: the "mixies" we already know about, but a refrigerator is a "fridgie." So far, they do not have a nickname for clothes washers, but "the washie" is probably not far from the lexicon of daily life.

But marketers know that this middle class is conservative at heart—they are the largest purchasers of ethnic art and artifacts, and largely keep alive the historical craftsmanship of India's traditional weavers, potters, jewelry makers, and folk artists. Nothing is more welcoming to the middle class than homes filled with dhurries, pillows, giant ceramic pots, and sculptures of Indian gods. They are often part of the silent political support system of the Hindu nationalist BJP party—an incongruity given their liberalism in material matters. As much as they adore the playthings of Western culture (not to mention the salaries), they realize that India is a unique, ancient, and very valuable culture, and they are not about to see it thrown to the marketing wolves of Coca-Cola and KFC.

In short, Raj and Mati are Western in ways but Indian in spirit. To visitors reading the icon publications of this culture—*India Today* and *Business India*—it is easy to identify India's middle class with the values of the movers and shakers of Delhi or Bombay, who are so beloved of the glossy ads and long-winded interviews.

However, being "wheaten-skinned" and Rolexed, Diored, and Guccied to the teeth is not the middle-class Raj and Mati way. The luxury BMW life is for the nouveau riche, the *arrivistes*, the politically connected, or those awash in dubious income. It is these who, by Raj and Mati's estimation, are the worst aberration of India; they are even more extravagant in drawing attention to themselves than the gurus with the fulgent beards or Afro hairdos who cater to the directionless dowagers from the West. In India the potted-plant, marble swimming pool, colonnaded home, gilded overstuffed furniture life is called Louis Farouk, Bengali Banal, or Delhi Decadent. Vast wealth reminds middle-class Indians of the dictum that in India today it is impossible to get rich honestly. Raj and Mati prefer modest innovation—that curious blend again of the conservative and the liberal.

Rural middle-class Indians are more traditional. They are cut from very different cloth than the urban bourgeoisie. Many have enjoyed a meteoric rise through the Green Revolution in agriculture. Others long ago acquired their status and now preserve it by money lending at up to 40 percent a month to farmers in need of seed crop or bridge loans to cover the time between planting and harvest. They love their houses brimming with ultra-budget consumer goods, soaps, cleansers, cookies and snacks. They hate change. They are also likely, through their rapacious dowry demands, to fuel a long-lasting demand for middle-priced, middle-quality, middle-of-the-image consumer durables.

Resentment against the urban middle class runs high in many rural communities. Locals say that city dwellers consume too large a share of government revenues, natural resources, and energy, while the country's food producers are neglected. Rural electricity is available for only a few hours each night, but air conditioners hum around the clock in cities. The farmers also see the markups in the prices of their produce in city markets and wonder why those big profit margins should go to someone else. To this they unwittingly make their own contribution by paying no taxes on agricultural income, enjoying subsidies in both buying supplies and selling goods, and withholding supplies from government procurement centers and the bazaars until the price is high. Except in the matter of their wives' traditional saris (which they would not dare to think of ever discarding), they dislike strong colors.

These are the two major middle classes. There are others—smaller, often stratified along religious lines; for example, the entrepreneurial Gujaratis, the money-managing Chettiars of the south, and the Jains and their unostentatious, quiet accumulation of wealth.

India did not have to create its middle classes. Under British administration, a corps of Indian civil servants kept the offices of the empire running. There were mercantile *babus* (traders) who amassed fortunes and acquired status dealing with imperial Britain and other Western nations. There were powerful indigenous industrial families who played important parts in economic, social, and political development for the greater part of a century before Independence in 1947. Long before Mahatma Gandhi, India's manufacturing dynasties had already established the strong capitalist base that is the origination point of any middle class—and the political vituperation of those who do not make it there.

The *babus* and industrialists, administrative and political services are the modern avatar of the early *ksatriya*, or warrior caste, of the original caste system. They are not the Brahmins or men of religion who were at the top, but the aristocrats whose original creator-of-the-wealth role switched from wealth transfer by territorial conquest to wealth transfer by industrial conquest.

Today, India's new middle classes are challenging the class and caste structure of all of old India, but especially that of the industrialist class. They are convinced that technology, small businesses, and medium-scale manufacturing are the key to a quicker ascent up Asia's value-adding ladder. They want travel abroad made easier so that they can learn these things from Malaysians, Singaporeans, and Thais (who heavily court tourists in India's upmarket media). They want the right to hold international credit cards. They want more business class seats on domestic flights and the income to afford better hotels when traveling.

Modern India is changing. It is not just a country of the Taj Mahal, the beggars, and the cows; development in India by looking at what and how much people are purchasing, not the charm of their local sights. Selling by brand name on television, billboards, or in glossy magazines began with soaps and toiletries; proceeded to basic foods; branched into motorbikes , household appliances, decorator bathroom fixtures, and fashionable clothes; and now has introduced patently Western soft drinks, snack foods, alcohol, and tobacco.

Jawaharlal Nehru would be appalled—especially if he knew how much more attractive these things are than the idealistic socialism he thought was the surest way to perpetuate Indian civilization. Whatever India's economic future, the new ways in which its urban middle classes perceive and use economy and the media are altering politics invisibly and with finality. The Congress party's 1996 electoral humiliation was caused by all of those television images of local pols building palaces for their relatives with the money that was supposed to be used for bridge repairs and roads. Multiply that by a thousand similar stories—which is what television election coverage did—and you have a sea of new faces in office with a corresponding change in ideas. In percentage terms, middle-class India is not large—less than one-quarter of the country. However, combined with media skills that are unavailable outside their sector, Raj and Mati have— and know they have—the ability to alter the older political linkages that are based on caste, region, and religion.

Raj and Mati are nearing critical mass with their very different sets of values. They rely on images, mediagenicity, substance, new ideas, realism, and unsentimental truth mixed with reverence for the meaningful. India's political elders are seen as feudal materialists who have neither a sense of justice nor a true belief in the old cultures. Raj and Mati sum up India's politicians in a quip: yesterday all over again.

All of this has fairly momentous international implications. Earlier generations—intellectuals for the most part—saw all problems in East-West or North-South terms. They failed to notice that the most powerful and effective movements for the environment, human rights, and feminism were growing in the industrialized nations as an inevitable part of their evolution, and not as yet another vehicle to oppress the masses. To this day, India's socialist intelligentsia is dumbfounded by the Western notion that culture can proceed from things other than labor and product. They do not know what to make of the information economy and value-added ladder. Still swathed in its old merits and scorning those that are new, the old way of India is a speck of dust hovering in the air as a great migration now masses and begins to move beneath it.

CULTURE AND CUSTOMS

The Social Effects of Indian Child Rearing

However, the old way is still very much there. India is a very conservative culture, and nowhere is this more evident than at the taproot level of a people: how they cook and how they raise their children.

Family and caste are at the core of Indian society. Yet the family is not a particularly loving social unit. Marriages from time immemorial have been arranged and are based on family convenience, not individual feelings. Witnessing a dowry negotiation is one of the most ghastly materialistic experiences a visitor can have in the country. Sometimes the couple does come to love, but most often there is a living legacy of frustration, bitterness, and long-unanswered needs.

This is in part because Indian society is so rigid and hierarchical that it allows for very few safety valves. When dealing with an unhappy marriage, the men usually drink to excess and the women usually gossip to excess. Marriage counseling has never really taken off. The traditional husband is, in his eyes , anyway, "Raja" or King. You hear this word all the time in Hindi love songs and movies. Rarely does this Raja ever turn out to behave magnanimously like a real king; more often, his relationship to his wife is a constant stream of instructions as though to a servant.

The woman is indeed supposed to serve her husband as a servant does a master. Women in India are, in fact, third-class citizens. The children are second-class. Partly because of the abyss that separates men from women, the Indian baby is overindulged, constantly handled, and every whimper brings a response. The Indian mother gives her baby endless and loving nurture. The father is as distant to his child as he is to his wife, having little to do with the infant. He adopts a stern and aloof role as the child grows older.

Unquestionably, the nurturing mother is the dominant authority figure in the Indian family. The mother-child relationship is the basic nexus and the ultimate paradigm of human social relations in India. In the other major Asian cultures, the father is acknowledged as the supreme authority. In India, the mother tends to become the ultimate authority—and thereby becomes the eventual target of defiance.

This can be traced to the way in which the mother manages the growth of her children. The close tie between mother and child, and especially mother and son, has several profound consequences for the Indian view of power. The all-nurturing responsiveness of the mother is the source of the ubiquity of the narcissism that is such a hallmark of Indian men. The Indian infant's first experiences are of complete bliss and the feeling that the world automatically responds to his or her every wish. He or she needs only to cry for wishes to become realities. The male child is led to feel that all of this is possible because he is exceptional, special, and deserves being the center of the universe.

When the shock of separation occurs following the arrival of a new baby, the male child does not seek autonomy and individualization, but strives to recapture the wonders of that first idyllic and blissful state of being one with the universe. Female children tend to isolate themselves. For males, being abandoned by the mother in favor of younger siblings is made more complicated because the child also learns his role in the *jati*, "the collectivity" that includes family, occupational group his father belongs to, village or neighborhood, and caste. He begins to learn that he must yield his individuality to the jati without gaining much attention in return.

The first and most basic reaction to all of this is withdrawal, believing that to be alone must be the supreme ideal. But withdrawal is frustrated by the desire to be recognized again as being exceptional, the center of everyone's attention. Hence the Indian male's propensity for aloofness, for being uneasily social when what he really wants is to be the center of attention again. This is termed secondary narcissism by Indian psychologists.

A key feature of secondary narcissism and the place one has in the jati is that the individual is little troubled by the feelings of guilt that arise from having one's conscience fixed by a demanding authority figure. The Indian way of manifesting goodness is to express moral values and to be free of aggression. Indian moralizing is more an act of self-expression and self-absorption than a serious attempt to impose standards on the community. Indeed, Indians can be oblivious to the problems of the larger world and feel no urge to correct injustices; they are completely engrossed in their own moral dicta. Morality comes to mean little personally but very much in the abstract, as for example in the case of karma, in which morality consists of living one's life according to the circumstances of one's birth and immorality consists of stepping outside the birthright's boundaries. Beings who suffer have earned it through bad karma and are to be held in contempt rather than pitied.

That the Indian child has a very distant relationship with the father and must learn to yield completely to family and caste authority explains Indian passivity toward authority. Young Indians learn that it is best not to fight for their rights or to protest mistreatment. The road is smoother if they submit to parental and caste authority. Early in life they develop the ability to feel no shame in bowing to authority. In doing so, they retain the dignity of their own inner goodness.

The shock of growing up, of losing touch with one's mother, and of having to settle for the impersonal collective identity of the family and the jati creates a sense of confusion about the true meaning of right and wrong, success and failure, praise and shame. The Indian child must operate under a complex body of taboos, rituals, rules, and contradictory ideas that can inhibit action and encourage withdrawal and introspection.

Not surprisingly, this leads to escapism. They yearn to be free of all external constraints and to become unified with the great, harmonious forces of the universe, to re-experience the exhilaration of infancy when they were one with the environment and could totally command the loving mother. This is the origin of the adoration of the guru, a kindly guide in seeking perfection in the inner self according to the rules of Dharma or the path to freedom and enlightenment. The rules of Dharma are purer than everyday jati rules.

Starting with their religious training, Indian children are presented with a universe of gods who are simultaneously creators and destroyers, men and women, both honest and treacherous. Then come all of the rules about the dangers of defilement and pollution related to the caste system. They learn that the physical world is filled with hazards. They conclude that it must be the spiritual world that is pure, for that is the only thing that can be mastered by the self on its own.

Finally, and devastatingly, the Indian child learns that in spite of all of the wonders associated with the nurturing, loving mother, women are considered socially and spiritually impure. As children learn the caste and non-caste pragmatic rules about avoiding impurity and the need for cleanliness, they are hit by the discovery that, according to the caste system, their own mother is considered unclean, a likely cause of contamination, a secondary level of life that can drag you down to their impure level. This gives rise to a mistrust of women that is second in psychological impact only to their mistrust of the world. It is these two mistrusts that have shaped much of Indian culture.

Because Indians elevate the mother into such a basic symbol of authoritarian warmth, they grow up ambivalent about authority in general. On one hand, they expect authority to be nurturing, sympathetic, supportive, all-embracing, and concerned with harmony and group cohesion. On the other hand, authority is associated with all that is negative in the Indian view of the nature of women: self-centered and fickle, a source of pollution and harm, and indifferent. It is hard to think of a more apt exemplar than Indira Gandhi.

However, long before Mrs. Gandhi, Indians had already linked the word *mata*, "mother," with the sacred cow that is the mythic image of India as a land and a culture, *gau-mata*. Gau-mata is the symbol of nation-motherhood: succoring, gentle, the antithesis of violence—everything that the cow is but the woman is not. Much of the Hindu reverence for the cow comes from combining *hindutva*, or Hindu self-identity, with idealized imaginings of what the human woman should have been.

Out of this contradiction comes the practice of *sati*, or the widow's self-immolation on her husband's funeral pyre. The woman's Raja now being dead, she has no further function or identity, is a pollution on the community, and should destroy herself in an act of final reverence for her husband. Sati's unconscious rationale is the idea that the husband's death was due to the wife's poor ritual performance and thus was her self-created fate.

Given that they hold women to be beings of power who are also corrupters and destroyers, men have strong ambivalences about sex. This is evidenced culturally by the contradiction between cheerfully erotic art on one hand and idealized celibacy on the other. Folklore has it that men are weakened by the loss of semen, yet a man needs the comforts of a dutiful wife. Indian men separate their fantasies about women from their actual sexual activities. Consummation is a problem, impotence common, the divorce rate next to nil, and pornography of the violent Western type is unheard of.

India's Major Religions

Through the centuries, India has accepted countless religious groups. Some 3,000 years ago, the Zoroastrians, or Parsees, were driven out of Persia and fled to India for safety. They were joined by a religion imported by Aryan invaders who blended their own beliefs with local ones into a hierarchical, ritual-bonded, power-religion named Brahminism. Splinters off Brahminism became Buddhism and the religion of the Jains. Eventually, Brahminism evolved into today's Hinduism.

Meanwhile, Syriac Christians arrived in the first century A.C. on the lips of one of Jesus's own disciples—Thomas (no longer as doubtful as he was on the day of the Resurrection)—forming the factual basis for the medieval legend of the Christian kingdom of Prester John. Centuries later, Islam arrived and stayed, inspiring the Indian Sufi movements and the Hindu-Islamic blend called Sikhism. In recent centuries, Jews from Spain, Portugal, Russia, and the Middle East came to India in search of religious tolerance and expanded economic opportunities.

Today, all of these mix with age-old village shamanism, astrology, and new-age spiritual ideas.

Zoroastrianism. Zoroaster, also known as Zarathustra, was a Persian prophet and philosopher who lived (by most accounts) in about the seventh century B.C.

Zarathustra preached a doctrine of morality and monotheism. At one time his religion spread across the Near and Middle East, but religious persecution forced its adherents to flee to India. The word Parsee derives from "Persia."

The Zoroastrian holy book, called the *Zend-Avesta*, offers prayers to Ahura-Mazda, the one and only God. Zoroaster spoke to God as "friend to Friend" and taught that even the wicked are eventually saved. The righteous go directly to paradise, while the wicked first must be purified by fire. (This belief formed the basis for the Christian doctrine of purgatory.) The greatest virtues are pure thoughts, good words, and righteous deeds. The worst evil is the lie.

The unitary Zoroastrian god Ahura-Mazda is "clothed in the most glorious of all glorious lights"—as apt a description of a sun god as ever worded. Ahura-Mazda's earthly symbol is fire, which perhaps originates in a very early belief from which the 17th century B.C. Aryans also borrowed when they adopted their divinity Agni on their way through Persia. (The English words "ignite" and "Iran" come from Aryan roots.)

Zoroastrianism's spiritual dualism between the forces of good and evil was the first religion to identify these earthly behaviors with godly origins. Truth and goodness among people strengthen Ahura-Mazda in the struggle against Ahriman, the force of evil. This concept has embedded itself deeply in Western mythology, by way of Zoroastrianism's strong influence in ancient Rome, just as a later offshoot of Zoroastrianism named Mithraism was borrowed from extensively by early Christian theologians when defining the relationship between a good God and the existence of evil. Much of the Catholic liturgy originated in Mithraic ritual.

Today, India's Parsee community has about 85,000 members, concentrated in Mumbai and Gujarat. Parsees are found in the highest echelons of business and finance—two are seen every day in Indian life: Tata and Godrej, the founders of two of India's largest industrial enterprises.

A fire is kept burning in Zoroastrian temples at all times as a symbol of sacred purity. The Fire Temple at Udvada, about a hundred miles from Mumbai, where the sacred flame was brought from Persia, has been burning continuously since 1741.

Hinduism. Hinduism is the most ancient of the world's major religions. Its origins are lost in the mythology of the Indus River Valley, around 1700 B.C. Hence Hinduism has no single founding figure like Buddha or Mohammed.

Central to Hinduism is the doctrine of the transmigration of souls and the doctrine of *karma*—the fundamental law of cause and effect by which the deeds in one's present life are rewarded or punished in the next life. Karma can be improved by living a life based on ethical values and the pursuit of knowledge, meditation, and devotion to God. Hindus believe that all experiences in life contribute to the knowledge of the soul. As the soul evolves and gains knowledge, it may reach salvation, or *moksha*, at which time the cycle of birth, death, and rebirth ceases.

The earliest written records of Hindu theology are the four *Vedas*, or Books of Knowledge, which appeared over the course of a 1,000-year period, from 1500 to 500 B.C. They contain a collection of prayers, hymns, rituals, and mythological and philosophical commentaries. Hindus believe that there is one Divine Principle, with a myriad of gods and goddesses representing various aspects of the Supreme Being. The Supreme Being, or Creator, is known as *Brahma*; the twin manifestations of Brahma are *Vishnu*, who is the Preserver or manager of the universe, and *Shiva*, who is the Destroyer.

Hindu cosmology includes the sacrifice of the Supreme Being from whose limbs sprang the four *varnas*, or classes, that form the basis of the caste system. From the mouth of Brahma came the *Brahmins*, the class of priests, scholars and diviners. From the arms of Brahma came the *Kshatriyas*, the class that includes warriors, soldiers, administrators, and nobility. From the thighs came the *Vaishyas*, or traders, farmers, artisans , and people in business. The *Shudras*, which include peasants and craftsmen, emerged from the feet. A fifth caste, known as the *Untouchables* (today more often called *Dalits*) developed at a later time and includes those involved in menial or degrading jobs. (Mahatma Gandhi attempted to uplift the image of the Untouchables by naming them *Harijans*, which means "Children of God.")

Around the sixth to fifth century B.C., a number of philosophical treatises called the *Upanishads* incorporated discussions on the meaning of life, the microcosm of the soul, or *Atman*, and the macrocosm of the world spirit, or *Brahman*. Ultimate Reality involves the blending of the Atman and the Brahman. Hindu literature also includes numerous epic stories about gods, heroes, and saints. The *Mahabharata* depicts the story of a great battle in northern India. It includes the *Bhagavad Gita*, a poem in which Krishna explains the duties of a true warrior to Prince Arjuna. The *Ramayana* tells of Prince Rama's exile in the forest and his journey to rescue his wife, Sita, from the demon-king Rawana. Hinduism has produced a prolific and profound literature in many genres, including epic stories, systems of philosophy, and theoretical treatises on fine arts and music.

Around the beginning of the Christian era, when India's contacts with other countries increased, the Hindu system evolved into multifunctional groups of castes and subcastes that are still apparent in modern Indian society. The peak period of Hindu cultural influence and its spread into the rest of Southeast Asia was the Gupta period, from 320 to 550 A.C.

Buddhism. Buddhism originated in India in the sixth century B.C. as a reaction to the institutional excesses of Hinduism—the behavior of the Brahmins who had become exclusionary and greedy, not the ideals of the belief system itself. A young prince named Siddhartha Gautama was born into a royal family. It was predicted by astrologers that he would become either a universal king or—if he encountered misery in life—a universal teacher. His father trained Gautama to be a prince and kept him confined in the palace to shield him from the miseries of the world. Despite such precautions, Gautama made secret excursions into the world outside the palace and there saw misery in the form of an old man, a sick man, and a corpse, and release from the world's travails in the form of an ascetic.

At the age of twenty-nine, Gautama guiltlessly absconded his home, patrimony, duties, parents, wife, and son to wander alone in the world seeking spiritual enlightenment. After studying under several gurus, and six years of fasting, study, and meditation, he achieved enlightenment while sitting under a *bodhi* tree (a species of ficus that was a sacred tree in Indian popular religiosity long before Gautama). He thereupon became known as *Buddha*, or the Enlightened One.

It is hard to avoid seeing every facet of the above profile of Indian male psychology being enacted in the life of Gautama Siddartha. Indeed, there has been much study of the actual historical circumstances of his life, and they differ in some fairly substantial respects from the mythic version above.

It is important to know about India that notable humans are turned into legends, and on that level they are stripped of the factual details of their life and re-clad with India's traditional mythic features, whereupon they are elevated into the realm of the gods. The name "India"[1] came not from the Indus River but from an Aryan warrior named Indra whose exploits during his tribe's incursions into the Indus River region earned him such renown that he was mythified through the chain of legend and demigod until he finally became the chief of the gods and thus bequeathed on the land his name. It is not difficult to perceive in all of this the modus operandi of a wandering tribe in unknown territory using myth to elevate itself to the top of the local hierarchy, much the way Westerners did with Christianity in Africa and the Pacific islands.

The chief doctrinal tenet of Buddhism also reflects the psychological profile above. In the Four Noble Truths of Buddhism, the first Truth states that all worldly life is imperfect and filled with sorrow and suffering. The second states that suffering is caused by craving, desire, and ignorance. The third states that suffering will cease if earthly desires are eliminated. The fourth holds that suffering can be overcome by following The Noble Eightfold Path. This path involves training, disciplined morality, and the contemplation of Nirvana. Nirvana is a state of bliss and emptiness beyond the limits of the mind and can be achieved by those who overcome desire, hatred and delusion.

Buddhism is a religion of equality. It preaches nonviolence and spiritual harmony. It recognizes no idolatry nor the fourfold caste system of Hinduism. There is no central god figure in Buddhism because they believe that the ability to find spiritual enlightenment lies within all people. It has no church or formalized church services. Temples, called *viharas*, are open at all times for people to meditate, leave offerings, or sit in quiet contemplation. Its affairs are managed democratically by a body of monks called *bhikkhus*, who assiduously (at least in some cases) attempt to attain the same sort of understanding that Buddha did.

Buddhism does not advocate a life of strict abstinence. Buddha believed that there are two extremes in life. One extreme is the indulgent life, which is given over to material pleasures. The other extreme is asceticism, or self-torture, which is painful, unworthy, and useless. Buddha guided his followers toward the Middle Path, which leads to insight, wisdom, serenity, and enlightenment.

Buddhism suffered greatly under Hinduism during and after the Chandragupta period. Hinduism essentially co-opted Buddhism's message and merged it into its own system; it transformed the Buddha (who said gods were basically useless) into an incarnation of the god Vishnu.

In recent time, Dr. Ambedkar, a great leader of the Untouchables, urged his followers to escape the slavery of Hinduism by embracing Buddhism *en masse*. He and 500,000 followers converted in a mass ceremony in 1956. Today, 3.5 million, or over 90 percent of the Buddhists in India, are converts from his followers.

Jainism. The name "Jain" comes from *jina*, meaning "one who has conquered the senses." The Jains are a strict group that, more than any other modern Indian religion, resembles the belief system of the early Indian ascetics who renounced both the world or material things and the ancient Brahminist religion of rituals and idols.

The founder of the Jains, Mahavira, articulated a doctrine of karma that was more cosmologically based than the psychologically based view of the early Brahminists. The human self consists of a soul enmeshed in physical matter. *Moksha*, or salvation, occurs by liberating the soul from matter so that it becomes pure and able to attain perpetual bliss. Karma is a specialized form of matter flowing into the soul through the body's senses. Cruel and selfish acts result in unhappy karma-matter, which results in unhappy rebirths. Good acts are free of karma-matter. Suffering sponges away bad karma-matter from the soul.

Jains avoid harsh words and insults, for these represent verbal violence. Jains build animal hospitals and shelters to express their love for all creatures. Jain lay people practice a spiritually serene life of prayers, fasting, and often vows of celibacy. The life of a Jain monk is rigorous. The two sects are the *Digambara*, or "sky-clad," and the *Svetambara*, or "white-clad." Digambara monks renounce everything that is not connected with the self. Since clothes are not connected with the self, they go naked. Svetambara monks wear only white. They cover their mouths with gauze to avoid accidentally swallowing any insect, and sweep the ground in front of their path so that they do not step on any insects.

Jains will not take up occupations like construction or farming because small creatures will be killed while digging the soil. The 3.5 million Jains in India today work at nonviolent commercial occupations, notably banking.

Islam. The founder of Islam, Mohammed, was born in Mecca, Arabia, in 570 A.C. Divine revelations came to him in the desert while he was leading trading caravans. But his preaching infuriated influential people in Mecca, which forced him to flee to Medina in 622. Known as the *Hegira*, this flight marks the beginning of the Islamic era. Eight years later, Mohammed returned to Mecca at the head of his armed believers. Mohammed died in 632, two years after he had made Mecca the headquarters of his religion.

The word Islam, derived from Arabic, means submission to the will of God and complete obedience to His law. According to Islam, there is one all-powerful, all-pervading God called Allah. Islam teaches that people are Allah's greatest creation, although they are misled by evil spirits. By following the teachings of Mohammed, people can be guided to the truth.

The religion Mohammed created is simple and easy to follow. The Five Pillars of Islam require profession of faith in Allah and belief in Mohammed as His true Prophet. Prayers must be performed five times a day, alms must be given to charity, and fasting is required during the month of Ramadan. At least once in a lifetime, the devotee must make a pilgrimage to Mecca, which is called the *hajj*.

By 651, the series of divine revelations made to the Prophet were compiled into a book called the *Koran*, or *Qur'an*, which remains the ultimate authority in political, economic, legal, and ethical matters of Islam. The *Koran* emphasizes moral responsibility, autonomy, and the dignity of the individual. It dictates strict social rules and a specific course of behavior for social events including marriage, birth, death, and inheritance. There are specific injunctions against the use of alcoholic beverages and the consumption of pork.

Islam preaches the brotherhood of all believers and equality of men before Allah, irrespective of color, race, or class but not gender. Much of the legal discrimination against women began two to three centuries after the founding of Islam, when the interpretation of the faith was in the hands of male scholars. They developed a set of guidelines known as the *Shariah*, which became a supplement to the *Koran*. The Shariah forms the basis of

Muslim legal and social codes, and provides advice for every social or religious decision.

Mohammed taught that God had finally and completely revealed Himself only to him. Mohammed felt that other historical messengers like Moses, David, and Jesus had received only partial revelations, and that their followers should be tolerated as "people of the book." All others were categorized as infidels, who were to be put to death if they refused to convert to Islam. Mohammed's inspiration led hordes of Arabs out of their homeland "with Koran in one hand and sword in the other" to reduce *dar-ul-harb* (country at war) to *dar-ul-Islam* all over the Middle East, North Africa, and the Iberian Peninsula in the seventh and eighth centuries. The rapid spread of Islam threatened the Christian countries of Europe and resulted in many battles and long wars, the most famous of which are the Crusades.

Islam has no priests and no formal church hierarchy. The Prophet was succeeded by a *Caliph*, who is the spiritual and temporal head of the Muslim community.

The followers of Islam are divided between two sects—the *Shia*, or *Shiite*, who believe that the caliphs have to be blood relatives of the Prophet, and the *Sunni*, who do not. The Sunnis are broken into four other sects: the *Hanafi*, the *Maliki*, the *Shaff'i*, and the *Hanbali*, named after prominent Islamic theological scholars. The school most dominant in Southeast Asia is the Shaff'i.

In the twelfth century A.C., a new sect called the *Sufis* developed. They are mystics who believe that salvation is attained through personal devotion to God. Sufi missionaries brought about large-scale conversions in India and Southeast Asia during the thirteenth century. Islam spread even faster in the fifteenth and sixteenth centuries in large portions of Southeast Asia. Today, it is the dominant religion of the people of Malaysia, Brunei, Indonesia, and the southern Philippines.

Sikhism. Sikh beliefs derive from the wisdom of the Divine Guru (spiritual teacher), Guru Nanak (1469–1539). This founder of the Sikh religion was born a Hindu but became dissatisfied with it. He explored Islam, but was no happier with that. After experiencing a supreme illumination something like what the Buddha experienced, Guru Nanak announced that God was neither Hindu nor Muslim. He devised a system of thought that blended Hinduism and Islam.

His beliefs were preached by nine gurus who followed him. The tenth Guru, Gobind Singh (1675–1708), declared that he would be the last guru and that, in the future, the book of Sikh Scriptures, called the *Guru Granth* or the *Sacred Book*, would be the guru.

Guru Nanak rejected the division of society by caste or god. He substituted his own view of a humanitarian and egalitarian society in which men and women have equal status and everyone is eligible to be a priest. Sikhs believe that God created the world and human beings to inhabit it, but that people can become too attached to the pleasures and concerns of the world, and thus become distant from God. People become self-centered, which leads to human suffering, including the endless cycle of death and rebirth. Rituals, ceremonies, and asceticism are useless. Only through purification of the heart and meditation can one achieve the ultimate union of love with God.

To protect the faith from oppressors, Guru Gobind Singh militarized the religion and created the Pure Order of Men (*Khalsa*), who pledge loyalty to the faith. As a public sign of their loyalty, the men were required to wear uncut hair (later covered by a turban), comb, sword or dagger, and wrist guard. The disciplinary code for Sikhs includes abjuring alcohol and tobacco, eating meat slaughtered according to Muslim rituals, and sex with Muslims. Sikh men take the name Singh ("lion"—traditionally an Indian name for kings) as a second name, while Sikh women take the name of "Kaur" (princess). In India, not everyone with the name "Singh" is Sikh, but all Sikhs use the name "Singh" as either a second or family name.

A Sikh temple is called a *gurudwara*. Sikhs tithe to their *gurudwara*. The *sangat* (gathering together of people) is an important part of Sikh religious practice, since they believe that God is among them when they gather religiously. Icons and rituals are rejected, and the ceremonies for birth, initiation, marriage, and death are intentionally kept simple.

Although Sikhs form 60 percent of the population of Punjab, their homeland, they make up only about 2 percent of the overall Indian population. The high proportion of Sikhs in India's armed forces, business, upper management, and politics is due in part to the nonexclusive and humanitarian character of their religion. They also form one of India's largest diaspora communities, and can be found in perhaps every country in the world.

Colonial Christianity. India was one of the earliest homes of original Christianity. The Syriac Christian community in southern India—notably in Kerala—is more authentically Christian than the colonial Catholicism exported to India from Portugal, and Protestantism from Britain and the Continent. The antiquity of the Syriac Church leads to fascinating tidbits of Keralean lore, such as the ubiquity of Jewish-sounding names like David Solomon. The origins of these names are from the Aramaic language, the language that Jesus spoke.

Catholic and Protestant missionaries, and later schools, arrived with the Portuguese and British. The Catholics were stupefyingly intolerant, and their forced conversions resulted in uncountable deaths and much of the early formative hostility to the West. The Protestants were more benign but remained largely a British religion. Indian adherents often converted for business or political reasons, and then deconverted when they got what they wanted.

Caste and Social Strata

India's earliest culture had its distant roots in the incursion of nomads into India from the Steppes of Central Asia and Persia during the two-millennium era roughly bridging 1700 B.C. and 300 A.C. From the nomadic Tungusic tribes of Central Asia came the practice of civilizing oneself by absorbing the civilization one conquers. From Persia came the idea of organizing social complexities using a system of social stratification called *pistra*, which grouped people into priests, warriors, and workers. In India this became the *varna* system, which subdivided the third category into what we might today term labor by brain and labor by brawn. This system also separated *jati* ("lineage") from *jataka* ("occupation") and gave a higher social value to people's ritual function than to their economic function.

Most people are aware that, in the limited *varna* of the rural community, caste ritual existed to perpetuate social order in a world of frequent physical uncertainty. It is less well recognized that caste had an economic preserver role as well. A society unified by occupational ritual would, according to this view, prosper despite famine and invasion, for it would manage the information needed to keep society going. The rising class of merchants added the idea that order occurred when there were sharply defined commercial functions, and civic functions should be based on these commercial functions.

The original Indian urban organizational pattern was a central religious shrine surrounded by an economically protective enclave of entrepots and then more distantly by housing districts, each in turn clustered into tribal or expatriate community social groups, all of which in turn were surrounded by the agrarian waste. The civic hierarchy of spiritual icon to trader to producer is the economic organizational pattern that has etched itself indelibly into the Indian mind. The only thing that protected the local shrine to the community's prosperity from the formidable, fecund, and fierce beyond the fields at urbanity's outer edges was an inner architecture of protective enclave upon enclave of self-sufficient units—the *jatis*.

Hence the caste unit replaced the tribal unit as the most important identity, and with it came the clothing, housing, and cuisine styles that identified one's role in the urban site. Today's 3,000–odd castes are a demonstration of how Indians have historically chosen information stratification as their adaptive mechanism to accommodate new technology and influence. Each caste came to control the inside information for a socially necessary function—in effect, castes monopolize technology by turning it into a privilege. The free flow of information and resources is restricted. Governance becomes the task of managing an array of self-defined units. The role of women became the medium of caste purity, and therefore economic viability; hence the large number of restrictions on their behavior and duties.

Caste supposes the desirability of assured but low-level prosperity. The modern world has very different attitudes about the relationship between assurance and low-level anything. Today, caste preservation has become a focal point of whether India can accept externally imposed change. The present rise of India's middle class, the internationalization of India by television, and the decline of the Congress Party will probably do more to erode the edifice of caste than all of the legislative fiats of the Nehru era and the Scheduled Caste laws of the last two decades.

Sublimated Pride: Lessons From Colonial India

When the British imposed themselves over the huge Indian subcontinent, they assumed that Indian society was impervious to technical and economic progress. Hindus, living within a rigid caste system and following ancient traditions, seemed to authorities such as Lord Cromer as "people living on a lower plane," who were ill-suited for the adoption of new industrial forms and technologies.

Such sentiments came naturally to the Europeans, who were shocked by the political decay as well as massive and deplorable poverty of the society they now commanded. They did not reckon with an India that, in the years dating at least to the time of Alexander the Great, attracted the brightest minds of China, Korea, and Arabia to study mathematics, medicine, and philosophy. In the industrial arts, particularly the manufacture of spices and textiles, India developed strong export markets as far away as the Roman Empire. After the fall of Rome, Indians also established strong commercial ties with their Byzantine, Persian, and Arab successors, forming a wide-ranging array of trading partners in Europe and, most particularly, the Middle East. By the thirteenth century, Indians also had developed world-class spinning wheel technology, and some of their products, such as Kashmiri shawls, were prized even by the emperors of China.

India's influence in Asia grew from early trading ties established by fourth-century Dravidians with southern China and much of Southeast Asia. These traders brought with them not only products, but also irrigation techniques and cultural influence, first in the formats of Buddhism and Hinduism, and later Islam. By 1500, an estimated 1,000 Gujerati merchants had settled in Malaysian Melaka, which emerged as a critical center for trade in spices, foodstuffs, handicrafts, and textiles from Arabia to Indonesia and China. By this time, Southeast Asia, in at least cultural and economic terms, was essentially a part of a "greater India."

But various forces, some political and some cultural, began to retard India's technological and economic progress. Under the Mughal empire, which came to power in 1526, the suppressed Hindu elites clung increasingly to the religious and caste systems as a means of excluding the new rulers from dominant social institutions and maintaining their own superiority over other Hindus. "Although the Muslim ruled the infidels," notes historian Romila Thapar, "the infidels called them barbarians."

The growing influence of the caste system sharply limited the progress of a market-based economy. High-caste Indians stayed largely outside the commercial sphere altogether, and virtually every activity was broken down into ever more specialized categories. Overall, the lack of mobility and an unwillingness to break the caste patterns hindered the progress of many of the very classes such as artisans who in Britain, continental Europe, and Japan played critical roles in commercial and industrial development. Under the caste system, interest rates for the Vaishyas and Shudras were twice as high or higher than rates for the Brahmins, who generally disdained new commercial ventures.

The enormous relative wealth of India also deflected interest in foreign trade, which was often a critical element in spurring both technical improvement and changes in the social order. The Mughal emperor Akbar, noted an Italian traveler in 1624, was a "great and wealthy king" whose tax revenues at the time were more than fifteen times greater than those available to Britain's James I. Even as late as 1757, the British conqueror Lord Clive compared the silk-producing city of Murshidalvad in Bengal, now little more than a small village north of present-day Calcutta, favorably to London in size, population, and wealth of its merchant class.

India's loss of economic control began first at its periphery. European power grew, but Indian traders, lacking the aggressive backing of their state, were reduced to serving as middlemen for newcomers such as the Portuguese, whose state actively promoted their activities through both missions of exploration and direct military action.

The European states also increasingly took advantage of their growing technological lead, sometimes improving on innovations and knowledge that originated in India. The very ships that were used by the Portuguese explorer Vasco da Gama to circumnavigate Africa employed both Indian navigational technology and a pilot from Gujarat whose experience with sailing African waters exceeded that of his European counterparts.

Perhaps even more critical was the widening gap in spinning technology. As late as the eighteenth century, India's textile industry, using the traditional spinning wheel technology, was still competitive enough to export products to Europe as well as to serve a vast domestic market. But, by the early nineteenth century, technological improvements pioneered by the manufacturers of Manchester—as well as new restrictions on the import of Indian textiles—were bringing on the virtual annihilation of an entire class of native weavers whose bones, as the British governor general would report in 1835, were "bleaching the plains of India."

The British hegemony, which started in the latter half of the eighteenth century, transformed India far more than such peripheral trading diasporas as the Dutch or the Portuguese. The empire needed modern ports and cities to service its expansion, and within a century British-developed cities such as Bombay and Calcutta had all but eclipsed the older centers of urbanization; they remain the leading centers for Indian economic life to this day.

British commercial dominance also overcame the last elements of influence held by Indian merchants throughout Asia, essentially detaching the subcontinent from direct access to its traditional markets. Even more important, British imports, most particularly textiles, swamped Indian markets, devastating the huge village-based economy that, as recently as the early nineteenth century, had been exporting its products to England.

Soon one of the world's oldest trading civilizations had become little more than a satellite of Great Britain. The imperial interest controlled major industries from jute to coal mining and treated the Indians as if they existed purely to further British commercial advantage. Between 1834 and 1934, roughly 30 million Indians were sent out as indentured servants to work on the empire's plantations, in the mines, and on other projects, often being subject to the most deplorable conditions.

India's overall domestic economy received similar one-sided treatment. Despite the favored position of British industrial products, India ran a huge trade surplus with the imperial metropolis and the rest of the world. By 1914, these surpluses were essentially propping up the entire financial structure of the empire itself. British interests carried away the profits from India's vast natural resources and agricultural products ranging from cotton to opium. Bullion earned in India found its way into the coffers of London and from there was reinvested in the expanding British world economic network.

Eight decades later, in 1991, Indians watched their bullion yet again board an aircraft for London—yet again to fuel an economic system that India had not mastered. It happened yet again because they held it in disdain rather than try to understand why it held such power. Today, the Raj and Mati generation realize that the decline of India was not brought about by outside forces, but because of the many internal limitations described in the paragraphs above. This is why India has changed for good. It is again looking to the marketplace, over which it once was such a master, to reassert itself in the future.

PRACTICAL MARKETING

Merchandising

The world of Western-style merchandising is fairly new to India. Cigarette companies had long used point-of-sale techniques, and Hindustan Lever and Nestle have used European-inspired aisle and island techniques for about 15 years. But in general, "everything sells, so why bother?" was the rule of the Indian marketplace until about 1992–1993.

Merchandising became a high-profile element of the marketing world in the late 1980s, when Procter & Gamble came to India and bought up considerable amounts of shelf space by paying several times more for space than arch rival Hindustan Lever paid. At the same time, Pepsi entered with a full-fledged handbook on merchandising that field reps actually had to read. Then India's Titan broke new ground by becoming the first Indian retail products company (watches in their case) to introduce its range to the market. (In India, a product "line" is usually called a "range.")

These altered the equation of the retail world. Today, most companies budget at least 15 percent of their total marketing costs to merchandising; this compares with 1994, when the average was 5 percent. Now specialized merchandising businesses have sprung up, and ad agencies have spun off separate divisions to handle this work.

In India, merchandising has been shown to push sales up by 50 percent for impulse products like cigarettes, chewing gum, soft drinks, and chocolates. In other product categories, "offtake" (in India this refers to purchases that the customer did not plan on making when entering the shop) can go up by 15 percent.

By late 1996, as a proliferation of new consumer-good labels arrived to jostle for space on the shelves, merchandising had become understood as a critical marketing tool. The term "merchandising," as recently introduced into Indian business school classes, is "the attractive display of a product at a shop in a manner that is consistent with the brand image, the objective of which is to increase point-of-purchase sales." This is a little more narrowly construed than elsewhere and tends to reflect the sense of segmentation and sharply defined boundaries that are part of so much of India's social history.

Indian marketers tend to see the term "merchandising" used in connection with consumer goods where impulse determines purchases at the point of sale—soft drinks, snack foods, and cosmetics being good cases in point. As global labels jostle for attention in the point-of-purchase marketplace, foreign companies setting up shop in India often find their years of experience in merchandising overseas not working in unfamiliar social territory. It takes a certain amount of mental rearranging to get used to the idea that the term "new product" is itself a new idea. For a long time merchandisers thought that their task was overcoming price barriers when in fact it was overcoming the "being-accepted" barrier.

Today some of the newness has worn off. Normally price-conscious customers are noticing the display itself as much as the product. This is true not merely with the low-price items like cigarettes, beverages, and chewing gum that usually register the sharpest sales increases as a result of merchandising. To the surprise of many people who thought they understood the money conservatism of the average Indian, today a range of expensive products have boosted sales using the same techniques that work so well with low-end products. Some examples are expensive lipsticks (Revlon is a classic example), tires (Apollo Tyres and JK Tyres), contact lenses (Bausch & Lomb and Ciba Vision), sunglasses (RayBan), and pricey home appliances (Usha, Philips).

One reason is that today fairly few customers come in with the intention of buying a particular brand—they are largely after a product. Hence a good deal of conversion via persuasion happens in a shop. One result has been a proliferation of stickers, danglers, and posters—to the point that by late 1996 they are either pass or at least not registering the sharp increases they did in the 1994–early 1996 period. At the time of this writing, their success has been replaced by custom-made racks, dispensers, and storage packs. In other words, the Indian consumer's sophistication cycle is proving to be a fairly quick one.

One result is that manufacturers have found it necessary to divert more and more of their "adspend" funds to merchandising, taking it from elsewhere in their ad budgets. This trend was first noticed in October 1995, when Pepsi Foods' snack foods division decided to move significant amounts of money from its television advertising budget into costs related to merchandising paraphernalia—special baskets, chip-station stands, and wire racks hit shop shelves in November and December of that year and have been there ever since. The focus was on gimmicks that appealed to children. Indians have a soft spot for the wheedling of children. Pepsi's sales doubled in two months.

In Indian merchandising's fairly brief history, visibility has proven to be a critical factor. Indian companies themselves did not take long to co-opt ideas introduced by transnationals. Delhi-based sewing machine and fan company, Usha International, introduced "Usha Corners" in 1996. These consisted of dispensers with the brand name prominently displayed and were introduced in some forty stores all over India. Initially, each dispensing unit (price: Rs 4,000–5,000 or $114–$142) was distributed free; later the dealers would have to pick up the cost.

In Bangalore—a metro never slow to spot a trend—electronics company BPL Ltd also set up "BPL Corners." Their self-standing display units were designed in-house and are fabricated locally—a big plus in the business sections of the local newspapers. BPL has now created a separate division for this purpose.

Retailer compliance is unpredictable. When Hindustan Lever launched Le Sancy soap in 1992, it gave every retailer a jar in which to store the soap, which was wrapped in a transparent foil. Not long after every bar was visible (the retailers did not think that customers would buy a product that they could not see, so they stripped off the fancy packaging), the perfume had faded (the jars were left open for long periods, sometimes in the direct sun), and the retailers were mixing products other than Le Sancy in the jars in an attempt to give slow-movers a classier image. Two years later, Le Sancy was relaunched—in a paper box.

Hence most companies have devised their own quality control methods. Kellogg staffers make the rounds of their outlets once every two weeks. Pepsi sends its merchandising teams out into the stores every two or three months—more frequently during the peak holiday seasons. Armed with scissors, cellophane tape, dusters, hammers, nails, pushpins, thread, and point-of-purchase material, these Pepsi "clean teams" tidy the shelves, dust the racks, put up new posters, and rearrange the bottles so that the Pepsi brand name faces the customer. Pepsi refers to such merchandising as "our silent salesman."

The Rise of Merchandising Specialists

In India's increasingly competitive market, an increasing number of companies have established specialized merchandising agencies to dress up their products at retail shops.

In Delhi alone, at least a half-dozen of such businesses sprang up in 1996 alone. Several advertising agencies across the country also jumped on the merchandising bandwagon. For example, the Bangalore-based Maa Bozell advertising agency first looked at the merchandising business in 1992 but waited until 1995 before it finally set up a separate company for the purpose, Ramms India. In September 1995, a second branch was opened in Delhi, and, in November, three outsiders were recruited in Mumbai to handle the business there. Ramms India claims that it has more business than it can handle—its turnover doubled from Rs 3 crore to Rs 6 crore ($857,000–$1.71 million) in just one year.

As the merchandising business grows, niches are already emerging. The magazine, *Retail Design and Merchandising*, notes that in Bangalore innovativeness is a key selling point. Ramms India, on the other hand, is working the more traditional ground of uniform image perception. Ramms India's philosophy is that every store and display should have certain standardized elements like colors and packaging.

As yet unproven is whether pure merchandising is a certain route to profits. One of the reasons is that there is only so much one can do with product display in India. India's great majority of retail shops are badly constructed—they move into four bare walls and a roof. There are as yet no store architects in India, so everything else must be done essentially cosmetically. Most merchandising agencies are a long way from the success stories in the above examples. Many in fact do a shoddy job and have little sense of merchandising beyond cramming as much of their product on the shelves as they can.

Although it is difficult to estimate how much the agencies are charging for their services, a rule of thumb is between Rs 10,000 to over Rs 1 lakh ($285 to $2,857) to go into retailers promoting a specific product in exclusivity. The price range depends a lot on their reach. However, as long as there are so few merchandising reps in the market, the sky is the limit, but the marketer must beware.

Gender Images in Advertising

In Indian most media serve fairly sharply defined audiences and are quite candid about being a long way from being secular and democratic. Women are depicted in a very different way than would be acceptable in the West. Simply put, most Indian males have not examined the implications of the fact that one-half of humanity is female. Here is a synopsis from the Malaysian columnist Alina Ranee about the way the heroine in a Hindi in-flight movie was depicted:

> Within a 10–minute period, the (unmarried) heroine was embraced seven times, cast shy glances at the hero three times, went down on her knee in apology once, and carried a water container on her head. . . . In true Hindi movie style, the woman in question indulged in much hip wiggling and breast jiggling during the dance routines. She pouted and fluttered eyelashes and coyly hid behind the nearest available object when the hero's "chase" act threatened to go over-board.

Similar imagery, though less crudely put, prevails in most Indian ads in which the assumed buyer is a woman. This is thought necessary because the "ideal" buyer is assumed to be a male buying a gift for the woman and the "real" woman actually doing the buying is really herself in his role. Hence, buying a product whose use is mainly female is presented as a way to yet again flatter a male. Even in pleasing herself she is not supposed to be pleasing herself; that is the man's role.

Largely due to international television and women's conferences, Indian social critics are beginning to emerge from their long era of lamenting the moral invasion of Indian culture as the result of West-infested media. Relatively few have begun to look sharply at the stultifying roles that women are given and the loss to society of so misusing their talents. Instead, male critics are more likely to focus on the impact that women employed in the media are having on women at large.

Indian women are underrepresented as active participants in events that affect them. Discrimination against candor, especially when it comes from women journalists and media executives, exists to a degree that would be considered unacceptable in the West—and, for that matter, in Japan or Hong Kong. The situation is sharpest in the regional press, where gender bias is articulated in quite blatant terms.

The depiction of women as passive is one of several interconnected problems faced by media and professional women whose work involves marketing foreign consumer products. The media in general tend to represent elite interests as moneyed and male. The great majority of non-upper caste women are underrepresented in print and in the visual media. Most advertising confines its women figures to (a) born in the middle and the higher classes, (b) living in urban areas, and (c) noncritical consumers. One result is that women discriminate among women using much the same criteria that men use when discriminating against women: their "weak" physiques and their "inability" to comprehend worldly affairs.

Women as entrepreneurial types—as opposed to widows or favored daughters—are latecomers in just about every field of business. This is largely due to social and religious taboos. Male domination keeps the vast majority of women out of business and away from the media. In rural areas, even where community radio or television is available, "women should have no spare time to watch TV" is a common statement from the men crowded around the televised cricket match. Programming created in Mumbai executive offices ignores the material that should most reach women. Information about personal health, family practices, and intelligent consumerism is often scheduled during the hours when rural women are occupied in things like fetching water from the community spigots or scrounging up enough firewood to cook with.

The language and content of India's public media tends to be fawningly elitist. Hackneyed themes, stereotyped patterns, and artificial and monotonous presentations are all traceable to the dominant interest groups that have taken hold of the media. India's elite has remarkably parochial experiences, interests, and perceptions—Doordarshan, wits have long said, is wealth set to music. The average Indian does not see India identified as a cultural mosaic but as an ancient epic forever in replay.

Rajya Sabha member Bharati Ray complained about the politics of representations in the media: "Most portrayals that attract our attention are dominant values of the privileged social groups." She has also criticized the portrayal of women in advertisements: "While men are projected as users of products, women are shown as extensions of products or as a form of consumer goods themselves. The indirect influence of the pictures we see as advertisements accelerates our process of socialization in a particular way of thinking, by selective reinforcement of certain values and attitudes."

The aggressive entry of women into the electronic media in the last two or three years has raised numerous questions about the role and ownership of those media. In the Indian press, women account for only 8 percent of the overall share of jobs. The future of the employment of women in media is not encouraging. Employers are reluctant to employ women not because of the general bias against them, but because of the higher costs involved in employing them by way of maternity leave and the undesirability of assigning them to certain places and types of work.

Mrinal Pande, of the *Hindustan Times* group of papers, summarized the situation of women in the media well: "There is an impression created that women do not prefer difficult shifts. This occurs because no one had decided to make the workplace a suitable place for them to work on those shifts," she said. In editorial meetings, "women are expected to be deferential to their 'gray-haired' colleagues." One expression of this is women's virtual silence during these meetings. The impression conveyed is that women are not interested. She also said that "effective participation of women has not been ensured, from the level of the desk to the management ranks."

Examples of Indian Ad Strategies

What lessons does the legacy of creativity in Indian advertising hold for today? In July 1996, India's *Business Today* magazine polled six of India's most distinguished ad people to find out. They were Mike Khanna of Hindustan Thompson Associates (HTA), Prem R. Mehta of Ammirati Puris Lintas, A.G. Krishnamurthy of Mudra Communications, Ravi Gupta of Trikaya Grey, Sam Balsara of Madison-D'arcy Masius, Benton & Bowles (DMB&B), and Tara Sinha of Tara Sinha Associates. Each was asked to nominate ten Indian campaigns they considered unforgettable. *Business Today* identified the Big Idea behind them that worked, and why they became classic. The ideas and the campaigns were as follows.

Provoke Reactions. Assertion was the key to the 1984 "Lalitaji" campaign for Surf detergent powder manufactured by Rs 5,883 crore ($1.68 billion) Hindustan Lever Ltd. This was a comeback campaign after rival Nirma attacked Surf's soft underbelly with a lower priced product in the highly price-sensitive household cleansers market.

Although Hindustan Lever was clear that what Surf needed was credibility to regain its market share, the creators of the campaign—Usha Bhandarkar, Lintas's creative director, with her colleague Anita Sarkar of Padamsee—realized that trust in the product could only be built through a character whom the target consumer could admire as well as identify with.

Shunning fantasy, the team turned to market research to find out just which quality of the product they should highlight. They discovered that the housewife's quintessential sense of thrift had to be appealed to. (Household incomes had not yet shot up under liberalization.) Hence the testimonial had to come from an anonymous housewife, not an achiever. The problem was that this did not sound like the kind of person who usually creates a strong impression. Searching for a solution, Bhandarkar remembered that Indian women love to "pat themselves on their back" when they strike a good bargain. Hence that is exactly what the Surf spokeswoman had to do—pat the Surf user on the back.

Bhandarkar drew up a two-page profile of Lalitaji. Among the details she noted, "Lalita is an upper middle class housewife, aged 32, who lives with her husband and six-year-old son in a two-bedroom flat in a cooperative housing complex in a Bombay suburb. Her husband is a senior accountant with a pharmaceuticals company. His salary allows the family to spend money on more things than just the basic essentials. Lalita is a careful spender. Although she is a disciplinarian when it comes to her son, she is also an indulgent mother. Her son is naughty, although generally well-behaved.[2] Lalita and her husband are often complimented by their neighbors for having brought up a well-mannered kid."

The campaign portrayed Lalitaji as a sensible housewife who does what is best for her family. Bhandarkar built a person who exuded confidence and had a personality of her own, who was in control without having to be a harridan, and who forced a reaction—and, by extension, remembrance—from viewers.

Provoking an extreme reaction was on Abhinav Dhar's mind, too, when, as creative director of HTA he conceptualized the Rs 16 crore ($4.57 million) Pepsi Foods' "Pepsi-Cola" campaign in 1992. His brief was to establish that Pepsi had taken the country by storm. He decided to provoke his viewers by putting together a pastiche of scenes, shot by film-maker Mukul Anan, from different regions of India. Each was a typically local situation—marchers singing slogans in Calcutta, classic Karnatic music in a South Indian temple, a traditional wedding in Punjab, monks in a Buddhist monastery. In these he would get the people to shout/sing/intone the Pepsi slogan. Each of the scenes came dangerously close to sacrilegious spoofs of local culture, and evoked either strong resentment or high approval—yet very few forgot the ad.

Astonishment Works, But the Advertising, Not the Product, Must Astonish. Without a pedigree of quality or even a claim on palpable differentiation, Gopi Kukde, art director of Advertising Avenues , and his team of Ashok Roy and Gautam Rakshit had no associations to draw on for their 1984 campaign for Onida television sets, owned jointly by the Rs 103 crore ($29.4 million) Monica Electronics and the Rs 327 crore ($93.4 million)

Mirc Electronics. They decided to flaunt the absence of ready feel-good connections with the product and searched for a negative impact instead.

The client's brief wanted the brand pitched as technologically superior to its rivals. Their feeling was that to externalize this edge with a litany of product features or a hi-tech ambiance would end in either a dense undergrowth of jargon or a vapid, "me-too" campaign. Provocation was essential to evoke response to the brand. One of the possible routes was to unashamedly exploit envy.

The symbol that emerged was the devil. However, this devil had to be a Western devil with horns and a tail rather than an Indian *raksha* (a fierce, devouring human-eater). It had to be cute rather than scary, wicked rather than evil. However, imagination and serendipity made for a more evil-looking devil than intended. "When we started shooting," says Kukde, "our inexperience with devilmakeup made the devil scarier and more evil-looking than intended."

The script for the first ad was never seen by viewers. Doordarshan trashed it on religious grounds. It opened with the devil escorting a shadowy figure with a halo on his head to the patron saint of heaven. "Here he is, my lord," said the devil. Asked the saint, "Whom have you brought?" Answer: "All his life this man has envied his neighbor." The saint strikes the man's name off the golden book while the devil takes his halo away and pushes him into the void. A vanishing scream echoes and the devil cackles, "Why envy when you can buy an Onida?"

The story line of every ad with the devil focused on apparently negative human characteristics. The idea exploited titillating shock while at the same time Onida TV appeared pristine pure. The campaign worked because appealing to negative instincts—and not just to refined sensibility—can make for a memorable ad.

Surprise. Surprise was the chief weapon wielded by Piyush Pandey, creative director of Ogilvy & Mather (O&M), and his associate creative director, Sonal Dabral, for their campaign for Cadbury, which repositioned the company's chocolates as products for adults, not just children. Their strategy highlighted the streak of irrational childishness in everyone that makes a fondness for chocolates in adults acceptable. They then translated this into a memorable campaign that climaxed with the commercial featuring a wild, uninhibited, impromptu dance performed by a girl.

Make the Consumer Aspire to the Impossible. Application of market research findings by former Lintas CEO Alyque Padamsee was behind one of India's longest-running campaigns—the convention-shattering commercial for HLL's Liril soap, which featured the signature image of a girl under a waterfall. The campaign began in 1975 and turned model Karen Lunel into one of the most recognized faces in India. The campaign broke new ground by being the first soap commercial to show someone bathing out of doors.

The client's brief demanded that the product be placed on an aspirational—and not a utilitarian—pedestal. Padamsee decided to weave a dream image around Liril that would not stop at the limits of the possible, or even the plausible. Instead, it would be an extravagant fantasy in which the setting would match the leaps of imagination a daydreaming housewife might have. Research revealed that the only time a harried middle-class housewife—the targeted customer—had to herself was in the bath. Says Padamsee, "She would daydream about a film hero like Amitabh Bachchan whisking her away on a white horse while she hummed melodies from the latest Hindi films."

Latching on to the housewife's need for release from drudgery, Padamsee affixed his ad to the image of the nymphet bathing in the waterfall. This was an escapist fantasy for the middle-class housewife. What could be further from her real life?

In a different campaign, the same concept—extreme individualism of a degree not quite attainable—was also the focus of Ambiance's 1987 campaign for the soft drink Thums-Up, then owned by Parle Exports. Slated to replace the earlier and successful "Happy Days Are Here Again" campaign created by Trikaya Grey, the campaign required a wholly new approach. Elsie Nanji, Ambiance's creative director, and her team decided to focus on the individual—to forge a sense of identification rather than stir up the good feeling that the togetherness of the earlier campaign had generated. The success stories for the different ads contained a wish-fulfillment element designed to conjure a sense of magical achievement that viewers could aspire to but not necessarily reach.

Advertise the Idea, Not the Product. This is the Indian variation on selling the sizzle, not the steak. Cigarettes, for example, are not advertised through surrogates. The genesis of the "Made For Each Other" campaign's slogan referred to a perfect match between filter and tobacco. It has, over the three decades since its inception in 1963, risen to the status of companionship between a man and a woman turned into a brand identity, much like the Marlboro Man does with the Cowboy West.

Syeda Imam, creative director of Contract Advertising, recalls that the objective was to give the brand a strong visual identity that would need "few words and no cigarette pack pictures"—in other words, advertise the idea, not the product—"So we decided that if the advertising was to work, the catch-phrase had to be taken out of the context of smoking, and transferred to a different setting, from where it could become part of common parlance."

This logic led to the focus on the concept of togetherness. When Imam was organizing the photography, the first-choice photographer was not available. Loath to bank on an unfamiliar photographer to get it right the first time, she decided to keep her options open: "To make sure I would at least have some good shots, I got the stand-in photographer to shoot a whole lot of scenes. When the contact prints came in, that's when it hit me—we could keep this going for years." Imam succeeded in creating a masterpiece of memorability by identifying the one feature that would endure—a connection with human relationships.

The same ideas played a part for Nexus Equity's managing director, Rajiv Agarwal, who headed the team that masterminded the Raymond Textiles 1992 "The Complete Man" series. This campaign likewise shifted away from the product toward an idea—to break through the commoditization of branded textiles as well as other commercials in the genre. The overworked machismo-with-sex-appeal formula needed a replacement. Agarwal zeroed in on the sensitive, multifaceted "Nineties Man" and transferred that image to the qualities of the user rather than the product. The result presented an idea rather than a brand of textiles.

Creativity Does Not End at the Storyboard. The irreverent, iconoclastic 1989 campaign for Nestle India's "Maggi Hot and Sweet Sauces" began life as the idea of using two comic characters—based on the BBC Smith and Jones series. Denis Joseph, executive creative director at O&M, masterminded the campaign. In it, the two characters would argue over the sauce, make stomach-churningly bad jokes, and, in the process, plant the distinction between the brand and ordinary tomato ketchup in the viewer's mind. Recalls Joseph: "There was a *Mad Magazine*'s Don Martin influence in it. I dreamt up various scenarios with Martinesque titles like *One Day On A Beach* and *One Day In A Prison*."

But Joseph knew that the best side-splitters could not be generated by funny one-liners alone. What he wanted was a near-lunatic sense of humor—one that would visualize the joke not just as a punchline, but also as a visual gag: "If they were to work, they had to be zany. And there was only one person I knew who could give that feel: Prahlad Kakkar." Kakkar in turn hired the craziest writer he knew—Jaaved Jaffrey—to write the scripts. Jaffrey, summoning all of the gag-writing ability at his disposal, wrote an assortment of encounters, with titles like *One Day at a Cricket Match*, *One Day Just Like That*, *One Day at Night*, and so on.

Kakkar realized that the client would never approve the scripts as written, and that the only way to sell the ads was to present them as they would finally look: "The way in which the situations spun themselves out of control was what made the difference."

Kakkar shot scratch versions of eight different scripts, using the rule-of-thumb that the unit had to crack up in laughter during the shooting for a particular sequence or it did not pass muster. Jaffrey and television actor Pankaj Kapoor—then riding a crest of popularity after his serial *Karamchand*—proved extremely effective with the ads, which ran under titles like *Jailbreak*, *One Day at the Saucepital*, and *Amnesia*. Nestle gained a classic campaign by accepting that creativity cannot conform to the requirements of conventional marketing.

Draw Associations with the Unexpected. Another lasting lesson came from Bajaj Auto's hanky-dabbing 1989 campaign for its scooters: shift the context of the campaign to ground that no one has covered before. What is the one image that no scooter-manufacturer had ever tried to link its product to? This is what Rahul da Cunha, director of da Cunha Associates, and his colleague, Prashant Godbole, creative director at Contract, asked when they were senior copywriters at Lintas India.

The answer was lump-in-the-throat patriotism. The idea occurred when da Cunha and his team free-associated Bajaj scooters with their users—the average middle-class Indian—and, further, with the hinterland from whence this consumer had sprung.

The competition, LML Vespa, was snapping at Bajaj's heels, and Bajaj could not compete in a feature-to-feature comparison. The campaign strategy was to pump up positive values—family-scooter, trustworthy, pride of nation to strengthen the bond between brand and consumer. Performance features were left out entirely.

The sheer audacity of the notion meant that it had to be cleared by Bajaj Auto chairman Rahul Bajaj himself. The Bajaj marketing team was decidedly iffy about such a soft-sell approach for a distinctly utilitarian product. Says da Cunha, "None of us knew how it would work out. But Rahul Bajaj saw the spark in the idea and approved it immediately."

What did Rahul Bajaj realize that his marketers did not? That the ad would elevate the product beyond the generic level and establish an emotional relationship with the consumer.

A second crucial decision that da Cunha took was not to predetermine the content of the commercial with a rigid script. Instead, he briefed filmmaker Sumantro Ghoshal to translate a selection from about 200 slice-of-life situations dreamed up by the creative team. Since the objective of the campaign was to appeal unabashedly to the emotions, only by running canned sequences by a sample of viewers could he gauge whether they had fulfilled their goal.

Ad Relevancy and Marketing Mix

There are many successful global brands with global advertising campaigns, but in India a global campaign must be tested in every market before it is run.

Usually, international marketing directors and international account managers are sick of hearing, "Our market is different." However, India is a complex country with regional divisions that are the equal of its better-known caste divisions. It is a country where marketing mix and advertising do not translate directly from textbooks.

The India advertising experience is that advertising's biggest role is in:

- making the ordinary extraordinary;
- making the unfamiliar familiar.

Hence, the role of advertising in the marketing mix is crucial to:

- Inducing consumers to take a fresh look at familiar brands in familiar, established categories; Cadbury's Dairy Milk is a good example.
- Making new products, thoughts, and ideas relevant; Titan is a good example of making a new idea (the watch as an expression of style) relevant.

In India, the view that attitude toward advertising is the single best predictor of sales effectiveness is not fully accepted. "Likeability" is not necessarily "the quality of being amusing or entertaining." Ogilvy & Mather of Mumbai considers it to include "relevancy or giving useful information or helping to solve a problem."

Nor is clarity alone always enough to sell a product. In a mature product category, putting the proposition into the headline (or its equivalent on television) does not create involvement. People do not turn on the television to learn the latest in product offerings. In the 1990s, advertisers often felt that all they had to do was be seen. Audiences were so captivated by the newness of the medium that they even endured its then long commercial breaks.

However, in today's multichannel environment, television viewers know that they do not have to put up with what they do not want to see. The three ways most often employed to get their attention are:

- Involving them with what you have to say, as when you have a new product idea that is inherently superior, surprising, or fulfills a strong need.

- Involving them with how you say it, communicated by the strength of the advertising idea.

- Sheer exposure through buying heavy media presence and making your advertising impossible to miss.

The last is obviously expensive and not every brand has the budget to allow it. Even if you have the budget, you can double the value you get for it by making your advertising involving and memorable.

The role of advertising is critical in a product's marketing mix. It should never be neglected. But also never to be neglected is that the advertisement must be relevant to the consumer.

REGIONAL AND RURAL ADVERTISING

The ad agency picture in smaller towns cannot—as it is in Mumbai's ritzy ad circles—be characterized as a rustic backwater. Far from the recording studios and pubs of Mumbai, Chennai, or Delhi, advertising agencies in small towns across the breadth of India have a grasp of local markets that the big agencies don't.

Pune's Notre Advertising, for example, closed 1995 with billings of over Rs 12.5 crore ($3.57 million), largely due to a strategy of concentrating on medium-sized centers. Notre's ten locations in west India are the largest network of second-rank and smaller cities in India.

Other small-town agencies have likewise performed well, recording some of the fastest growth rates in the industry. In 1994–1995, the average growth rate for Mumbai agencies was 72 percent, Delhi: 47 percent, and Bangalore: 46 percent. In the same period, Notre grew by 114 percent, television ads in Baroda by 119.8 percent, Shakun Advertising in Jaipur by 133.6 percent, and Tomyas Advertising in Trichur by 247.0 percent.

If these growths are startling, the sheer number of small-town agencies is more so. The Indian Newspaper Society (INS) handbook lists over 110 ad agencies operating outside the metros and larger cities such as Bangalore, Hyderabad, and Ahmedabad. However, this counts only agencies accredited by the INS to place advertising at the 15 percent commission and with a sixty-day credit period; there is no all-India estimate for agencies operating beyond INS accreditation. A look through the Yellow Pages of Nagpur yields seventy such agencies, Coimbatore has over forty-five, and Baroda over forty. The number of these that are full-service as opposed to one-person operations varies considerably.

One-person operations are a hindrance to larger operations in smaller cities where professional advertising is thought of in terms of an ad agent rather than an agency. Most advertisements are written by the clients, who call in a single-person agency to take the copy to the local newspapers, which then compose and release it. The is split between client and agent. In this milieu, the idea of someone from outside telling clients they need advertising strategies and proper creative direction for which they must may pay higher fees is a formidable obstacle.

One bread-and-butter clientele for many small-town agencies is recruitment and tender ads for public-sector undertakings headquartered in their towns. The agency TV Ads in Baroda began with these and has since grown beyond. This firm chose the name in 1973, long before television commercials were possible, hoping that the agency's future lay there—ironically, the agency has never done much television work due to the lack of television (and even radio) production facilities in Baroda. Even more important is the lack of the consumer goods' clients with the kind of budget for television advertising. West Indian clients after a television market look more to Mumbai than New Delhi for their services; southern Indians turn to Chennai.

The INS also lists affiliates devoted to marketing issues. For example, in Gujarat, the firm Z-Axis has databases related to marketing issues for Gujarati centers that include rural areas. Since Gujarat contributes 30 to 40 percent of the subscriptions to India's ebullient shares (capital) market, firms such as Z-Axis are a bellwether for economy-watchers.

Smaller regional agencies face problems of infrastructure, people, and the absence of large mainstay accounts. Of these, infrastructure has been the easiest to deal with given the advent of new information technology and better phone lines. Up-to-date, if not always state-of-the-art, desktop publishing equipment is within the price range of most agencies. This has greatly simplified press ad design and composition, and gives many the tiny nudge of profitability that enables them to invest further and covert new clients. Today's media software enables smaller agencies to do reasonably sophisticated media planning at more competitive local rates than large firms from the metros. Hence there has been strong investment by smaller agencies in infrastructure (Notre states Rs 45 lakh—$128,000—in the first quarter of 1996).

Audio-visual and translation work, however, remains a perennial problem. Here the demand is not great, so services are imported as needed from the metros.

Finding qualified talent is also a perennial problem. Experience outside the metros is not considered as professional. The normal solution is to induce and train family members (TV Ads has used this method) or recruit and train local talent (the approach used by the Pinkcity agency in Jaipur). Shell Agency in Nagpur searches for promising trainees in local art colleges or management institutes. Those who follow a "locals-only" policy argue that it is the best way to staff a small-town agency. Indeed, these firms tend to have lower staff turnover, which may be attributed to the fact that the job prospects for small-town school graduates are not likely to be great outside the region. Other firms recruit talent from personnel services such as Dignity Professionals, while still others, particularly those nearer to the metros, use big-agency operatives who are willing to moonlight.

The most keenly felt problem of small agencies is their difficulty attracting the big-spending, ad-savvy clients that headquarter in large towns. Smaller cities often endure the fact that big companies with large turnovers locate their manufacturing bases, and sometimes even their corporate headquarters locally, but conduct their marketing operations from the metros. Hence market-driven advertising goes to the metro agencies. On the opposite end of the scale, local businesses that grow large enough to reach the metros switch to metro-based agencies.

Small firms have tried several solutions to these problems. Opening more branches is the most common response, and several have started offices in metros, calculating that even a small share of the metro client budgets can multiply their billings significantly. Others organize on a hub concept under the assumption that no client wants to be more than a day away. Still others opt for a network of local representatives.

A broader based attempt to solve this problem is the networked agency system. India Link is a consortium of twelve medium-sized agencies across the country (including metros) that have banded together for regional support. The aim is to provide the higher penetration of a national network advantage to clients while preserving the lower costs of locals. Each member is remunerated separately for national campaigns. An added virtue is reducing the risk of losing the client to a metro agency. Some members want India Link to become a holding company for what would amount to a national agency with a strong small-town penetration and "feel." Small-town agencies are attracted by access to larger clients and budgets, yet they like the idea of retaining their ability to focus on local operations. As clients move from saturated urban markets into lower population strata towns, they realize that small-town agency support makes sense.

All of this has prompted some metro-based agencies, for example, R. K. Swamy/BBDO, to form local links of their own. One area where local knowledge can be especially lucrative is election campaigns. With the overall political outlook seemingly headed in the direction of short-term and local instabilities, elections are likely to occur more often than every five years. Here small agencies can benefit considerably for alliances with metro agencies.

Another feature of the smaller independent agencies is their tendency to operate related side businesses as income-levelers. Some examples are marketing consulting, screen printing operations, business centers, specialized travel agencies, rural marketing, market research, and training. Income from subsidiaries like these is becoming important as 15 percent commissions become increasingly rare.

Overall, the potential for small-town agencies is improving and is likely to continue that way as the middle class becomes broader and more affluent. Small agencies are realistic about their strengths and weaknesses. They would rather be leaders in their own domain where they have an edge over the metros.

The Hoardings Market

In the early 1990s, 60 percent of India's premium hoardings (billboards) sites were rented on an annual basis by liquor makers. Liquor advertising and the equities market supplied 80 percent of the industry's business. By 1995, liquor advertising was in bad repute, being totally banned in several states, with pressure groups in others vowing to follow. The hoardings industry was scrambling—mostly unsuccessfully—to fill up its looming blank spaces.

An unexpected savior emerged in 1995 with the arrival of hi-tech multinational advertising. The entry of the multinationals reduced the risk on investing in hoardings technology. The MNCs were used to high-quality advertising venues and were willing to pay for them. Vantage, a contracting agency with forty of the top fifty ad spenders on its client list, was the first to take the technology route, and it did so in a big way. It signed with the world's leading large-scale computerized imaging technologies—Metromedia Technology (MMT) and Vutek—to provide advances like front- and back-lit frames and printing on vinyl, which has an outdoor life of five years with no color loss.

These steps resulted in an entirely new hoardings clientele. Coke, Pepsi, Reebok, Exide, and Bajaj Auto have begun to appear in a venue where they were rarely seen before. This occurred despite the very high cost differential between the old hand-painted hoardings (Rs 5 to Rs 6 per square foot) and the hi-tech alternatives (Rs 150 to Rs 350 per square foot). Cost notwithstanding, everyone in the hoardings business feels that technology is changing the hoarding business forever, in a positive direction.

The scope of the new technology came as a surprise to many in the business. Mumbai's 1 Up Ads agency has put up laser billboards for some ten clients. These billboards operate for four hours in the evenings, each telling a 30–second story about the brand being advertised. Though expensive, it is an exclusive medium for 1 Up's clients.

To others, these are just gimmicks for those few clients with really deep pockets, and therefore a ripple rather than a wave of the future. Most agencies agree that high-tech advertising is unlikely to make significant contributions to their billings for some time to come. Some advertisers look at the new hoardings medium with outright skepticism.

The reason for such diverse opinions is that there is virtually no reliable data available on the opportunity-to-see (OTS) market that hoardings address. Procter & Gamble, for example, relies on a data-based approach toward the media. But since it is next to impossible to accurately measure the number of people a hoarding makes an impact upon, no one can say what a fair price for hoarding might be. Hence, many hoarding vendors bill on a cost-plus rather than an ad-reach basis.

Many advertisers feel more comfortable with television, whose reach can be quantified anywhere in the country. Godrej Soaps, Godrej Foods, and Blue Star are three consumer product categories whose marketers are not keen on hoardings. The general manager of business development of a Mumbai agency sums up the advertiser's dilemma: "There are various studies like the ABC and the National Readership Survey available for the print media which give advertisers a good idea of the impact an advertisement in a particular print journal will have. That is not true of hoardings. There is only one somewhat dated study available, the Oscar study for Mumbai."

The Oscar study is the Outdoor Site Classification & Audience Research survey, a felicitous acronym if ever there was one. The intent was to survey all sites in Mumbai, determine their actual use, and classify them on the basis of OTS. Despite its promise to be the first organized research by an independent body in India to give a scientific basis on which a client could decide where to advertise, the survey was far from successful. One reason was the limited scope (restricted to Mumbai) and lack of updates. Another was that there is skepticism about how correctly OTS can be gauged—counting the number of people crossing a site does not necessarily mean that the message has registered with them. Moreover, ad creativity plays an important role in being noticed.

There is another effort to organize the operations of this industry, made by the consumer goods giant, Hindustan Lever. For nearly twenty years HLL has followed what it calls the Integrated Hoarding Plan (IHP). The company has identified some 1,300, same-sized hoardings across the country. The idea was to affix identical posters on all of these hoardings and change them every month. This worked for nearly twenty years before being abandoned in 1993 because it took at least six months to conceptualize and put up fresh posters across the country when HLL brand launches were arriving much faster than that.

Many efforts to put some hard numbers into the business are now on the drawing boards as the hoarding business picks up. OHM, India's fourth largest advertising agency, is planning to buy or lease hoardings on a large scale. This is the next logical step for an agency that previously confined its role to helping clients rent them out. OHM has a fifteen-member team selling hoardings all over the country. With about forty active clients, the agency hopes to double its 1995–1996 hoardings billings of Rs 20 crore ($5.71 million) in 1996–1997.

Although the vacuum left by the ban on surrogate liquor advertising and a slump in the equity market have yet to be filled by new billings, the industry views the entry of MNCs who seem to have faith in the medium as refocusing the direction of the industry. While India's adspend on hoardings was Rs 350 crore ($100 million) in 1995–1996, the 1996–1997 figure is anticipated to be Rs 450 crore ($129 million), about 15 percent of the country's total adspend.

Direct Marketing Services

A growing number of multinationals have turned to direct marketers to sell their new and sophisticated services. When Citibank decided to launch its credit card in India, its biggest problem was that its offices were confined to a few select cities—hardly enough to make a nationwide splash. Citibank did not try to set up an elaborate marketing chain, but instead contracted local direct-marketing firms to sell the card. The card carved a niche for itself in a shorter span of time, at a lower cost, and with fewer headaches.

Other companies—Sterling Holiday Resorts, and Hutchison Max among them—have also tapped specialized direct marketers to promote and sell their services.

Direct marketing (DM) is not new to India, but the application of DM activity to the services industry has resulted in a mushrooming of direct-marketing firms—over 150 such ventures were in operation at the end of 1996. The industry was worth Rs 20 crore ($5.71 million) in 1995, and its proponents project that it will multiply two to three times each year up to the year 2000.

Perhaps so. But it cannot be argued that the strongest attraction of DM is its penetration/cost-efficiency. In marketing a product in India today, a company must budget upward of Rs 75 lakh ($215,000) to merely set up a full-fledged marketing cell devoted to the product—and more on running it. If the company turns to a direct marketer, all it must part with is a 21 percent commission for every item sold. DM firms can survive on such modest commissions because they handle many products. Their overheads are so low that a new DM firm needs startup capital of only about Rs 5 lakh ($14,285).

Cost-effectiveness is not the only factor to DM in India. With cut-throat competition replacing the protected environment in the Indian market, companies find it difficult to retain their market share as they simultaneously try to break into new areas. Multinationals like British Airways, Leo Mattel, Bank of America, and Fujitsu all realized that they needed local market knowledge that sometimes DM companies could provide better than ad firms.

Ad agencies themselves realize that with so many new services and concepts invading with unprecedented speed, India's market has revealed certain limitations to traditional advertising. The market is so crowded with new products that there is severe competition for shelf space—shelf space in the heads of consumers as well as India's myriad of tiny shops. Moreover, traditional advertising is not as effective with services as it is with products. An advertising blitz can create awareness, but a distant sales spiel over the radio or television does not communicate how a seemingly complex service in reality makes accomplishing a need very simple. Pagers and cell phones have been made familiar by ads, but getting past the intricacies of their use to the convenience they represent is best done personally.

Direct-marketing firms generally offer a mix of resource databases, technology for sorting information, and (typically) a 50– to 250–person sales team relying heavily on interactivity and one-on-one parleys. When a direct-marketing firm is hired, it shortlists its target customers on the basis of income, tastes, and earlier consumption patterns, using its database in consultation with the client company. Once the promotional strategy is established, sales teams approach target groups to describe the product or service, record the response, and persuade to buy.

When Citibank hired Andromeda Communications to sell its credit card in the suburbs of Mumbai, Andromeda decided on a two-pronged approach. At the qualifying level, Citibank launched print advertisements, and, based on the responses, Andromeda's sales personnel made a list of potential subscribers. At the sales level, Andromeda personnel made direct calls on offices in the area, describing the virtues of Citibank to executives. During these calls, promotional literature was left behind and Andromeda staffers followed it up until they received a definite response.

This is painstaking but produces results. Hallmark Cards, the famed greeting-card manufacturer (in India they are home-based in Pune), reported a 20 percent rise in sales after hiring a DM firm. Modi Xerox, Pagelink, and Snowcem also praise the results of their direct marketers (but decline to release figures).

Ad agencies have responded to this new niche for their services by joining it. Mumbai's Genesis Marketing, once part of an advertising agency, was turned into a DM company on its own to market holiday packages, computer-based products, and financial services.

Although most of the DM activity is presently in product industries, major moves are expected in the service sector when more multinationals enter with their new consumer services. Foreign insurance companies have long since made quiet agreements awaiting the day when that sector is liberalized.

For most multinationals, the key asset of a DM provider is its knowledge of the audiences to be targeted. Qualified DM companies maintain large databases of potential customers of different products and services. DMs tap different sources to replenish their databases, some of which may not be as solid as others. Confidence in the nature of a DM's resource base is of utmost importance to any client before contracting for their services. For example, when Colgate-Palmolive launched a new toothpaste, its DM approached the All India Dental Association for its list of dentists, who were then solicited by mail, phone calls, and personal visits. There are non-DM companies that specialize in targeting and acquiring just this sort of database. Hence, any client of a DM should know whether the DM has acquired its information first- or second-hand. When acquired first-hand, DM information can be as good as the often more costly established-market-research firm data. It is these data which will set the tone of a client's marketing strategy, and hence due diligence must be done to independently validate a DM's database claims.

There is no end of wrangling between DM providers and advertisers as to whose information works best. DMs claim that a face with a person attached is remembered better than a televised face followed by another televised face. That is half-true. The more apt Indian marketing truism is that DMs excel on the ground while ad agencies excel over the air.

Value for Money Versus Money for Value

In India you are not marketing to placeless consumers, but to the same consumers in a lot of places. The classic question of whether to position brands in the value-for-money (VFM) or the money-for-value (MFV) category is complicated by the additional question of how to position them.

When India's economy began to liberalize, like many Asian countries it was heavily targeted by luxury goods producers, especially European fashion and beauty accessories firms jostling for position in the money-for-value (MFV) market. Those and other luxury gift items like fountain pens and liqueurs have now settled into their boutique markets in the large metros, duty-free shops, and their traditional five-star hotel venues.

Some, such as Giorgio Armani, realized that for volume and balance they needed value-for-money (VFM) variants. Hence Armani's second-tier label, Emporio, went into affluent-city medium-scale outlets. Armani is a case of MFV successfully migrating downward. The reason for the success is that Armani's marketing people were very careful about the way they migrated: They presented a VFM product in an MFV setting.

In India, most brands that start in the VFM category tend to stay there—"brand stick" is a way of life exacerbated by caste purchasing patterns. Those who try to upscale VFM brands to MFV buyers have generally had mediocre to poor success. Image migration generally goes only one way. (In intercaste marriages, males marrying down-caste is accptable, but women marrying down-caste is not.)

Migration potential is keyed to what VFM and MFV mean locally—what works for Armani in Mumbai and Pune will not work in gritty industrial Surat 400 kilometers away. In India, VFM means a good, practical, reliable product for the money, though not necessarily because of pure price point over competing products. Rather, value is "a perceived good deal"—"This wasn't the lowest price but it was a good deal." For household commodities, marginally larger sizes at the same price tend to sell better than same-sized products with one discounted. For household durables, reliability is valued higher than price or image value, such as striking design.

With MFV brands, product appeal changes little no matter where you are. Extrinsic value tends to be more important than performance, except with items to be used in high-profile situations, such as fountain pens. There performance must match very high expectations. Schaeffer fountain pens, for example, are much preferred to Parker's because of the Parker's perennial problem with inking smoothly when drawing vertical lines.

A major task of advertisers is to create an MFV image for VFM products. They have been able to stake a legitimate claim to belonging to both worlds. Advertising commentator Tara Sinha points out that one of the big successes with this strategy was devised by the Videocon television maker's "Bring Home the Leader" campaign. Videocon launched its premium-priced "windows" television with this slogan, knowing that its greatest sales volume by far would be its cheaper models. However, "Bring Home The Leader" induced buyers into believing that any Videocon television was a leader. Today, Videocon retains its top market share position despite several international brands with more advanced features all across their product range. The same thinking can work in reverse. When Nissan and Toyota in the United States found it difficult to move existing brands up-market, they developed the Infiniti and the Lexus.

Many international brands have entered India via the MFV route only to find themselves permanently niched there. Others, like Proctor & Gamble's Ariel, Levi's jeans, and Daewoo's Cielo automobile, realized that they had to generate the volumes necessary to keep the trade interested by broadening into the VFM market. The approach taken by Ariel and Levi was to use the same brand for cheaper line extensions. Levi's kept its sub-branding from weakening the label's image by making sure that the sub had the same fit-and-finish quality even though the price point and fabric differed—the "I got a good deal" factor in operation.

Skillful MFV-for-VFM promotion requires experienced staffers at the local retail level. Local means "in that area or town," since local conditions vary so sharply in India due to income differences from type of industry, dominant local caste agglomerations, and political alliances. The following lessons can be drawn from recent VFM and MFV experiences in India:

1. Brand image is an important factor even in India's value-motivated society.

2. People buy more than intrinsic VFM—they seek extrinsic MFV in economy products. Nirma detergent, with its Surf/Persil-derived advertising, is an example.

3. MFV positioning has wide appeal even if the product is out of reach of the average buyer. Ariel lead-markets higher priced products first even though they will be little purchased; its image then rubs off on the VFM variants.

4. It is risky but not difficult to migrate from top-down, but moving from bottom-up is tough and may often be impossible.

MARKETING CASE STUDIES

Bata's Retailing Model

Nearly 60 years after the Bata shoe company opened its first store in Calcutta, the company has built a chain of 1,000 proprietary outlets and another nearly 600 franchise stores throughout India—and a huge overseas empire as well. Bata is nearly every Indian government official's idea of what a good Indian business should be.

Bata sold 500 million pairs of shoes in its 1995–1996 sales year. Despite this, the company lost 40 crore ($11.4 million). In the intense soul-searching exercise that followed, Bata decided to revive sales by focusing on its main strength, its retail network.

Bata is the only shoe company in India that is both a manufacturer and a retailer (indeed, very few companies of any kind fit this description). Bata's retail network is the largest in the country. Managing such a huge chain is both complex and expensive. Nearly one-quarter of Bata's total work force of 5,000 is employed in retailing and wholesale. This work force accounts for close to one-half of the company's Rs 227 crore ($64.8 million) overhead, and in turn contributes to almost one-half of the company's turnover.

Bata's stores vary in size from 700 to 10,000 square feet and are located mostly in prime urban areas. They can be broadly categorized into three tiers that cater to the top, middle, and lower segments—named Super Stores, Family Stores, and Bazaars. A unique aspect of Bata for the overseas consumer-goods company is that a particular locality will have within a short distance of each other three or four Bata stores, each catering to a specific type of product ranging from exclusive to everyday wear. Bata will not say so publicly, but there is a caste/class aspect to its clientele in any particular type of store.

The top Super Stores—an example being the Theatre Road Bata shop in Calcutta—normally display the leisure and sport shoe range and other high-value merchandise; Bata's down-market Sandaks or Signors range will not be found here. Says manager Sanat Basu, "People come here looking for brands like Hush Puppies. It would be ludicrous to offer them anything else." The Super Stores are staffed by a managerial staff—there is not a unionized soul to be seen.

Next come the Family Stores, offering a mix of various brands. Depending on turnover, these are classified into A, B, and C outlets. Finally there are the discount Bazaars shops, which are huge open showrooms packed with products at steeply reduced prices. There are just a few in any particular city, but they do brisk business. Bata in effect acts as its own discounter and remainderer.

Bata ruled the shoe market from the 1940s to the 1980s. Now it is being given a run for its money by a range of smaller companies like Metro in Mumbai, Lakhani in north India, and, more recently, Liberty, Mesco's, and Phoenix. The shoe trend over the last 15 years shows big brands fading slowly to newer, more affordable products in a swiftly changing market.

To an extent, Bata's sales erosion is due to its own errors. Most analysts list three: downgrading quality, inability to adapt quickly to changes in design, and pricing. In the case of women's shoes, for example, Bata was slow to respond to the market for fancier styles that the Metro company capitalized on. Bata had hoped to dominate the sport shoes market with its North Star and Power brands, but it was undercut by cheaper shoes by Lakhani, Action, and Phoenix.

Surprisingly, Bata's strong retail network has a few liabilities. Bata's policy of preferring directly managed stores to franchised units has lead to high overheads. Originally, given lease contracts and archaic rents in the older stores, the policy made sense. Now real estate prices have soared and the old leases are coming up for renegotiation. Bata has found the cost of operating old stores ever more marginal and the cost of opening new stores prohibitive.

Bata's response was to reposition its stores as up-market fashion outlets, stocking high-value merchandise for men and women, with an emphasis on leisure wear. It outmaneuvered its own Power and North Star brands by launching the premium Ambassador label, and introduced the international brands Adidas and Lotto, which are considered prestige brands in India. It launched designer stores such as Marie Claire and Bata For Her with glitzy store fronts and blazing neon signs. Bata also diversified into accessories and garments.

This has been good for Bata's image, but sales did not respond as well as hoped. According to outside analysts, buying footwear in India is a family affair, and a single-product store does not really work well for that market the way an all-product store works. The mass-market customer who normally shopped at Bata found the prices out of reach.

The exclusive store strategy also faced competition with the arrival of Benetton and Reebok. Adidas and Lotto both pulled out of their deals with Bata, dissatisfied with both their margins and their sales. Adidas is now on its own and in September 1996 was advertising that it was looking for franchisees. Squeezed at both the high and the low ends of its market, Bata's market share fell from around 16 percent in the 1970s to around 10 percent in 1996.

Bata has devised a new strategy focusing on wooing back its mass-market customer base. Store fronts display huge discount signs with numbers like 50 percent. Even Bata's premier show rooms are discounting, something that was unheard of in the past.

The degree to which this can remain a long-term policy is not clear. It has certainly helped Bata clear inventories and also kick-started sales. The first quarter of the 1996–1997 financial year recorded an 11 percent rise in sales.

The key word in Bata's present sales lexicon is "volume sellers"—the bread and buyer lines, which include their canvas and PVC range, children's school shoes, and sporty Hawaiis.

Another new word is "merchandising." Bata stores were never particularly well-stocked—broad, yes, but not deep. Shops received inventory directly from the factories. When the company opted for a merchandising approach, a separate division was set up in tandem with a distribution wing that directed the supply movement. The merchandising wing's responsibility did not resemble what many non-Indian shoe retailers might call a merchandising wing. Bata's wing was assigned to follow up on feedback from the retail outlets, and replenish the necessary product in appropriate volumes—in other words, more a distribution arm. Not surprisingly, the system did not work particularly well in practice, largely because "the movement of supply was poor," in the words of a shop manager.

Bata's strategy of refocusing on retail was also expected to help cut costs in Bata's ad budget by harnessing the already visible stores as an ad vehicle. Bata is a household name, and the company felt that they were an advertisement just "being there." Bata eliminated print ads and put its money into store-front and in-store advertising, largely through point-of-purchase materials and displays. Bata trimmed its annual media ad costs from Rs 10 crore ($2.85 million) to less than Rs 8 crore ($2.28 million).

Bata also implemented the RM-80 inventory format in which a particular shop sends daily sales reports to the inventory department so that replenishment can take place immediately. RM-80 proved unpopular with employees, who felt that "the new scheme is nothing but an extension of the invoice records we were already keeping. It just means more paperwork, which takes at least a couple of hours' time, after the store closes, and yields no practical benefits. Supply continues to be in driblets. Merchandising usually sends over what's at hand when it is really required."

Bata's future strategies also include redoing existing stores, combining smaller retail stores, and better space and display use.

All this said, customers will tell you that, "the reason why newer shoe companies are doing better is because their salesmanship is better. Bata salesmen need a more customer-friendly approach."

Some shop managers in Super Stores earn between Rs 15,000 and RS 20,000 ($428–$571) per month, a very high income in the retail world of India. Middle-range store managers can earn up to Rs 12,000 ($343) a month, with the bottom-segment shop managers earning around Rs 7,000 or Rs 8,000 ($210–$229) a month. These salaries are the legacy of wage agreements in the company's plusher past, when it was one of the best paymasters in the industry. Today, Bata's bills for salaries, commissions, and wages total Rs 95.2 crore ($27.3 million).

Taking a long look at Bata's retail power, both Reebok and Nike wooed the company for a tie-up, which was bagged by Nike in September 1996. Nike will sell its shoes only in the Super Stores and Family Stores. Nike has identified ten strategically located Bata stores located in the metros and mini-metros where special Nike Corners will be set up.

Coca Cola's Problems and Solutions

India's markets are characterized by long distances, huge populations, and difficult politics. The capital and time commitments that Coke and its bottlers are making around the region are evidence that the company knows that it is involved in an endurance run.

The downsides to continued rapid growth in India are formidable. Coke often does not have the control it needs to make merchants follow the rules. The company also is bumping up against intense difficulties in expanding the distribution of its products because of primitive infrastructure—Coke often finds its cases of Coca Cola being ferried down narrow streets on large tricycles.

The company also faces extensive requirements on transfer of food-processing technology as a price for entry. Local regulations limit its ability to deliver in certain places at certain times. Picking business partners and hiring enough local employees are serious challenges. And, as one of the premier symbols of American consumer culture, Coke faces the prospect of political backlash from nationalists.

Coke is convinced that the rewards outweigh the risks. Hence Coke is splashing out training programs for everyone from senior local executives to route drivers. It is buying refrigerators and trucks, upgrading electrical wiring so that more stores can install coolers, and offering millions of samples of Coke to consumers who have never tasted it.

The problem is, the underdeveloped marketing areas in India are so vast and served by such poor infrastructure that Coke cannot rely on its experience elsewhere to foresee solutions to problems. In more developed markets, Coke bottlers distribute all of the product directly, giving the company complete control over its goods. That is not feasible in India, where a high percentage of Coke products goes through independent wholesalers. It is difficult to control the quality of such things as coolers, product display, and pricing.

Finding the right partner has also proved troublesome. Coke acquired India's top soft-drink company, Parle Exports, for an estimated $40 million. That gave it the top local soft-drink brands and access to Parle's fifty-four bottling plants. Thanks to that deal, Coke-owned brands have nearly two-thirds of the market, far eclipsing Pepsi.

But the Coke-Parle alliance was fated for trouble. In 1994, Coke accused Parle of breach of contract for making soft-drink concentrate without consulting Coke. Parle executives claim that they were making soft drinks only out of old, leftover stock. The issue became a full-blown war, with Parle's chief executive exchanging harsh words with Coke's chief of Indian operations. Coke executives point to the company's 65 percent share of the soft-drink market as proof that the matter has been resolved.

In the summer of 1996, Coke finally won permission to inject $700 million into its Indian operations, making it one of the country's largest foreign investors. Coke's first step will be to build twenty-five new bottling plants over the next several years. Coke is likely to bring an anchor bottler into India, Singapore-based F&N Coca-Cola (Pvt.), Ltd., as its partner.

To win Indian hearts and minds, Coke aggressively invests in cultivating a local image. It was the official soft drink of World Cup Cricket. Local television spots did away with actors and used Indian cricket fans to promote Coke products. Coke's ad campaigns show signs of learning what is hot in local trends and then find a way to connect with it.

Wherever it goes, Coke brings a missionary zeal to selling its product. Coke's teams around India spruce up shops, spreading the gospel that good retail presentations increase sales. The company hosts massive gatherings of up to 15,000 retailers to showcase everything from the latest coolers and refrigerators (which Coke loans out under strict controls) to advertising displays. Its salespeople go house to house passing out free samples to potential new customers. In New Delhi alone, they handed out more than 100,000 bottles of Coke and Fanta last year.

Politics presents a tricky obstacle. Coke is very mindful that it was forced to withdraw from India in 1977 by Indira Gandhi's demands for access to the company's secret formula—a plot for her real motive of Indian nationalism. Today Coke keeps its eye on the rumble of antimultinational sentiment from Hindu nationalist parties. One level of political emotion is the number of smashed Coke bottles at BJP rallies. With BJP's reputation declining, so is the number of smashed bottles.

Up-Marketing Suzuki Motorbikes

In late 1992, the joint venture between manufacturer Suzuki Japan and marketer TVS India needed a new retail strategy. Faced with mounting losses and an industry recession that saw their market drop almost 16 percent, TVS-Suzuki devised a comprehensive turnaround plan based on a three-prong strategy. It worked so well that others emulated it. It is now the standard model for the motorbike industry.

It was clear that new-look products alone would not pull the company out of the trough. Even though they had a market share of 35 percent in mopeds and 12 percent in bikes (huge unit numbers in India), there was no excitement or emotional attachment to their products. More worrisome was the fact that TVS's smallest market share was in the larger cities.

TVS-Suzuki began by segmenting their product range in the premier 100-cc motorbike category (known as the "Indo-Japanese bike segment"). They researched and designed in-house the "Samurai" and supplemented it with "Scooty," a Vespa-genre model that was the company's first effort in the ungeared scooter segment.

Next to be revamped was the appearance of their retail outlets in India's then ill-defined midmarket midcity arena. The role model was Titan Watches' move from workaday wristwear to high-class image-consciousness. Taking a look at the upscaling ad formats in India's midmarket magazines, TVS-Suzuki asked themselves why motorbikes couldn't be sold the same way as fine-quality watches and clothing. They were well aware that customer perceptions of shopping for a two-wheeler were "not a great buying experience," as one interviewee put it. The oily rags littering showroom floors that more accurately resembled back-shed repair places may have had something to do with the image.

Repolishing showroom appearance spurred TVS-Suzuki into completely redefining its retailing strategy. The blue, red, and white TVS logo was standardized for every dealer. They either custom-designed or redecorated their retail outlets in a uniform sporty look. The service areas in each showroom (an unavoidable necessity in India's many cramped, narrow older buildings) were upgraded to company specifications regarding tidiness and a sense of everything in its place. Dealers had to change all of their computer software and hardware.

But the deciding factor in the fast-growing industry was the service component. By extending its corporate identity to after-sales operations, TVS-Suzuki focused on its long-term goal of market leadership. Until then, most sales operations were the last time the customer dealt with the selling company; most service was done in messy, ill-lit shopfront operations run in the main by teenage bike fans who were known to exchange the old parts in their own bikes for the new parts in a customer's.

TVS-Suzuki put the onus for quality service on the dealers themselves, giving them a unique incentive in the form of a no-discount policy all across their dealer network. A countrywide seminar introduced the 300–odd TVS dealers to the new look and the economic significance of the complete overhaul of their system, operation, and showrooms. TVS- Suzuki chose their top-rung dealers to showcase the concept.

On its part, TVS-Suzuki invested close to Rs 3 crore ($857,000) in the first year to boost the pace of the program. To reinforce their switch to more traditional consumer selling, the company recruited dealers with no prior experience in two-wheeler sales but considerable experience with consumer sales. To ensure that dealers did not neglect customers' post-purchase needs, this quality-of-service was made a major criteria in evaluating a dealer's performance. They also set up a consumer satisfaction survey every six months.

Hence, while TVS-Suzuki subsidized the costs of the branding operation in terms of signboards and long-term loans to upgrade showrooms, the bulk of the investments came from the dealers themselves. Their increased investment costs to meet the new corporate identity standards ran as high as 60 percent.

Company executives worked alongside shop floor managers to implement the change to TVS-Suzuki manufacturing principles; the parent firm also monitored the spare parts and their sales.

This program upped the ante for TVS dealers. It was too much for some, and approximately eight dropped out of the TVS stable. Today, the top rung of dealers are "landmark dealers," while in late 1996 at least 70 percent of the entire dealer force conformed to corporate identity standards.

The results are impressive. From selling just 3,000 bikes a month in 1992, by late 1996 the company was logging sales of up to 13,000 a month. Their aim now is to reach 600,000 units annually. The company is now looking at introducing a range of traditional scooters by early 1998, in addition to 200-cc motorbikes. All of this points clearly to how upscaling to middle-class standards in a low-class product can result in high-class sales.

More Than Packaging a Designer Coffee

Tata Cafe has jumped into the instant coffee market with novel packaging and a tantalizingly low price. Will it sell?

Inherently tea junkies, Indians drink considerably less coffee. Many cannot afford the price of coffee, especially the instant variety, compared with the cost of tea. Big-brand coffee manufacturers have discovered that, beyond a point that is about 1.5 times the per-serving cost of a popular beverage category, a competing beverage hits a real cost wall: Consumers are perfectly happy to go without, no matter how good it is. Instant coffee has always fallen in the 2.25 multiple and higher range compared with *chaiwallah* ("tea hawker") tea.

The March 1996 arrival of Tata Cafe, an affordable "designer" instant coffee, has marketers watching carefully. Tata Cafe offers the same amount of coffee at one-half the usual price—a clear face-off with tea. While market leader Nestle offers its Nescafe at Rs 52 per 50 grams, the same amount of Tata Cafe has been available to consumers across northern and western India at Rs 27.50 ($0.79) since March 1996. Tata is mum on how they have arrived at this price.

The instant coffee market in India is a tiny 6,000 tons (down from about 8,000 tons in 1993–1994 due to a sharp spike in coffee prices after this period). This is a Rs 60 crore ($17.1 million) market. Its leaders are Nestle's Nescafe (in the market since 1964) and Brooke Bond Lipton's Bru (since 1968), which together account for over 90 percent of the market.

The years 1993–1996 have seen the coffee market get very active. On the new products marketing front, the launch of Coorg filter coffee in 1993, which uses 100 percent pure coffee, broke new ground. In 1995 came Golden Roast, a 47 percent chicory and 53 percent coffee mix, which was reportedly very favorably received in a southern test market. Tata Cafe has a unique advantage in that it owns its plantations. Competitors admit that this is a big hedge against further price rises in the world coffee market.

Another factor in Tata's favor is that they have introduced a uniquely marketed product at a time when the market, after having shrunk by over 30 percent, is ready for reflation. Tata Cafe hopes to garner a high share of this new market. The main reason for the unique packaging concept is that Tata knew that if it was to enter a market which has been dominated by two products for three decades, Tata would need something dramatic to get a toehold. They chose both pricing and packaging.

Tata realizes this is going to be a long operation. Nescafe and Bru are so strong that it will take a lot more than a price break to win steady customers in the market. Tata needs a huge and sustained marketing effort—a brand-building exercise that will drive up their costs tremendously in the first few years. Their basic premise is that the company is being very aggressive in order to toehold the market and inch up this price fairly soon.

Tata disagrees that their pricing is sensational: "We are offering our customers the benefit of buying coffee from a company that is fully integrated all the way to the plantations. Our advantage of lower production costs is passed on directly to the customer."

All of this is very fine, but what is fascinating about Tata's approach from the overseas marketer's point of view is not the way the company has priced or packaged its product—the foregoing could have been photocopied from an international marketing textbook. To these visible marketing efforts Tata added an unseen one: its extensive taste testing in all of India's major markets. Months of blind tests all over the market resulted in a flavor database unique in Indian marketing history. Tata devised what amounts to a map of flavor profiles for different parts of India that were instrumental in the company arriving at the distinct flavor of Tata Cafe. The lesson is that while debates go on and on about taste versus price, Tata went out to find out what customers really liked and why.

Chefs in a Can

The concept of the doggie bag is unknown in India. Among Muslims, a dog around the house is *makruh* (defiling), and Hindus regard dogs as the karma of a particularly vicious previous human life.

So doggie bags are definitely out of the picture in the restaurant business. Still, restaurants whose customers often leave full but want or are famished for more are leading the way into what one might call the Paul Newman market by canning their most famous menu items.

In 1996, ITC's Welcomgroup, whose flagship Maurya Sheraton Hotel & Towers houses one of Delhi's best restaurants, launched a selection of items from its menu in vacuum-sealed cans. Their Dal Bukhara is Rs 150 ($4.20) for 450 grams.

This is ordinarily a slow-cooked dish. It took months of painstaking R&D and test-marketing before it was allowed on the market. With a shelf life of up to a year, the restaurant's first offering, the Dal Bukhara, will be sold through the group's hotels and in select stores throughout the country. Next in line for launch is *phirni*, a luscious sweet dish. Are you hungry yet?

Customer-Smart Fashion Retailing

When couture couple Yashodhara and Sanjay Shroff opened their high-fashion store Ffolio in Bangalore in 1991, they created an innovative niche: a one-stop shop for a comprehensive collection of clothes from the country's best-known designers.

This retailing strategy has taken Ffolio's top line (the Indian term for gross profits) from Rs 50 lakh ($141,000) in 1991–1992 through Rs 85 lakh ($242,800) in 1993–1994, Rs 1.5 crore ($428,500) in 1994–1995, to ($714,000) in 1995–1996, a healthy return on their initial investment in the 5,000 square feet store of Rs 25 lakh ($71,400).

Ffolio cultivates its clients through a variety of intimate events that give the opportunity for one-on-one interactions with clients and their favorite designers. In its first two years, Ffolio hosted coffee-mornings every month, privately showing a designer's collection before a hand-picked gathering of 40–odd buyers. Customers felt wanted. This was the origin of Ffolio's pamper-the-customer marketing philosophy. Yashodara observes, "Our clients are always flying to Mumbai and Delhi, and the merchandise is essentially the same everywhere. We provide a personal touch that makes them want to shop nowhere else."

The Shroffs used the occasions for two-way communication in which the customer's preferences influenced future buying decisions. A 30–minute fashion show followed by a chat with the designers often translated into on-the-spot sales of Rs 2 lakh ($5,700) and more.

To avoid these becoming a cliché, Ffolio stopped these fashion shows as other stores picked them up. Instead it focused on one big-bang annual event. To keep the interactive nature of its promotions alive, Ffolio now stages wine-and-cheese play-reading evenings. The players wear clothes created by the designers, who are the focus of the evening. Sales are closed afterwards.

Since its high-priced designer ware is not off-the-shelf products for casual or impulse purchase, Ffolio must constantly keep customers interested in its wares. Central to that objective is its always-evolving process of tracking customer preferences. At first the Shroffs kept in touch with customers quite simply through their coffee-morning shows and comments in their guest book. However, as Ffolio grew, the Shroffs needed a more scientific, less subjective, monitoring mechanism.

In October 1995, Ffolio set up a separate marketing team with the mandate of tracking customer expectations, measuring the store's ability to meet them, and developing new clients. Most customer calls are buying-motivated, but a sizable number were simply feel-good social calls. Today, Ffolio's marketers are quite literally more outgoing. Members of the team network the city's social circuits and update customers about new showings at Ffolio, match products to customers' evolving preferences, and record them in the store's database. Each promotional event is followed by a survey to assess customer perceptions on a particular aspect of Ffolio's service, such as price or attention to customers. Ffolio surveys work with the "scale of one to five" rating system.

Having started Ffolio as an innovation rather than a "me-too," the Shroffs are now plotting expansions that will reinforce their uniqueness. On the drawing boards is a Ffolio chain with three more stores due for Hyderabad, Pune, and Kochi in late 1996 and early 1997, as well as a second store in Chennai. To broaden Ffolio's reputation beyond the high-spending customer, Ffolio has begun to market-segment its products. While the premium designer brands continue in the Rs 3,000 to Rs 40,000 ($85–$1,140) range, Ffolio has also launched the premium label Bandhej, with outfits in the middle-class Rs 800 to Rs 3,000 ($23–$85) range.

The post-1997 step will be diversifying Ffolio beyond clothes and repositioning it as a life-style store. The Shroffs are adding a design center to their Bangalore outlet to retail books, music, and art. They feel that they will grow stale if they do not expand quickly.

High-Profile Newsletters

Company newsletters are gaining importance as their value as an effective internal communication tool is being recognized. One unexpected result is that in-house corporate media have inculcated a sense of corporate participatory democracy that would have been unheard of just a few years ago.

The intended result was somewhat different. As Indian companies, both public and private, grew, they saw the importance of more open internal communications. One assumption was that keeping employees happy by giving them a sense of involvement would have a spillover effect on their relations with the public media and with the government—a sort of double-edged blade in positive public relations.

The result was a proliferation of in-house newsletters. Those that already existed were pizzazzed to be more employee-friendly. One switch was from pats on the back for past accomplishments to clearer information on what is happening right now. American Express revamped its newsletter, *Amexpress*, to give more information to sales agents about a particular program. Its writers explained in detail what technological and corporate thought went on behind the scenes before introducing the AmEx training programs that the sales staff reading the newsletter was just about to undergo.

Other companies added spiffy color and design elements to improve their look and appeal. The National Institute of Information Technology—not especially noted for its spiffiness—originally published *NIIT Times* as a quarterly with no decorative elements at all. Now it is a monthly speckled with spot color and plenty of photos. To source attention-getting articles, NIIT appointed correspondents in regional offices across India and abroad. Now *NIIT Times* blends weddings and birthdays with the literary efforts of its more creatively inclined staffers. Employees are delighted to read quotes from and see pictures of themselves, and would-be poets and story-tellers are ecstatic to see their bylines in "real print." Some say that this is as good as a raise, though unions shop stewards are not quite so sanguine about that.

Most company newsletters face the age-old problem of distinguishing themselves from others. The National Thermal Power Corporation (NTPC) decided to target children by teaching them the do's and don'ts of electricity. The company produced a comic book entitled *Mote, Chotu and The World of Electricity* in English and Hindi in which an "Uncle" from

NTYC takes the winsome pair Motu and Chotu plus their friends through the maze of electrical artifacts around the house and in industry. Children do not get this kind of didactic tool in school texts, so NTPC found itself fielding unexpected requests from science teachers. The idea proved such a hit that a Hindi daily in Rajasthan now serializes it.

Another increasingly popular internal medium is video magazines. NIIT's video magazine NTV went from an irregular series to a bimonthly for division heads to play during their monthly meetings. Each approximately 40–minute video addresses major cultural and professional events within the group.

Bausch & Lomb's in-house video magazine tries to "edutain" its employees using an annual theme. The 1996 theme was based on Olympics Fever and was titled "Go for Gold." B&L also publishes an in-house magazine in which the employees vent opinions. B&L encourages them to share a voice in whatever the company does. The magazine is heavy on news, reports on meetings, and behind-the-scenes summaries of company-related stories in the public media.

Hindustan Lever's *Hamara* newsletter goes out to 15,000 employees and has a pass-along readership that is estimated at 43,000. At a commendable multiple of 2.86, this is nearly twice the 1.78 pass-along ratio popular magazine ad-reach is based upon. *Hamara* is supplemented with an online version, *CC Mail*, that is quick to put together, instantly distributed, and has no printing costs. *CC Mail* makes a determined effort to give their online newsletter a pizzazzy look that is geared to the presentation effects of the scrolling screen as distinct from flip-over paper pages.

A good deal of thought goes into the names of in-house journals. Maruti Auto's *Gatirang* refers to speed and color (although wits were quick to point out that Marutis are more famed for the latter than the former). *Moonbeams*, Procter & Gamble's in-house, refers to the company's Man in the Moon logo. Pepsi's in-house, *A-ha!*, does double-duty, repeating the punch line of one of the company's soft drink's ad campaigns, and also reflecting the flavor of the journal—pun intended—which is jolly, loose, and fun-filled.

Other companies put out different media for different moods. Airfreight has three in-house journals—*Channel A* is a monthly journal for all employees, *Brainstorm* is for managers, and *Fast Lane* is for customers, media people, and industry colleagues. Of the three, *Brainstorm* is avowedly experimental. It involves employees directly by soliciting them to debate issues that are important to the company. Each issue raises a corporate issue via an article about it and employees are invited to reply. When competitors

Elbee and Blue Dart launched a new airline, *Brainstorm* helped senior management get feedback on what the employees felt about it. Airfreight's *Channel* A then helped them discuss Airfreight's competitive service idea called Jumbo Box with employees to de-bug the system as much as possible before announcing it.

THE INNOVATIVE RECRUITMENT ADS MARKET

For Indian ad agencies, recruitment ads are not a sideline business. Delhi-based Arms Communications reported total billings of Rs 17 crore ($24.2 million) in 1995, of which Rs 85 lakh ($2.4 million), or 5 percent, came from recruitment advertising. For another Delhi-based firm, Anthem Communications, 5 to 8 percent of total billings are expected from appointment ads.

Companies have increased their recruitment ad budgets substantially as they try to locate top-quality talent. TCS spent about Rs 60–70 lakh ($1.7–$2.0 million) on recruitment ads in 1995, a leap of about Rs 10–15 lakh over 1994. By 1996, C-DoT had doubled its figure of 1991. Ranbaxy's ad budget for recruitment ads in 1995 was Rs 65 lakh. NIIT's recruitment adspend went from Rs 40 lakh in 1995 to Rs 60 lakh in 1996.

Indian recruitment ads have a unique style of their own, one that is much slicker than other Asian ads. They have little affinity with the staid boxes that all but vanish amid the blur of cookie-cutter relatives in the newspapers. Their copy is as appealing as a consumer product, and most have a strong visual element. They also make a strong corporate statement. They sell the company as a brand in addition to appealing to people's knowledge and skills.

In 1996, for the first time in India's ad history, the Abby (Advertising Club of Bombay) Awards for Excellence in Advertising included a category for recruitment ads. The gold medal went to Delhi-based Contract Agency's ad with the line: "What kind of company gives you time off to have a baby, even if you're a man? You won't just find a better career at NIIT, you'll find a better quality of life." The silver medal went to Anthem Communications' ad for Oriflame Natural Cosmetics, which showed a mother with her children and the line, "Welcome to the second most rewarding career on earth."

FABULOUS FLOPS

What makes products fail in India? There are usually several contributory reasons, but most flops can be traced back to a mistake in the marketing mix, getting it wrong on one or more of the four P's—Product, Promotion, Price, and Place. Following are some examples:

- **Two heads are better than one** is what the marketing whiz kids at Ajay Home Products had in mind when they launched the D'Tach toothbrush. Its unique selling proposition (USP) was that the head was detachable (the toothbrush came with a spare head). It made no impact in the market. Why would anyone need a toothbrush with two heads? Market verdict: Product Flop.

- **Catch them young.** Refrigerator and air-conditioner major Voltas introduced Little's Big Hug Sipper, a feeding cup for babies. There were no obvious synergies with the existing lines of business, but Voltas felt that it was no babe in the woods when it came to marketing unrelated products. Market verdict: Promotion Flop.

- **All cats are gray.** Polar Industries thought it had a great idea: decorate ceiling fans with cartoon characters. The bright fans, styled Cool Cats, would appeal to children and look good in their rooms. The company forgot that the basic function of a fan is to rotate. When it did, all of the colors dissolved into a gray blur, and so did the USP. Market verdict: Product Flop.

As marketing professionals seek a raison d'être for their new launches, flops are more and more common. Increased competition has brought an increasing number of them. Some companies, desperate to seek a market-mover's advantage, often do insufficient homework on the market demand for a "me-too" product. Others do canny research based on other people's mistakes, but then overlook marketing basics.

With regional television such a growing market, phased roll-outs are gaining currency and companies do not have to take big gambles on a simultaneous national launch. Casualty rates are high, but companies are not going under because of a single flop, as happened periodically in the 1980s. Well-known brands are disappearing from the shelves because of corporate restructuring, mergers, and buyouts.

The product itself is often the key cause of failure. Pune-based two-wheeler manufacturer Kinetic Engineering thought that it had hit upon a great idea: Why not combine a television set and a computer terminal? The company spent two years and some 3,000 software man-days to develop Merlin. They invested around Rs 1 crore ($285,000) promoting it. After poor sales (2,500 sets in the first year, 1992), the company realized that

Merlin would never be a wizard of an idea. A year after its launch, Merlin was gone.

The problem with Merlin was that there was a market for televisions and a market for computers, but few wanted the two together. Indian marketers call this the "shoehorn-with-toothbrush product"—you can use both, but not at once.

D'Tach, the two-headed brush from Ajay Home Products, was launched in Mumbai in December 1992. It was trying to introduce the replacement concept in toothbrushes that had worked well with shaving systems. By April 1993, before repeat purchases could show whether it had succeeded or not, it was taken national. In the first six months after launch, D'Tach sold 200,000 pieces. But from June 1993 until it was withdrawn at the end of the year, additional sales notched up a dismal 5,000. Replacement heads, which came in a set of two for Rs 1 (2.8¢), were a nonseller. The total expenditure on D'Tach was around Rs 1 crore ($285,000) including a Rs 30 lakh ($85,700) launch budget.

Indian marketers often quote a study done by The University of Pennsylvania's Wharton School of Business, which indicated that 23 percent of brand failures can be attributed to a bad idea. So why do companies come out with new and untested products?

One reason is that companies sometimes see what they perceive to be a niche in the market and develop a product without asking whether there really is a market in the niche. Another is that product differentiation in crowded markets often leads to inadequately researched concepts. In 1991, Hindustan Ciba-Geigy launched Cibaca lime gel toothpaste. It offered users squeaky clean teeth and a tangy, tasty flavor. Unfortunately, despite its "14 genuine herbal ingredients," Cibaca flopped. The fact that there were other tasty gels available was less important than the fact that while people like lemon flavor in foods (especially sweets), while brushing, citrus jarred the tastes. The lesson was that while product differentiation is important—for any brand to succeed, there must be some uniqueness about it that sets it off from others—more important is the fact that the uniqueness must be relevant. Hindustan Ciba-Geigy executives apparently did not think to ask their children what they thought of it.

Another problem occurs when trying to create a new market. Margarine, for example, is a successful product category in the West. But the two brands, Spredit and Merrigold, launched in India a few years ago made no headway. There is a structural problem with the product in India: The refining standards of sunflower oil in India are poor. Margarine soon disintegrates and sours. Artificial flavoring, which makes margarine such an acceptable product abroad, is not allowed in India.

Nor has iced tea ever been much of a success in India. Nestle tried to market its Paloma brand in the 1980s and Nestea in the 1990s. They both left consumers cold because Indians prefer their tea hot; they cannot relate to iced tea.

Packaging and product name also come in for their share of failure rates. Packaging disasters litter the snack food category. Lite Bite potato wafers failed because faulty packaging could not keep the chips crisp.

Packaging is a big cost component in lamipacks and flexipack marketing. When some snack food manufacturers cut corners on quality, customers were turned off to the entire category.

Product names can also cause headaches. Paras Pharma launched a cold rub named D'Cold in 1994. The adult version was sub-branded Majorub, which sold well, but the sub-brand for children named Dingorub was too reminiscent of Australia's wild dogs to attract mothers of children.

Famous names attached in an attempt to promote mundane products do not also always work, either: Hadlee dried peas (promoted by cricketer Richard Hadlee) could never overcome its dried pea image no matter who claimed they were great.

Jaisalmer cigarettes, from Godfrey Philips India, faced a geographical identity problem when the brand was launched in 1990. In Delhi it rose to sell 500,000 sticks (the Indian term for a cigarette) a month, but had to be pulled out of Mumbai because the cost of distributing was too great for the quantity sold. The problem was the name. "Jaisalmer" is a famous north Indian landmark, which had little brand identity in Mumbai. Although GPI plans a national relaunch, if it does not succeed in the south, the brand will be pulled.

Failure of the product is one of the four P's that is relatively easy to understand. But promotion failure (which includes brand positioning and advertising) can be more frustrating to understand. There are enough promotional disasters to give some hints, though. One example was Milk-food Yogurt. The name Milkfood was a successful ice cream brand in northern India, so the manufacturer felt comfortable in opting for the line extension into yogurts. The product died on the test market. Analysts say the problem was that the advertising projected yogurt as a superior form of curd (buffalo-milk yogurt, which is much higher in butterfat content than cow's-milk yogurt). Consumers mistook it as a gel form of ice cream. The problem arose because of the Milkfood name's association with ice cream. Retailers worsened the problem by selling it as a deluxe ice cream, adding to the confusion. Moreover, the yogurt cost Rs 5.50 and Rs 6.50 for different variants, compared with a vanilla ice cream cup of the same size at Rs 4 ($0.11). Consumers balked at the premium, and those who did buy it thought that they were getting something else. Prices were slashed to Rs 5, but that did not help. An adspend of Rs 1 crore ($285,000) in three months went down the drain over the simple mistake of advertising communicating one thing but the consumer perceiving the product as something quite different.

The same problem occurred with Ritz Bits from Britannia Industries. This was projected as a snack food item for teenagers that had the nutritional benefits of biscuits. But to the teenager, Ritz Bits had too many attributes of "boring old biscuits" while mothers looked upon it as "junk food." Britannia said of the failure, "We had positioned it as a snack but it was too heavy to be a snack."

Inadvertent identity confusion plagues the men's toiletries category. From the mid-1980s on there has been a steady procession of launches—Park Avenue, Premium, Nivea, Fa, Denim, Saka, Instinct, and many more—but the overall market has not grown beyond Rs 200 crore ($57.1 million), one-quarter of the total cosmetics market. A market research executive observed, "In India, nobody knows the difference between a body spray, a deodorant, and an anti-perspirant, so why should they buy any of them?"

The experience of Fa is a good example. This cosmetics and personal care brand is owned by Henkel KGmA of Germany. Fa was launched in 1990 in collaboration with the Goa-based Menezes Cosmetics with a launch budget of Rs 45 lakh ($128,500) for Fa's first two products, a cologne and an eau-de-parfum. In 1993, Fa introduced a deodorant and a soap, and raised the advertising budget to Rs 1.5 crore ($428,500). Later, a roll-on deodorant was also launched. Yet the products had no special identity that could be communicated to consumers; they remained part of the herd. Menezes lost Rs 4 crore ($1.28 million) and withdrew the range in early 1996 with a swan song ad campaign whose main purpose was to clear the Rs 60 lakh ($1.7 million) worth of stocks still on the shelves.

Positioning also dealt a poor hand for the Bajaj motorbike model KB 100 RTZ. Bajaj introduced a hi-tech, robotic-looking cheetah as the model symbol for the RTZ. The slugline in the commercials was "ride the cheetah." Everyone knows that cheetahs go fast, but the KB 100 RTZ went more like a tabby cat. Zen Communications director for planning and development, Pradeep Narasimha, painted no fancy spots on the reason for the disaster: "Promotion that raises expectations the product can't meet leads to disaster."

Another positioning failure came from Top Ramen, a challenge to Maggi noodles from Brooke Bond Lipton India Ltd. Top Ramen's birth was hardly auspicious: It failed at launch when the taste proved unwelcome to Indian palates. In the first relaunch, it did not do much better. Now Top Ramen is billed as "smoodles," which even top advertising executives admit says nothing.

If product and positioning have served up their fair shares of disasters, so too has place. Distribution remains one of the weakest spots in India's marketing world because it interfaces with some of society's most entrenched and conservative elements, the *babus*, or petty traders. (*Babu* has many hidden meanings in India; it can mean what the French derisively term "*petit commerçant*" and can also mean "coddled brat.")

When Nestle launched its chocolates range, its elegant promotional campaign was the talk of India and won several awards. The product too was up to the mark—most Indian sweets' manufacturers ruefully say that Nestle does not know how to make a bad candy bar.

But their campaign, which included Crunch, Milkybar, and its premium milk chocolate namesake brand, Nestle, flopped in the sales department. What went wrong? The company insisted that its chocolates be stored inside refrigerators; otherwise, they would melt. This ruled out the vast majority of India's prime outlets for small food items—the country's legions of tiny kiosks. Moreover, chocolates are an impulse buy—if they are not visible, they do not move. Nestle eventually had to reformulate its bars to match the conditions imposed by the retail end. Fortunately for Nestle, it had the money and expertise to do so; others are not always so lucky.

Another product that got the place element wrong was Henko detergent, owned by Henkel of Germany. Launched in 1993, it was expected to challenge Hindustan Lever and Procter & Gamble. Today, Henko has a mere 2–5 percent of the market, depending on the region. Henko did not nail down its distribution channels carefully and today remains an also-ran even in its strongest market in the south.

Pepsi has had distribution problems with its Ruffles chips. The company assumed that since bottles were breakable and chips were fragile, the Pepsi distribution system could be used for both. But chips got mashed by the sturdier (and heavier) bottles. Pepsi had to find an independent distribution system.

Distribution is something that new companies can easily fall foul of. In their effort to woo dealers and retailers, companies can easily promise margins that are unsupportable by sales levels. New entrants have real problems with the established clout of the market leaders, who can red-flag a rival product by refusing to release their own best-selling wares to distributors who carry rival products. (In India, the term for "red-flag" is "blackball"; bad-mouthing is "blaggarding," short for "blackguard.")

Finally, there is the parameter of price. That brand success or failure depends to a large extent on this parameter is even more true in India, where $100 a month is a good subsistence. However, India's very vastness turns price into the handmaiden of both product and positioning. Yet the product still has to clearly offer value for money.

Lack of clear benefit plagued the launch of Jet Fighter, an insect repellent in vaporizer form, in late 1993. The dispenser was priced at Rs 240 ($6.80, very high by Indian hardware and home convenience items) while the liquid repellent refills went for Rs 60 ($1.71, also high). Aside from price, there was not much to distinguished Jet Fighter from the market leader, All Out. But All Out costs Rs 135 ($3.80) for the dispenser and Rs 65 ($1.85) for the liquid repellent. The customer saw no trade-off in paying Rs 100 ($2.85) more for Jet while saving a meaningless Rs 5 on refills. Jet Fighter bombed, taking down with it an advertising and promotion budget of Rs 75 lakh ($214,000). Jet was reincarnated as Jet 45 with the dispenser priced at Rs 145 ($4.14). The price of the repellent was kept the same so the differential reduced to just Rs 5, but the image damage had already been done.

Price problems hit Walls ice cream the same way. In March 1995, the price of Walls' Solo ice cream bar was raised from Rs 2 to Rs 3, and its Cornetto from Rs 16 to Rs 18. Sales immediately took a licking. By September, Solo was back to its Rs 2 price.

In the male toiletries market, price is often a major factor because consumers do not understand the product benefits and so tend to judge it on price alone. M.N. Mehta, executive director of J.K. Helene Curtis (makers of the Park Avenue and Premium range), makes this point very clear: "I can give it to you in writing that any after-shave or deodorant priced over Rs 200–RS 300 ($5.71–$8.57) for 100 milliliters, regardless of label, will bite the dust."

In price-sensitive domestic categories like edible oils, where there are both branded and cheaper nonbranded alternatives, increasing prices can bring disaster. The National Dairy Development Board's Dhara refined oil's volumes dropped from 113,000 tons in 1991–1992 to 49,000 tons by 1994–1995 solely due to a price hike that the government company still has not backed down on.

Puma, too, got its prices wrong. Market research done by Carona—the Indian company that manufactured Puma shoes under license—indicated that the top-of-mind brands were Nike and Reebok. Adidas came in high, but Puma was in the basement (in a country with no basements, the equivalent term is "figured nowhere"). Carona took the plunge anyway with a shoe priced at Rs 600 ($17.14). This was considerably higher than Bata's Power, which, retailing between Rs 200–Rs 300 ($5.71–$8.57), defined the market. The consumer, who had little brand recall for Puma, saw no justification in paying a premium for a seeming "me-too" product. Puma bombed. Bata's own upmarket sally—the Hush Puppies range—met with a similar fate. Hush Puppies has scores of colleagues with low market shares and growth rates caused by largely the same problem: too much price for too little difference.

Do marketing professionals learn from their disasters? Some have. Britannia followed up its Ritz Bits fiasco with Little Hearts, which were better targeted at teenagers, and it was a runaway success.

However, sad to say, most marketing managers seldom admit the flaws in their babies. Says Hindustan Ciba-Geigy's division head, Satish Kalra, "Marketing people never listen to what the consumer is saying. For every brand that fails, there is a consumer telling them why. The commonest bad excuse is, 'The product was before its time.' They all seem to think that a time will come for a relaunch and they will be vindicated. In actual fact, the result is more disasters on an already massive list."

NOTES

1. India's original name was Jambudipa, "the flower of the rose-apple tree."

2. In India, a "naughty" child is one who precociously asserts itself. It is usually referred to in fond terms. The term has no connotation of willfully "bad" or "troublesome."

5

Distribution and Sales

WELCOME TO YOUR *KIRANA*

The *kirana*, or street shop, will be one of a dozen or so practically identical stalls on both sides of a street through which autos careen past ox carts, sending dogs whining and chickens skrawking out of the way. There are no curbs or sidewalks, and in the monsoon it all becomes a rutway of mire.

The neighboring shops will be reserved for hair-cutters (one mirror, one razor, one comb), vendors of agricultural implements (many forged from sheet iron in the back) and purveyors of poisons: *chaiwallahs* selling tea but no soft drinks and *colawallahs* selling soft drinks but no tea (caste being ever present on an Indian street), and chemists who sell just about anything without need of approval from any physician.

Most customers buy for the moment, whether it be an analgesic tablet for a headache (yes, *one!*), a disposable razor, a cigarette, or the vegetables required for the next meal. Fronting the *kirana* will be an array of banana bunches dangling on strings from metal hooks. There may be as many as twenty-three varieties of bananas (called "plantains") ranging from a few varieties of dull-green, hard-fleshed ones used only for cooking to a fairly exotic species with a skin the thickness of paper and which tastes like perfumed honey.

Aside from the bananas (mostly well past their prime), there will be an array of oranges, mangos, mangosteens, papayas, and so on (likewise mostly well past their prime) in slivery wooden bins, a metal wire bread display with six shelves that hold dozens of jars of marmalades, and polyethylene sacks of cookies.

Inside it looks like retailer's convention reduced to the dimensions of a room roughly the size of a living room but twice as high. Nowhere is there a square foot of empty anything, except perhaps for the floor, where spare foot room often as not is partly taken up by two kittens or a pup lunching on Mom. Shelf space amounts to cardboard boxes with their tops cut off and stacked on top of each other, gaping cavernously for attention. Bags of Pampers and boxes of tampons hang from the ceiling on strings, onions vie for attention with a half-dozen brands of hand soap heaped on a plank nailed to another plank nailed to a wall. You can hardly find the counter (there being no cash register) behind the facade of coffee packets and bags of dried mango slivers and onion flakes. One wall will be a garishly colored escutcheons promoting milk powders or insta-noodle soups. In between are tins of peas; sacks of lentils, garbanzos, and red beans; and things labeled in Hindi or a local script that might be either pig's knuckles or sheep testicles—it is hard to tell from the pictures. Not without reason are many Indians vegetarian.

Around the periphery, brooms hang from hooks, fire extinguishers lie next to boxes of matches in boxes (a one-stop-shop for faint-hearted pyromaniacs?), tea, toothpicks, dried chilis in frilly bunches that any good photographer could turn into art objects, two-liter bottles of cooking oil, hopsack bags of sugar and semolina spilling their cargoes over onto the floor. Do not step in the spill of brown sugar, because the proprietor intends to sweep it back into the sack momentarily.

The entire affair is coated with dust, the grime of the roaring river of diesels just outside the door, and gecko (lizard) poop decorating everything like icing on a birthday cake from hell. Locals would not dream of shopping anywhere else.

INDIA'S DISTRIBUTION SYSTEM

There are some 2.5+ million shops just like this in India's 3,700 designated towns and more than 600,000 villages. About 350 million people live within a one-minute walk of one—as heartening a fact for consumer-goods manufacturers as keeping all those *kiranas* stocked is disheartening.

India's transport infrastructure—roads, rails, and vehicles—is a severe encumbrance to economic development. Given the magnitude of the problems and the constant burden of increased use, there seems little likelihood of improvement. The principle challenges to marketers are (a) the time distribution takes, and (b) the need for more warehousing than otherwise would be sensible.

Most overseas companies work with an established distribution house, since setting up a distribution network from scratch is expensive and fraught with reliability problems. Many Indian companies distribute their products through their own networks, although a sizable number (especially the smaller ones and new entrants) use the distribution houses. Some multinationals have set up their own networks, but most use distribution houses. Centralized purchasing for chain stores and supermarkets is only a recent phenomenon.

Distribution houses exist solely for distribution—they do not, for example, do marketing and often will not even provide the type of marketing information a sales representative can give. (The representativess themselves, if you can find them, are often much more approachable.) Despite the frustration of dealing with petty-minded and inefficient people who know they have the upper hand, these distributors are often the only realistic choice. In a large company selling fast-moving consumer goods (FMCG)s, there may be 500–600 distributors and about 1,000–D1,500 wholesalers serving up to 1.2 million retailers across the country, two-thirds urban and the rest rural.

The margins at various levels of the distribution network vary among companies and, at times, even among the same company's brands. A typical example of margins in a company manufacturing FMCGs is:

Manufacturer's price to distributor	Rs 100
Distributor's price to wholesalers	104–106
Distributor's price direct to large retailers	106–108
Wholesaler's price to small retailers	108–110
Retail price to consumers	120

These are low margins compared with similar systems elsewhere in the world. They mainly reflect India's cheap labor costs. For most other goods, the entire distribution chain adds a relatively low margin of about 15 percent, compared with the 25 percent margin of many other Asian countries.

Distribution Channels

All of India's marketing success stories feature superior distribution as a theme. After advertising, distribution is the most important line item in the marketing budgets of most Indian consumer-goods manufacturers.

India has over one million market intermediaries—wholesalers, stockists, distributors, and retailers. The distribution network is dominated by family-owned businesses. While urban areas have a complex range of distribution outlets, from large supermarkets and superstores to tiny neighborhood retail stores, most villages have a narrow selection of small shops which, as we saw above, provide a narrow and uninspired line of products using a display philosophy that makes chaos seem positively tidy.

Appointing a Distributor

There are no legal or commercial restrictions on appointing a distributor in India. The distributor is normally a wealthy individual in a town who entered the business several decades earlier or was born into a local distribution dynasty that started generations ago. Often he (and it will be a he) handles a number of companies (sometimes competing) and could distribute for, say, Unilever as well as BAT.

The distributor and the manufacturer sign an agreement under which the former is obliged to service a certain territory. This arrangement stays in place almost indefinitely (there are cases where a distributorship is passed down from generation to generation) and is rarely terminated for reasons other than financial or ethical improprieties.

It is important to note that, while an agreement specifies a certain geographical area that a distributor is obliged to service, there is no legal restriction on his supplying another territory. Any such restriction would run afoul of the Monopolies and Restrictive Trade Practices Act. However, a distributor does not in fact step outside his territory. If he were to do so, there would be nothing to stop a manufacturer from appointing several other distributors in his territory.

The Mechanics of Distribution

A distributor employs sales people who visit retailers and book orders. The manufacturing company, for its part, appoints a few sales people whose brief is to ensure that the distributor's people do a good job. Normally, all important retail outlets are visited each week by the distributor's people. The manufacturer's sales people usually visit all of their important outlets on a monthly cycle. They confer with the distributor's people and book orders.

Delivery occurs using a truly marvelous variety of conveyances, ranging from smoke-belching trucks and ox carts for upscale goods, to Bajaj threeweelers with a pickup-truck–like bin on the back instead of seats for passengers, and the ubiquitous rusted bicycle towing a rickety cart on wheels whose tires have been half-flattened to cushion the shocks of the road. One of the latter with a load of cheerfully bright Coca Cola boxes is a sight good enough to frame for the office back home.

Among most major companies manufacturing FMCGs (fast-moving consumer goods), the distributor's sales people cover about 60 percent of retail outlets. The rest are covered indirectly via wholesalers. These are more stockists than wholesalers in the Western sense, supplying and stocking on shelves products ranging from soaps to cigarettes, but not selling directly to the retailers—that is the distribuor's function. Small retailers and distributors from rural areas use wholesalers because they can deliver a wide range of products. There are two differences between retail outlets serviced, respectively, by distributors and wholesalers:

- In outlets serviced by wholesalers, there can be no "company push" of the kind that can be applied to retailers serviced by a distributor.

- Most sales made by distributors are on credit (normally of one week but ranging up to three); in the case of sales via wholesalers, retailers usually pay cash for the service.

Distributorship has relatively low overheads. The cost of a sales person to a multinational company can be eight to ten times higher than the cost of a sales person to a distributor. Distributors who feel that, for example, a rural area in their territory has good potential may decide to service it themselves rather than let a wholesaler have it. In such cases, the distributor often sends out sales people in buses or on bicycles to the rural area. Sometimes the distributor may invest in a van to service that portion of territory, although not so often in the case of fast-moving low-margin consumables as with durables with higher markups and fragility factors.

Establishing a distribution network with the necessary marketing muscle is an arduous task and may take years to perfect, but the rewards are manifold. The company has control over sales and marketing, and is comfortable in the knowledge that distributors will put in enough time and energy into promoting-its product.

The vast majority of small companies do not distribute their goods nationally. This is due to their inability to advertise in the expensive national media and to their lack of networks for setting up a national network. Thus, they confine their services to within a region.

A distribution house's success depends on the reach it provides to the principal and its capacity to operate on a small enough margin so that the marketer finds it more economical to use a distribution house rather than set up its own network. There are two types of distribution houses:

- Those that do it as a regular business. Such companies usually have a few of their own products and distribute for many other companies (Voltas and TTK are good examples of such distribution houses).

- Those not in the business of distributing other companies' goods but who do it on a one-off basis for a short period of time.

Firms usually seek third-party distribution agreements for the following reasons:

- They feel that they are much too small to attract an adequate number of distributors who will get their goods to consumers across the country.

- They do not have the know-how or experience to set up a nation-wide distribution network.

- They do not have sufficient funds to set up a distribution infrastructure on their own. Marketing costs are high, and are likely to rise as the need grows to create brand awareness.

- They want immediate reach to the consumer and do not wish to wait for the two to three years required to set up a network.

Naturally, many companies use distribution houses for the first few years after starting up but later set up their own networks after they learn the business. Some foreign multinationals have forged alliances with Indian firms that have an experienced distribution infrastructure already in place. The aim is to gain easy and inexpensive access to a wider consumer reach than the multinational can attain itself.

Companies using distribution houses have several complaints about them:

- The products handled by the distribution house are not always fully "compatible" (i.e., they do not go to the same retailers); the noncompatible products thus do not fully benefit.

- The distribution company's sales staff pay more attention to their own products while other companies' goods get short shrift.

- The distribution house can provide nationwide reach but does not attempt to convince consumers to try new or newly packaged products.

INDIA'S RETAILING WORLD

India's total number of retail outlets is estimated at one million in urban areas and 2.5+ million in rural areas. Of these, greengrocers and *kirana* merchants constitute 44.5 percent, followed by general department stores at 15 percent, cigarette shops at 7.8 percent, chemists at 6 percent, and bakeries and confectionery stores at 4 percent.

Manufacturer-owned and retail-chain stores are springing up in major urban centers to market consumer goods to the middle class. The number of outlets is growing at an average rate of 8.5 percent annually. In towns with populations of between 100,000 and 1 million, the growth rate is 4.5 percent.

Changes Coming to the System

Most international consumer-goods manufacturers seeking to market in India will encounter distributors of three types:

- independent small retailers with only one or a few outlets that they run themselves and offer local convenience but few discounts;
- mass merchandisers with huge professionally run department stores, in which choice is very broad and moderate discounts are given;
- large warehouse, high-discount operations, which trade off zero service for the widest selection and cheapest prices.

Historical Background. Today's consumer-durables boom has focused attention on the distribution end as manufacturers and retailers both innovate a variety of tactics designed to gain them some kind of control over the market.

Broadly speaking, India's retailing world has only recently developed from an independent-dominated market to one in which independents are a dwindling minority and mass merchandisers and discount houses divide up the rest of the market in roughly equal portions. Buying a television, refrigerator, or mixer used to be quite simple. You knew that there were three or four brands on the market and that each had two or three models to choose from. Where people bought them depended on the product and how expensive it was. Similar technology and lower priced products, like radios, mixers, and black-and-white televisions, were available in consumer-durables retail outlets, several of which could be found in any city. For higher end items, one had to go to the showroom run by a company's exclusive distributor, who sold both to the trade and to customers. There would be just one or two showrooms per manufacturer in each city, and they were usually in the swankier parts of town.

A Rapidly Shifting Contemporary Scene. Today, shoppers, especially those looking for consumer durables, face a much greater choice of retail outlets from which to choose:

- large outlets that stock all possible brands, mostly patronized by comparison shoppers;
- smaller chain-store outlets, where the choice may not be as great, but the before- and after-sale service is much better;
- shops that specialize in stocking all brands of a specific type of product, such as table fans or refrigerators;
- stores specializing in extended-payment credit.

Such a list of options reflects India's remarkable revolution in the distribution and retailing of consumer durables. However, outside the boom in the durables sector, the number and type of channels to consumers of other products have not been changing at quite the same pace. Myriad new brands and models, Indian and foreign, jostle for limited space. The dynamism of product innovators has not been matched by retailers. As a result, new distribution channels have become the most sought-after innovation in the consumer market.

This has translated into something of a free-for-all. The consumer market is full of players trying to control part or all of the distribution chain for themselves and exclude competitors. The most notable effect has been the erosion (and disappearance in some cities) of the former system of exclusive dealers; few have been sad to see these go.

The retailing community has accepted that consumers want to choose between a variety of brands. The slow evolution away from exclusivity began, ironically enough, in distributorships themselves. Manufacturers did not prevent distributors from stocking noncompeting lines from smaller manufacturers. Hence, a dealer could distribute Kelvinator refrigerators, BPL televisions, and Philips audio systems at the same time. The logic to this was that consumers got a full range to choose from while dealers could spread their overheads over several clients and product categories.

At the same time that this innovation was occurring, consumer habits were also changing. City congestion has been a fairly rapid phenomenon. Since about 1994–1995, consumers have begun to resist driving into cities only to endure parking problems and expenses. Suburban growth has brought a sizable class of consumers who want to buy where they live.

City-centeredness has brought problems for distributors as well. If a city has, say, thirty consumer-durables outlets, a manufacturer has to be present in at least twelve of them, spread more or less evenly across the city. Their solution was to convince small retailers to stock more from exclusive distributors. The conventional wisdom was that the distribution structure for durables would successfully replicate the manufacturer—wholesaler—retailer—customer hierarchy that India's FMCG products devised early on.

Sensing this trend, large distributors increased the size of their showrooms, opened new ones, and started selling aggressively to consumers directly rather than to the trade. Small retailers who had the means opened new outlets and upgraded the quality and variety of their lines. The structure became manufacturer—retailer—customer.

This quickly became a price-sensitive system. In India, customers shopping for durables generally decide on a model first and then shop for price. However, some manufacturers and retailers saw the need for an alternative to price-based buying. Their market research found that in fact the most important consumer concern was credibility. Quality concern turned out to be as important as price. Once a consumer had a successful experience with a retailer, the customer was very likely to return for most future durables' purchases. Hence retailers were encouraged—even trained—to market for strategic retention.

The result today is four types of retailers, differentiated by the number of outlets they operate and the brands that they stock:

- large multibrand stores with few locations, huge showrooms (often multi-floor), and boutique counters for different products;
- smaller multibrand, multilocation chain stores;
- single-brand, multiple-location stores such as manufacturer-controlled retail shops;

- specialty stores in which the retailer attracts the customer through value-adding services such as installation or after-sale service.

Multibrand Stores: The Example of Vivek & Co. Vivek & Co. in Chennai (Madras) is a good example of the first type of retailer. This company operates three huge stores in metro Chennai and one in Bangalore with a combined area of over 400,000 square feet. Vivek's average monthly volume is 600 refrigerators, 400 washing machines, 650 television sets, 1,000 audio systems, and 1,500 mixers. Its price policy is low, but not the lowest. Knowing that its customers are well aware of this, Vivek turned it to its advantage by holding an annual New Year's Day sale during which prices are cut to the bone. Vivek's volume on that day is equivalent to a thirteenth month of sales. In 1996, Vivek projected a turnover of around Rs 55 crore ($15.7 million).

Vivek clearly reflects current retailer thinking in its expansion plans. The firm is building three more large-format stores in Chennai, one of which will be reserved only for high-value consumer durables. This tactic could not be easily pulled off by a smaller chain. Moreover, Vivek recognizes the inherent dangers in too much bigness and is rapidly developing fifteen to twenty smaller stores that more resemble the typical chain-store format of around 3,000 to 4,000 square feet and broad but not in-depth product representation.

Vivek's motivation for this investment is that if they do not do it, somebody else will. Indeed, another 250,000 square foot megastore has just opened outside Chennai in the suburban market that Vivek has not much penetrated. Vivek's chain-store concept is also being aggressively promoted by Jainsons, which has ten retail outlets in Chennai and seven in other towns in Tamil Nadu. Jainsons seeks to distinguish itself through increasing specialization in higher end products, especially color televisions. Their thinking is that, given space limitations and so many more products appearing all the time, it makes sense for retailers to specialize in categories. Jainsons has opted for high-tech.

Moving back to the broader picture of India, there is a move by some stores to even more specificity than the example of Jainsons. A firm might, for example, specialize in only fans and air conditioners. The thinking behind this is that these are products bought at particular times of the year, while most consumer durables can be bought at any time. Fans and air conditioners follow the seasonal cycles of a torrid, dry spring; a cool and damp monsoon season; and a warm, more humid autumn. Other shops tend to specialize only in items that people buy when moving into a new house.

Here the customer is not necessarily after the cheapest fans but expert advice and installation/post-purchase service.

Product expertise is becoming a marketable fact. Most retailers know little about how the products they sell are made or what causes them to go wrong. While matters have not quite gotten to the factory-training stage for the average durable as yet, some dealers are being invited to sit in on dealer advisory panels set up by manufacturers to solicit information from the trade. The retro effect of this is dealers who know what is behind the plastic housing on the product.

If product awareness is one value addition, a far more potent selling point is retailers with in-depth knowledge of consumer finance—particularly the benefits of their plan versus the defects of others. India's more finance-savvy retailers are thus better able to qualify customers.

Consumer finance itself is undergoing changes. The problem most retailers face is how to establish the credit-worthiness of potential terms purchasers in a society filled with so much hidden income and a social stigma attached to discussing the source of one's income. Some retailers form relationships with collection agents to weed out risks. Given an inside track on a customer's credit history, retailers can take more calculated risks with terms. The next step in this area is using credit histories to prune bad and target good customers for direct-mail campaigns featuring products suited to their assumed discretionary income.

Hence Vivek, and others like it, have reversed the retailer's position by claiming both the retailer's and the distributor's margins. Manufacturers hate having to give in to the chains' demands for additional margins, and instead try to channel these into alternate forms of remuneration such as dealer gifts and increased assistance for publicity and promotion.

The foregoing is largely a metro and city retailing phenomenon. Outstation and rural retailers are still largely at the manufacturer's mercy. Manufacturers still demand advance deposits but take their own time sending inventory. Margins to the trade have traditionally been around 10 percent for retailers and 4–5 percent for distributors. Low as that is, many companies insist on cutting into it to fund their own promotional costs, lightly white-washed as "better exposure for the retailer" since the retailers' names are often in fine print in the ads. Small retailers can do nothing.

The Manufacturers' Response: Reference-Point Retailing. The manufacturers' view on all these changes is ambivalent. On the positive side, these retailing efforts ultimately result in increases in sales. Yet it is clear that they are losing a degree of power over their retailers. In India, power relationships are just as important as money relationships. Power is a very ancient form of trade, and in India the modern is often a rewritten form of the ancient.

What has switched the equation to the side of retailers is the great many manufacturers whose bottom lines are nowhere as good as the retailers'. Shortage of retail space has forced manufacturers into concessions of the 2 percent on net-10 type (which in India is often net-6).

Manufacturers are countering by turning more and more to proprietary showrooms. BPL Galleries, Onida Arcades, Videocon Plazas, and Voltas World are examples of "brand boutiques" that are more and more visible in larger cities. In these, manufacturers sell on their own terms, quite often co-opting the retailer-perfected goodwill base of services such as easy-terms credit and after-sales. The retailers are not pleased, and their complaints in the otherwise unexciting retail/distributor trade press is an endless source of revelation.

In order to avoid the semblance of direct competition between manufacturers and trade, the outlets are run by franchisees and their prices are not discounted. This phenomenon is called "reference-point retailing." The manufacturers' franchisees are guaranteed a return and hence are not effected by sales. Only top-end products are sold and the manufacturers are not unduly distressed if consumers inspect and get the complete details of their products at an exclusive shop and then buy it cheaper from a multibrand shop.

There are some clear marketing advantages to reference-point retailing. One addresses the fact that retailing is a very working capital intensive business in which many retailers discount heavily against each other to attract quick sales. A quality brand loses its quality image. When a manufacturer opens an in-house boutique, its products are displayed properly. Retailers turn the boutique prices to their advantage by using their highly visible prices, not the lower ones in the trade catalogs, as the reference points for discounts.

The Rural Picture. The descriptions in the foregoing apply mainly to the cities. For the rest of India, which has been so slow to change in many regards, retailing will likely remain not very different from the way it has always been done. Again, personal/power relationships dominate over price/volume concerns. The exclusive dealership seems to be making some inroads there, and as the market grows a few newer brands will likely find their way to the shelves. Rural dealers see that most of their turnover comes from a few brands. Most do not sense any real need to go to the trouble of dealing with many different companies. They are likely to continue with the same brands and sell them the same way.

Third-Party Distribution

As more new products are launched in the market, third-party contract distribution can be a useful, though not problem-free, means of market penetration.

Rather than waste time and money establishing their own sales teams and dealer networks, Indian consumer-products distributors have long outsourced distribution to either independent agents or alliances with established companies that distribute their own related but not competing consumer goods.

Most examples are fairly straightforward. Birla 3M, the makers of Scotch Brite, distributes via TTK, a Bangalore-based maker of Prestige pressure cookers and kitchenware. Wrigley's chewing gum is co-distributed with Parrys Sweets, an arrangement that serves the similar markets of an American multinational and a Chennai-based confectionery company. GEEP Industrial Syndicate, the Allahabad-based manufacturer of flashlights and batteries, is open to alliances to distribute the products of several other manufacturers; the first was Mount Everest mineral water. Reebok's distribution solution is slightly different: They appointed an independent logistics consultancy, the Mumbai-based Nexus Logistics, to act as their western India distributor.

The sudden popularity of contract distribution has come as something of a surprise to industry analysts. Many had written off arrangements like the above examples as unworkable. Indeed, the early 1990s gave news reporters plenty to occupy themselves with as several high-profile distribution arrangements collapsed. Voltas' distribution division lost the Kelvinator and Spencer & Co. refrigerator distribution accounts. The ubiquitous Parrys at one time also distributed the Horlicks and Britannia beverage supplements. TTK's range included Levers soap, Cadbury chocolates, and Sheaffer pens. Yet all of these companies suspended these contract operations to build their own distribution networks.

The recent resurgence of contract distribution arrangements illustrates a historical pattern that applies to other shared-business arrangements in India.

Contract distribution is in fact one of the oldest channels for the diffusion of branded goods in India. It originated during the British Raj, when English companies became interested in tapping the Indian markets. Their goods were first sold to local importers, but as volumes grew they started appointing agents who would distribute on commission. Some, such as Spencer's, had retail outlets of their own, but most were purely godownto-shopfront agents. After Independence, the concept was altered somewhat in that small local manufacturers represented the old British companies. The principle was the same: national distribution by a third party. The Voltas distribution network made possible the fame of brand names like Amul and Rasna.

Today, multinationals have refueled the old boom. Starting up on one's own distribution company—as Pepsi did—is a costly option. It costs roughly Rs 10 crore ($2.85 million) to start up a large consumer distribution company, and can take as long as a year to become smoothly operational and two years to become fully market responsive.

Most multinationals are unable to commit to either acquire a company or start one as a joint venture, nor do they want to go to the trouble and expense of setting up their own network. One problem they face is self-referential: They assume that, since they are competent marketing in other parts of the world, India should be no different in the long run. They recognize that distribution in India has particular problems such as the sheer scale of national operations and the difficulties to be expected from labor. However, they are often not prepared for the time it takes to solve these problems.

Hence many companies start their operations by piggybacking on another company until they are experienced enough to go it alone. A company tying up with GEEP Industrial Syndicate, for example, can instantly plug into a network of 1,550 distributors and 310 sales personnel who cover over 300,000 retail outlets. Wrigley's tie-up with Parrys has given them coverage in 250,000 outlets serviced by 1,200 dealers and 103 sales personnel.

A company need not necessarily be after mass market penetration to benefit from contract distribution. Premium-goods manufacturers that ordinarily distribute through select market-specific outlets can outsource their distribution through relatively lean operations that know India's regional markets.

Case Study: The Nexus of Nexus with Reebok. Reebok wanted to launch nationally but had only twenty-five executives, all in their Delhi office. They found a good match in Nexus Logistics, an independent logistics consultancy. Nexus itself was a new idea and had not yet achieved notable success selling to Indian companies. (Most Indian companies consider logistics to be a glorified form of dispatch operation.)

Nexus's Reena Singh approached Reebok on spec. Reebok showed her an empty warehouse and told her to take it from there. Singh worked out the optimal warehouse layout for receiving, stacking, and picking the many

Reebok models; trained people to work in it; and helped draw up the general logistics plan for the country. When the product was launched in Mumbai, she helped again. Nexus became so vital to Reebok's success that they appointed Singh their Western region manager. She continues to operate Nexus independently (it has other clients), but also does all that any Reebok regional manager would do.

Variations on the Theme. A success story of this type does not mask the fact that when companies look for partners they have to consider more than the mere numbers. Even with the mass market distributors, the type of distribution network matters as much or more than sheer market penetrability. For Wrigley's, the fact that the Parrys network served a similar product category mattered equally as much as their network size. Braun deliberately chose to form an arrangement with an Indian third-party distributor despite their access to the company's parent, Gillette, whose razor blades have one of the widest distribution networks in the country. However, Gillette's myriad mass market outlets were unsuitable for upmarket products like Braun, which needed more department store outlets. This was the market in which TTK's Prestige cookers sold.

For Birla 3M, the attraction of TTK went beyond their field force of 1,200 and coverage of over 16,000 retail outlets. Rather, it was the two firms' synergies in distribution. Birla 3M had looked at Lever, Wipro, and Godrej before settling TTK. One such synergy was the natural relationship between TTK's Prestige pressure cookers and Scotch Brite's cleanser pads. The partnership has been synergistic in other regards as well: Scotch Brite's sales have grown so rapidly that today they comprise 15 percent of total company sales.

Examples such as this underscore the need to look for hidden virtues in contract distributing to new markets. Indeed, new entrants into the India market may sense caution from distribution companies unless there is the possibility of a joint venture. This has to do with the low margins of 1 to 2 percent in the distribution business, which makes it unwise for firms to take on clients with new, unproved, or ill-defined markets.

Another cause of ambivalence can be the distributors' earlier experiences, or stories they have heard about agreements gone awry. Unless planned as long-term relationships, contract distribution can boomerang, leaving ill-will on both sides. The Voltas experience began to keep the business press busy after it agreed to distribute the Amul Company's products. This turned out to be quite profitable, so Voltas added Rasna, a minor brand selling in Gujarat; Mealmaker, the Kothari General Foods line of brands like Tang; and Volfarm, in which Voltas did the marketing as well as the distribution. Then Amul and Rasna decided that they had become large enough to sever the connection and go it alone. Voltas was left with no really successful product in hand, and the company realized that the returns from those they did have could not justify their now-huge sales and distribution infrastructure. The distribution subsidiary soon shut down.

Today distribution companies place strong emphasis on manufacturing their own line of products in addition to those they distribute. TTK, for example, has grown from distribution into a primarily manufacturing company. Of their total consumer-products sales of around Rs 340 crore ($97 million), distribution accounts for only Rs 10 crore ($2.85 million). Companies in this position agree to distribute outside brands mainly to spread their overheads. Distributors are convinced that a cardinal rule is to keep costs variable and to avoid anything that might prove to be quicksand if the supplier business leaves.

Cross-Product Conflicts of Interest. When working with distributors who also manufacture, it is important to carefully look for hidden cross-product conflicts of interest. The size of the retail outlets to be serviced is important, since a distributor might be tempted to spread its sales force too thinly or have them wasting their time chasing different types of outlets, leaving the new partner's products in a lurch. Some sales people will cope with distributing a consumer durable and a nondurable by focusing on the one with the highest commissions irrespective of price or volume.

Another cautionary is to avoid stretching the sales force. A rule of thumb is that a sales person can handle up to five different product lines, as long as the total number of stock-keeping units (SKUs) does not exceed about fifty-five.

Some Indian business analysts state that the biggest value of contract distribution lies in how it can change Indian companies' simple perception of distribution as an infrastructure necessity into a broader view in which it is an asset of its own that can be used to leverage their other—preferably new—products manufactured in India.

Multilevel Marketing

The multilevel marketing (MLM) system would seem tailor-made for India's underutilized work force of nonemployed women. MLM in India uses the same organizational formula as in the West: a sales force of independent distributors who sell products directly to consumers and earn commissions from the form of the difference between the distributor's cost and the selling price, plus income from a portion of the commissions earned by other distributors they recruit.

Given that MLM bypasses the retail chain, it would seem best suited for rural areas and remote suburbs. With shelves in India's retail stores already overflowing, innovative marketers (some not traditionally MLM distributors) have turned to the method:

- The $300 million Swedish cosmetics company Oriflame International was the first to introduce the concept in India in mid-1995. Oriflame India, a joint venture with the Rs 7 crore ($2 million) Delhi-based trading house Rollscon India, quickly built an MLM network of 5,000 distributors notching up sales of over Rs 10 crore ($2.8 billion) in 10 months.

- In March 1996, Modi Care, part of the Rs 784-crore ($224 million) K.K. Modi Group, started selling its range of household and personal care products in Delhi, with 800 front-line distributors forming the core of a planned MLM network, and an initial investment of Rs 20 crore ($5.7 million).

- The $6.3 billion U.S. household products company, Amway Corporation—with more than 2.5 million distributors worldwide—introduced its range of household cleaners, laundry-care, kitchen-care, and personal-care products at the end of 1996, investing Rs 25 crore ($7.14 million) in manufacturing and marketing operations.

- The $4.5 billion American cosmetics giant, Avon, will be taking the MLM route when it launches its skin-care range in 1997 with a first-year investment of Rs 7 crore.

All of these products target the same market. All have priced their products in the premium slot. Oriflame's and Avon's cosmetics are among the most expensive products in their genres, and Amway and Modi Care's products are in the top fifth of the price range in each category. Can the market support so many players with so many similar products at the same high price points?

MLM marketers in India are making the same assumption that has served them so well in more affluent economies: The real customer for MLM is not one of the minuscule (by Indian standards) 600,000 wealthy Indian consumers who is normally the target for premium-priced products. Instead, it is distributors who are the major customers of their own products.

Distributors of MLM companies in the United States sell, on average, only 19 percent of their products to new customers. Indian MLM marketers calculate that their percentage will remain about the same.

India's business press sees MLM as a quick, cost-effective channel for distributing products to customers, bypassing the logistics of India's warehouse-depot distributor/retailers. This is not news. These analysts also see some sharp downsides to MLM in the Indian arena.

For one, the MLM product profile is narrow: fast-moving consumer goods targeted at niche markets such as specialist cosmetics or premium fragrances. None of the major players cited above distributes products that need to be demonstrated—hand-held vacuum cleaners or illustrated books, for example—which gain from the personal interaction between customer and salesperson. Analysts regard MLM as a niche for Indian distributors who cannot easily get shelf space as a serious misreading of the true market—everyday garments and education-related items being two examples of missed opportunities.

They also have mixed feelings about the MLM method of presenting only one product line. To them the biggest merit of conventional retailing is that the consumer has so many options. Unless the MLM product is a novelty or the customer has developed a close relationship with the brand, analysts expect MLM to compete strongly against similar retail products only in areas where the retail products are hard to get to.

The strategy of selling many same-branded products simultaneously also does not cut much ice with Indian business analysts. Amway's MLM distributors, for instance, try to sell an array of floor-care, glass-care, and car-care products; laundry detergents and fabric softeners; and personal care products—all with the name Amway on them. Not that there is anything wrong with Amway—but it isn't Modi Care.

Modi Care plans to attack Amway's identity gap by flooding its distribution chain with its ten visually familiar (and scent-familiar) product lines from its portfolio of over 1,000 products, including the same array of detergent powders, fabric-stiffening iron-aids, multipurpose cleaners, shampoos, toothpastes, mouth-fresheners, and beauty soap.

The term "scent-familiar" should be broadened to include "shape-familiar" and "size-familiar." The concept "superjumbo = good deal" is new territory for Indian consumers. In a climate where spoilage is often associated with overbuying, there is a long-established aesthetic of just-enough which corresponds roughly to the Japanese mentality about just-in-time. The Indian housewife habitually purchases only as many vegetables as she needs for the next meal. They may well rot in the bin at the market stall, but they are not going to rot in *her* kitchen. It will be interesting to see what marketing analysts have to say when enough sales data are in to compare Amway's size mentality against Modi Care's just-enough mentality.

Product definition considerations aside, analysts are also asking whether today's product range is necessarily the only good one for MLM. Picking their way through the virtues and limitations of MLM, analysts have come up with some dos and don'ts for would-be MLMers:

- Products priced too low or too high will not offer the sense of good value at the heart of the MLM buying experience.

- The assumption that MLM works well only for consumer nondurables has never been tested with many other nondurable product categories.

- Nor has the assumption been tested that MLM will not work with high-value durables that normally involve testing rival brands— no one has put five televisions, five wet-dry vacuum cleaners, and a petrol generator on the back of a pickup before.

- Innovative products where there are few brands to choose from can most easily broaden their customer base through MLM.

- Existing MLM marketers are excellent candidates to introduce new products from noncompeting manufacturers to the marketplace.

Analysts also see some downsides to MLM at other levels than distribution:

- Matching manufacturing volumes to sales can be fraught with dangers since the MLM method's only forecasting tool is the number of its distributors.

- Too successful an MLM effort necessitates either big inventories to ensure that there is no supply shortfall or customer-alienating delays in delivery.

- There is little prospect for strong equity for the brand; absence of advertising limits brand awareness to only customers who distributors actually call on.

- With prices and discounts often being arbitrarily extended by the distributor to meet personal volume targets, the value statement of the brand is never certain.

- The MLM parent company is never in touch with its real consumers; hence it is vulnerable to the "see no evil, hear no evil" mindset of overly optimistic distributors.

- Tracking customer tastes, checking their perceptions, and monitoring satisfaction levels is impossible.

- There is an ever-present possibility that the MLM chain will break down due to distributors jumping ship or not selling enough to meet their income expectations and giving up.

- So long as distributors are also principal customers, erosion of the first will result in loss of the second.

Hence the conventional wisdom in India is that companies which invest only in MLM, without the back-up of a retail network, run substantial risks. The MLM-dependent company, never having built bridges with its customers, risks losing buyers unless its distributors are perpetually happy. Hence MLM will remain a niche channel like direct-mail catalogs or TV home shopping and will work best for well-funded major players. Its greatest opportunities lie in products to which the system has not been traditionally applied. This, however, means a substantially capitalized learning curve.

CASE STUDIES

Pharmaceuticals Distribution

The pharmaceuticals industry has seen numerous changes in the last few years. From a market dominated by a few multinationals, the industry now has 18,000 licensed manufacturers competing with over 50,000 branded products generating Rs 10,000 crore ($2.85 billion) in sales.

The industry relies on a brigade of some 40,000 medical representatives who go from doctor to doctor with briefcases full of pamphlets, samples, and, increasingly, laptop computers. These representatives usually have a Bachelor of Science degree (in some cases an MBA from a smaller institute). They call on up to fifteen doctors per day, getting a bare two or three minutes to impart their information to a particular doctor. The doctors are chosen by the companies' area sales managers on the basis of information garnered largely from retail chemists (pharmacists). Representatives operate in marked territories, have sales targets, follow up on visits, and ensure sustained prescription support. As long as an individual doctor makes pharmaceuticals decisions, there is likely to be little change in this system. The world of the medical representatives, however, is being stressed by a combination of problems:

- Recently there has been an explosion of me-too products prompted by the process-patent approach encouraged by the Indian government. For example, the Ranbaxy firm launched Cifran five years ago at Rs 19; today there are 132 substitutes available at less than Rs 5.

- The pressures of the job have produced a precipitous drop in the quality of people being recruited. With more than 5 lakh (500,000) general practitioners in the country, pharmaceuticals companies are keen to expand coverage. In their bid to recruit more representatives, selection criteria suffer.

- Doctors have a low regard for representatives, particularly in large cities where doctors dismiss them as lowly sales people with no real knowledge of the goods they are promoting. Many doctors feel themselves sufficiently informed by direct mailers from the manufacturers.

Doctors may show the representatives little respect, but representatives demand and get it from the companies they work for. This is largely because they are organized and unionized.

The process of unionization among medical sales representatives illustrates some of the attitudes related to union thinking all over India. The Federation of Medical Representatives Association of India (FMRAI) is recognized by some thirty companies. Instead of using the collective process to press for job-skills upgrading, FMRAI agitates to get their representatives deemed workmen the same way factory workers are, although the hours FMRAI wants also happen to be the hours doctors are the busiest and least likely able to see a sales representative.

FMRAI has also gone in for union action. In the northern and eastern zones, it barred pharmaceutical companies' management teams from entering their territories without prior notice. The state level FMRAI in Punjab issues a "green pass" that allows area sales managers entry into their territories and refuses to work beyond three in the afternoon.

The pharmaceuticals' management has brought a lot of their problems on themselves. Low motivation from representatives is related to policies like surprise territory checks and transfers on short notice—meaning that representatives are often suddenly uprooted from their families—have contributed to the FMRAI's present stance. Moreover, the companies have made few attempts at upgrading job skills. There has been little enhancement of their job profiles in keeping with the changing industry.

These are somewhat offset by pay packages. Most trainees start on an average of Rs 5,000 ($143) per month, along with daily allowances. Representatives with ten years' experience earn as much as Rs 15,000 to Rs 20,000 ($429–$571) a month—a very good income in India.

The fading reputation of the representative has led some companies to experiment with ways to bypass them. The results are still not in. Soon after FMRAI started agitating in its areas, the Cipla Company dismantled its operation and switched to direct mailers to its doctors. These were not as successful as Cipla expected, so the company went back to direct selling—only now using MBAs from smaller institutes given the cosmetic rename "product managers."

The Lupin Company, with about 635 representatives, opted for organized doctors' meetings. In 1995, Lupin hosted 250 meetings in 100 towns all across India, organized in association with local Indian Medical Association (IMA) bodies. Each meeting usually attracted thirty to thirty-five doctors. This approach was initially successful enough that several other companies copied it.

Lupin's was a halfway step in a changing consciousness which is beginning to see that it is no longer enough to simply promote products. Companies must be perceived as being involved with overall health care. This comes in part from the external factor of so many competing products involving much more complex molecules. The medical profession has come to see its role as product evaluator, which has replaced its self-image as consumer.

The more foresightful companies like Lupin participate in national seminars on generic issues such as TB and AIDS, and publish periodicals aimed at the 130,000 doctors on the mailing list. Glaxo has an online medical database. Medline has an online database of doctors. Wockhardt promotes drugs through medical symposia. Its Aminodrip (an intravenous amino acid) was launched at such a symposium in 1994. Ranbaxy has struck a balance in which medical conferences are organized by the area sales managers with local chapters of the IMA, which local sales reps in the area attend.

Some techniques do not do well. Joint conferences are often poorly attended—the more reputed doctors are too busy to come, and many doctors feel that they are just expenses-paid holidays with little scientific interaction.

Hence companies like Lupin are returning more wisely to representatives and training them better. But most companies need to do more to update their representatives. Most do not have a full-fledged training department—after an initial training period of three to six weeks, representatives receive less than a month of continuing education each year thereafter.

Some companies are taking proactive note of such concerns. When Ranbaxy launched Conviron TR iron capsules with a gastric delivery system, they prepared a multimedia presentation to demonstrate the working of the medicine. When the representatives made follow-up visits to doctors, they were given laptops with the same presentation. They were also accompanied by area sales managers to make sure they handled the message (and the laptop!) right.

The FMRAI issue about whether representatives are management or labor is irrelevant in the eyes of most observers of the medical representative world. The real issue is that representatives need less union restriction and more and continual upgrades to their skills. (This observation could indeed be generalized to much of India.) Chastened by the only partial success of their promotional techniques, companies see that they cannot do without the representatives. With more new drugs on the way, both companies and representatives have to work more closely, but personalized selling will remain the mainstay promotional tool.

The Tetrapak Jinx

What do you do in a category where nearly every product launched has failed? Cut the losses and close? Keep plugging away? Or launch something wildly different in the hope that it may change the rules of the game?

Welcome to the four basic questions of life in India's tetrapak market, one of the most casualty ridden in the country.

- Unilever chose the first option and killed its Lipton Treetop brand, despite the money and effort that had gone into it.

- Godrej Foods took the second, relaunching its Jumping product line, only to watch sales barely rise above a low hop.

- Parle Agro tried the third option with the launch of Joly Jely, a jelly-based drink that was completely different from anything else on the market. Unfortunately, sales were also like jelly.

Tetrapaks have proved themselves a difficult category—a situation that has not occurred in other Asian countries the way it has in India. Once tetrapak was touted as the way to rewrite the rules in the soft drinks industry due to disposability and ease of transport and storage. Yet with a total market size of a minuscule about 11 million cases—only 10 percent of soft drink sales—they are no threat to glass-bottled drinks. Even Parle Agro, which produced India's one tetrapak winner—Frooti, a mango-based drink—has never managed to duplicate Frooti's success with its other tetrapak drinks. At best, Parle Agro's other two mainstay sellers, Appy (apple) and Pingo (pineapple), ride along on Frooti's coattails.

However, based on these three, Parle Agro decided to try something completely new. The idea was a product that would break the concept that tetrapaks only contain fruit drinks. In one of the fastest launches in Indian marketing history, Parle Agro took barely fourteen weeks to take Joly Jely from product idea to shop shelves. The product was tested via trials among 2,000 people across the country, receiving a positive response of 89 percent; of these, 21 percent said they would prefer Joly Jely to any other drink. On the minus side, some customers complained that the product was hard to drink, which Parle Agro modified by reducing the gel content.

The 1996 launch in Pune took on the air of an election campaign. Parle Agro also invested heavily in trial and spot promotions. The company spent Rs 2 crore ($571,000) on the launch and another Rs 2 crore on advertising. Production costs came to Rs 5 crore ($1.42 million) for a stand-alone production line with a 150,000 cases (of twenty-seven packs each) capacity. The distribution went through the seven franchisees Parle Agro uses for Frooti.

Despite these efforts, market circles were skeptical of Joly Jely's ultimate success. They pointed to the very small customer base that is familiar with edible jelly, much less the idea of drinking it. They also pointed out that radical departures from fruit drinks, such as soya milk drinks, have failed just as miserably—despite the fact that soya milk sells well among Southeast Asians of Indian ancestry.

In the tetrapak market, 90 percent is cornered by mango-based drinks, 65 percent of which is accounted for by Frooti. Frooti so dominates the market that Parle Agro's competitor, Godrej's Jumping-brand mango drink, is billed Jumpin' Frooti by retailers.

The reason for Frooti's success is several-fold. The mango-eating base in the country is large. Drinking mango extract is common. Mothers mash mangoes for baby food. When tetrapak drinks became associated with mango drinks, they became associated with the all-natural drinks image. Moving away radically has made for unpredictable results. Tetrapak has inadvertently boxed itself into a niche market in which there is not much of a market in the niche.

Volume Fabric Retailing

The decor of Kumaran Silks' 19,000 square foot outlet is definitely commercial kitsch married to Kodambakkam art deco, but clearly the 5,000 shoppers who are sucked in through its portals everyday do not care. As a result, Kumaran Silks in Chennai is now one of the largest retailers in the country, with Rs 150 crore ($42.8 million) a year in sales. In the process it has apparently overtaken Nalli's, its venerable neighbor and the shop most associated with saris in Chennai. Under its single roof Kumaran has 150 counters, employs 460 sales people, and sells textiles sourced from every state in India. Silk accounts for 50 percent of the stock, and the rest is in handlooms and synthetics. When the firm expands into ready-mades (ready-to-wear) in 1996–1997, it expects sales to expand 25 percent to Rs 200 crore ($57.1 million).

Such success would probably have been beyond the wildest dreams of its founder, the late P.G. Chengalvaraya Chettiar, a weaver from the Padmasalyar weaving community of Kanjeevaram who set it up as a modest 30 by 40 foot shop. Ramamurthy, his son, attributes it simply to hard work and total commitment. "Being in the shop from morning to night, offering what our customers want, good quality stuff, competitive pricing, and, above all, receiving my customers warmly, paying attention to what they say ... this is the secret of Kumaran's enduring popularity," he says. It is a formula he has ensured has been learnt by his four sons, P.R. Babu, P.R. Subramaniane, P.R. Kesavan, and P.R. Kumar.

The sons take care of the sourcing from all over the country, and in doing so close attention is paid to customer preferences. "At the end of everyday, our counter sales personnel communicate what varieties move faster, and why certain others don't," says Babu, adding, "this is the best guide for our future buying." Ramamurthy has developed an impressive system of communicating this customer preference for color combinations, weight in silks, preference for zari and types of weaves to the store's 1,000-odd dedicated master weavers located in Kanjivaram, Arni, and Kumbakonam.

The master weavers, the dye suppliers, and the Kumaran family team then work together to make a small-scale prototype to evaluate the design and texture and then implement the final product. Recently, computer-aided design and color coordination has been introduced, affording more freedom to innovate on customer feedback.

The shopping crowds throng around the year, but peak in particular during the wedding season, from April to July, with a slight lull during the inauspicious period from 15 July to 15 August. "But from Pongal, to the wedding season, through Ramzan, Diwali, and Christmas, we have our loyal customers who will not go anywhere else for their shopping," says Ramamurthy. Kumaran does not spend much on print or audiovisual ads, preferring to depend on word-of-mouth publicity. "We bring out ten new sari designs every year during Diwali, and it is only then that we get these modeled, for fashion advertising, spending about Rs 10 lakh to Rs 15 lakh," says Ramamurthy.

Kumaran is proud of the width of its clientele. Ramamurthy points out that they have prices to suit every pocket. "We have saris from Rs 1,200 to Rs 40,000. I make profits on the big volumes, not margins." Another major advantage is range. While most of its competitors concentrate on saris, Kumaran also sells mill cloth (all major brands), suitings (fabric for suits), shirtings (the same for shirts), and blouse material, offering customers the convenience of shopping for all of their needs, in air-conditioned comfort, under one roof.

Kumaran's most important selling point is service. "Even a *ricksha wallah* (rickshaw puller) shops happily here, because he is treated well. No snootiness. Our USP is this personal touch. We don't want anyone ever to say that Kumaran has changed or that 'cared for' feeling has gone," emphasises Ramamurthy. The key factor in this is naturally the sales people—on a typical marriage season day, a counter person may have to attend to one hundred customers, taking them through the huge variety of textiles and patiently dealing with the confusion that such a range tends to cause. Understanding their importance, Ramamurthy takes good care of them, for example, by implementing free housing. And of course there is the constant presence of the family on the floor, adept at moving around and making sure that no one goes away unhappy or without buying something.

Ramamurthy is optimistic about the future. "But we will keep on building our customer base, by giving them what they want, with assured quality and affordable pricing."

Kerala's KINFRA Textiles and Apparel Park

"Bangalore is already crowded and we can offer sites and infrastructure at a far lower cost," explains G.C. Gopala Pillai, managing director of KINFRA. "If Bangalore can do it, why can't Thiruvananthapuram?"

That seems to be the driving spirit behind the plan of the Kerala Industrial Infrastructure Development Corporation (KINFRA) to build a new 50-acre International Apparel Park in the capital of Kerala state. KINFRA is assiduously wooing some of the country's top Bangalore-based garment exporters, notably Rajendra Hinduja of Gokaldas Exports, owners of two chains of ready-made stores named Wearhouse and Weekender.

The KINFRA Kerala venture is positioning itself head-to-head with the Karnataka Industrial Areas Development Board in Bangalore, which advertised ready built "industrial flats" for garment entrepreneurs at its proposed site in the Peenya Industrial Park in Bangalore. The advertised price was Rs 1,650 ($47.14) per square foot, the real price negotiable.

Hence the KINFRA Apparel Park proposed built-up areas at Rs 400 ($11.43) per square foot. The first few buyers were offered land at Rs 14 lakh ($40,000) for a one-acre plot, to be raised to Rs 20 lakh ($57,140) for latecomers. Units which commence production within a year of allotment of the site were to be reimbursed Rs 2 lakh ($5,714) as a concession.

Power being a perennial problem in India, KINFRA planned to get a dedicated 11-kilovolt power line from the Kerala State Electricity Board (KSEB) to offer its units electricity whose tariff, at under a rupee for a unit, would be cheaper than elsewhere in the country. However, plagued with a growing demand–supply gap, the KSEB could take some time to provide the power connection to the park, so KINFRA planned to install an on-site diesel generator.

KINFRA also touted another advantage in Kerala's literate women workforce. There is an acute shortage of skilled labor in Bangalore, with workers job-hopping from one garment firm to the other for often trifling increases in pay—the "move if it's more" attitude is common in Maharashtra and Karnataka's fast-industrializing areas. Kerala bills its labor force as cheaper and more literate. This from a state that has been fiercely Communist for decades.

To generate a pool of skilled workers, KINFRA planned to set up a training center in its Apparel Park. Girls from the local area would be trained free, but without any firm promise of employment. The idea was to offer entrepreneurs a ready-made bank of skilled hands to tap into once the park begins to function, scheduled for September 1997. To do the training,

KINFRA planned to draw on the resources of the National Institute of Fashion Technology (NIFT).

If it takes off as planned, the KINFRA Apparel Park will house thirty-six units, each with 200 machines offering a minimum production capacity of 2,000 pieces of ready-made garments a day. Each unit will typically employ between 420 and 500 workers.

Its bigger lesson is how spillover entrepreneurialism works in today's fast-changing India.

Appendix A: Useful Terms

acharya: religious teacher

adivasi: a tribal person, especially the hill people in the northeastern states

agarbati: incense

ahimsa: nonviolence

angrezi: general term for Westerners

apsara: heavenly nymph, equivalent to bacchantes

arak: liquor distilled from coconut juice

asana: yogic seating posture; also a small mat used in prayer and meditation

ashram: a center for spiritual learning and religious practice

asura: demon

atman: soul

avatar: reincarnation of Vishnu on earth

ayah: nursemaid

ayurveda: ancient system of medicine employing herbs, minerals, and massage

bagh: garden or park

baithak: reception area in private house

baksheesh: bribe; also a tip or donation

bandh: strike

baniya: a moneylender

banyan: labyrinthine fig tree traditionally used as a meeting place for teaching and meditating

bazaar: commercial center or market

begum: Muslim princess or women of high status

bhajan: song

bhakti: religious devotion expressed in a personalized or emotional relationship with the deity

bhawan (also bhavan): palace or residence

bhumi: earth, also an earth goddess

bidi: tobacco rolled in a leaf

bindu: red dot worn by women on their foreheads as an adornment

bodhi: sacred pipal or ficus tree, associated with the Buddha's enlightenment

bodhisattva: Buddhist equivalent of a saint

brahmin: member of the highest caste group; priest

bundh: strike

burkha: body-covering shawl worn by orthodox Muslim woman

burra-sahib: colonial official; boss; man of importance

bustee: slum or squatter settlement in a city

cablewallah: person who sells cable TV connections (often pirated from nearby legal ones) and who (on rare occasions) services them

camise: woman's knee-length shirt, worn with *shalwa* trousers

cantonment: military quarters

caste: social status acquired at birth

chai: tea

chaiwallah: tea seller

chakra: focus of power energy point in the body; also a wheel representing the circle of death and rebirth

chandra: moon

chappal: sandals; flip-flops; thongs

charpoi: string bed with wooden frame

chauri: fly whick, symbol of royal authority

chemist: licensed pharmacist

Chennai: new name for Madras

choli: short, tight-fitting blouse worn with a sari

chowkidar: watchman/caretaker

Congress (Indian National Congress Party): Founded in 1885, becoming a major force during India's independence movement. Congress dominant in Parliament and formed governments from 1947 to 1977 and 1980 to 1985, at which time it enjoyed its largest-ever legislative majority. In 1969 Congress split, and the ruling party became known as Congress (R) for Ruling; in 1978 it became Congress (I) for Indira (a label recently dropped).

coolie: porter/laborer

copies: locally made products deceptively sold in foreign packaging; scotch whiskies are notorious victims

crore: 10 million; colloquially, "crores and crores" means "zillions"

dacoit: bandit

dalit: "oppressed"; the term preferred by untouchables as a description of their social position

darshan: vision of a deity or saint; receiving religious teachings

dawan: servant

deva: deity

devadasi: temple dancer

devi: goddess

dhaba: food hall selling local dishes

dham: important religious site or theological college

dharamshala: rest house for pilgrims

dharma: conformance to duty and obligations of life as determined by *karma* and divine will

dhobi: clothes washer

dhoop: thick pliable block of strong incense

dhoti: white ankle-length cloth worn by men, tied around the waist and sometimes hitched up through the legs

dhurrie: woollen rug in geometric patterns

Digambara: "sky-clad" Jain monks who shun clothes as part of their ascetic discipline

diwan (also dewan): chief minister

Doordarshan: abbreviated DD, India's national government TV network, known for it stodgy and generally Hindu-oriented programming

dupatta: veil worn by Muslim women with *shalwa chamise*

durbar: court building; a government meeting

fakir: ascetic Muslim mendicant

fudged: popular parlance for decisions are made but nothing is done—equivalent to nonfunded mandates

gadi: throne

ganj: market

gari: vehicle, or car

ghat: mountain; landing; platform; steps leading to water

ghazal: melancholy Urdu songs

gopi: young cattle-tending maidens who served as Krishna's playmates and lovers in popular mythology

guru: teacher of religion, music, dance, astrology, etc.; in Hinduism, a religious teacher or guide; in Sikhism, one of 10 spiritual leaders and teachers, the first of whom was Nanak Dev, the last was Gobind Singh

gurudwara: Sikh place of worship

haj: Muslim pilgrimage to mecca

hajji: Muslim making or who has made the *haj*

hannah: elephant saddle shaded by a canopy

harijans: term introduced by Manhatma Gandhi for untouchables; literally "Children of God"

hartal: strike

Hinayana: literally "Lesser Vehicle": perjorative term given to the original school of Buddhism by the later Mahayana ("Greater Vehicle") sects

hindutva: militant Hindu nationalism

image magnet: the image value of having a shop in a large metro or megacity; also the value of living near one but not in it

imam: Muslim leader of congregational prayers; leader of an Islamic community

Ishwara: God; Shiva

jaghidar: landowners who possessed a *jagir* or grant from the government to collect revenues, rents, and other valuables from land

Jatakas: popular tales about the Buddha's life and teachings; *jataka* can also mean "one's geneology"

jati: caste status determined by family and occupation; the basic unit of the caste system; there are about 3,000 *jatis* in Indian society today

jawan: soldier

jhuta: soiled by lips; food or drink polluted by touch

-ji: suffix added to names as a term of respect

jihad: striving by Muslims to spread their faith

jina: another term for the Jain *tirthankaras*

Kailasa: Shiva's mountain abode (a mountain pilgrimage site in Tibet)

karma: spiritual merit or demerit that a being acquired in previous incarnation and being acquired in one's present existence

kavad: small decorated box that unfolds to serve as a portable temple

khadi: home-spun cotton; Gandhi's symbol of Indian self sufficiency

khan: honorific Muslim title

khol: black eye-liner

kirana: small street shop selling general cheap consumables

kotwali: police station

kshatrya: the warrior and ruling caste

kumkum: red mark on a Hindu woman's forehead

kurta: long men's shirt worn over baggy pajamas

lakh: 100,000; often used vaguely to mean "a large number of"

lama: Tibetan Buddhist monk and teacher

lingam: reverential phallic symbol representing the god Shiva

loka: realm or world (*devaloka* = "world of the gods")

madrasa: islamic school

mahadeva: literally "great god"; a common epithet for Shiva

maharaja: king

maharani: queen

Mahatma: "great soul"; nowadays used almost exclusively in reference to Gandhi

Mahayana: "Great Vehicle," a Buddhist school that broke away from the original Theravada form of Buddhism and subsequently spread throughout Southeast and East Asia

mahout: elephant driver or keeper

maidan: large open space or field

mandala: religious diagram containing mystically symbolic and often repetitive geometric shapes

mandi: market

mandir: temple

mantra: sacred verse

marg: road

masjid: mosque

mata: necklace, garland, or rosary

mataji: female *sadhu*

megacity: Delhi, Mumbai, Chennai, or Calcutta

memsahib: respectful address to European woman

metro: a city large than a million but not one of India's four megacities (Delhi, Mumbai, Chennai, and Calcutta)

mithuna: sexual union; also amorous couples in Hindu and Buddhist figurative art

moksha: blissful state of freedom from rebirth aspired to by Hindus and Jains; Buddhists aspire to a somewhat similar state called *nirvana*

mudra: hand gesture used in Vedic rituals, depicted in Hindu, Buddhist, and Jain art and dance, symbolizing the teachings and life stages of the Buddha

muezzin: the man calling Muslims to prayer (the Muslim word is *bilal*)

Mughals: descendants of Mongol, Turkish, Persian, and Afghan invaders of South Asia who conquered and for a time ruled much of the Indian subcontinent; sometimes written Mogul, Moghul, or Mogol

mullah: Muslim teacher and scholar

Mumbai: new name for Bombay

nadi: river

naga: mythical serpent; also a person from Nagaland in the northeast provinces

natak: dance

natya: drama

nautch: performance by dancing girls; also the dancing girls themselves

nawab: Muslim landowner or prince

nirvana: unwordable state of supreme bliss and release from the cycle of rebirths; similar to Hindu and Jain *moksha*

nizam: title of Hyderabad rulers

offtake: purchases a customer makes without planning to when entering a shop

om (also *aum*): verbal and visual symbol denoting the origin of all things; the ultimate divine essence; used in meditation by Hindus and Buddhists

paan: betal nut, lime, calcium, and anis seed wrapped in a leaf and chewed as a mildly addictive digestive; godawful taste

padma: lotus; also a name for the goddess Lakshmi

paise: one of the 100 *paisa* in a *rupee*

pajama: mens' baggy trousers

pali: original language of early Buddhist texts

panchayat: village council

pandit: honorific for erudite individual, sometimes taken as a personal or family name; various Brahmins such as the family of Jawahrlal Nehru are known as pandits

parikrama: ritual circumambulation around a temple, shrine, or mountain

Parsi (also *Parsee*): Zoroastrian

pir: Muslim holy man

pol: residential quarters

pranayama: breath control used in meditation

prasad: food blessed in temple sanctuaries and shared among devotees

PSU: Public Sector Unit

puja: worship

pujari: priest

pukka: correct or "proper"

punya: religious or spiritual merit

purdah: seclusion of Muslim women inside the home: the general term for wearing a veil

purohit: priest

qawwali: devotional singing popular among Sufis

raag or *raga:* series of notes forming the basis of a melody

raj: rule or monarchy

raja: king; also a wife's reverential name for her husband

rajput: princely rulers who once dominated much of north and west India

rakshasa: demon (*rakshasi* = demoness)

range: Indian equivalent of a product "line"

rangoli: geometrical pattern of rice powder used to decorate the entrances to houses and temples

rawal: Hindu chief priest

rickshawallah: person who operates auto or pedal powered rickshaws; something of a dying trade

rinpoche: revered tibetan Buddhist lama, considered to be a reincarnation of a previous teacher

rishi: "seer"; a philosophical sage or poet

rudraksha: beads in Shiva rosaries

sadar: "main" or "principal" as in *sadar bazaar,* "principal market" *sadhu:* holy man with no caste or family ties; also an utterance used to mean "holy" or "joyful"

saffron brigade: militant Hindu nationalists, often racist and violent

sagar: lake

sahgeet: music of any kind

sahib: respectful word meaning "gentleman," especially a European man

samadhi: final enlightenment; also the site of the death or burial of a saint

samsara: cyclic process of death and rebirth

sangam: sacred confluence of two or more rivers; also an academy

sannyasin: homeless, possessionless Hindu ascetic

sarai: resting place for caravans and travelers who once followed the trade routes through Asia

sari (also *saree*): drapey dress for indian women made of a length of cloth (usually 5, 7, or 9 yards) wound around the waist and draped over one shoulder

sati: when a wife sacrifices her life on her husband's funeral pyre in emulation of Shiva's wife; no longer a common practice, and officially illegal

satsang: teaching given by a religious figurehead

satyagraha: literally "grasping truth"; invented by Gandhi during his campaign of non-violent protest

Scheduled Castes: official name for "untouchables"

sepoy: an Indian soldier in European service

seth: merchant or businessman

seva: voluntary service in a temple or community

Shaivite: Hindu who recognizes Shiva as the supreme god

shalwa: baggy ankle-hugging "harem pants" worn by women

shankha: conchs used as a symbol of Vishnu

shastra: treatise or sacred text

shikar: hunting

shishya: young student

shloka: verse from a Sanskrit text

shri: respectful prefix to a name

shudra: the lowest of the four *varnas*; a servant

shulab: public toilet

singha: lion (sometimes *simha*)

soma: medicinal herb with hallucinogenic properties used in early Vedic and Zoroastrian rituals

Star TV: Rupert Murdoch's Hong Kong-based satellite TV network

sthala: site sacred for its association with legendary events

Surya: the sun, or the name of the Hindu sun god

sutra: (*sutta*) verse in Sanskrit and Pali texts

svetambara: "white-clad" sect of Jainism which accepts nuns and shuns nudity

swadeshi: literally "of one's own country," the term originated during the independence movement to promote further the use of Indian-made items, particularly cottage industry products such as hand-woven cloth; also rendered as "self rule" and "self-reliance"; also a synonym for Independence coined by Gandhi

swami: a holy man

tala: rhythmic cycle in classical music; in sculpture a *tala* is one face-length

tandoor: clay oven

tempo: three-wheeled taxi

thali: combination of dishes, chutneys, pickles, rice, and bread served as a single meal; also the metal plate on which a meal is served

thangka: Tibetan religious scroll painting

Theravada: "Doctrine of the Elders"; the original name for the doctrines of Buddhism

thug: member of a north indian cult of professional robbers and murderers

tiffin: light meal

tiffin carrier: stainless steel set of tins used for carrying meals

tilak: red dot smeared on the forehead during worship

tirtha: river crossing considered sacred by Hindus; the transition from the mundane world to heaven; a place of pilgrimage for Jains

tirthankara: "ford-maker" or "crossing-maker," an enlightened Jain teacher who is deified; 24 appear every 300 million years

tola: unit of weight (11.5 grams)

trimurti: Hindu trinity

trishula: Shiva's trident

untouchables: members of the lowest strata of society, considered polluting to higher castes

urs: Muslim festival

vahana: the "vehicle" of a deity: the bull Nandi is Shiva's vahana *vaishya*: member of the merchant and trading castes

varna: literally "color"; one of the four hierarchical social categories of Brahminism which evolved into the many Hindu castes of today: *brahmins, kshatryas, vaishyas, shudras*

vedas: sacred texts of early Hinduism

wallah: suffix to another word stating occupational identity, e.g. *dhobi-wallah, rickshaw wallah*; the technical meaning is "a man whose job it is" with the name of the job tacked on, e.g., "chaiwallah" or tea-seller

wazr: chief minister or vizier to a king

yaksha: beneficent or evil earthly spirit popular in folklore

yakshi: female fertility figure

yantra: cosmological pictogram often containing one's astrological chart and other mystic symbols

yatra: pilgrimage

yatri: pilgrim

yogi (female: *yogini*): priestly figure possessing occult powers gained through the practice of yoga

yoni: symbol of the female sexual organ set around the base of the lingam in Hindu shrines

yuga: eon; the present age is the *kali-yuga* or "black-age" of degeneration and spiritual decline, is the last in a cycle of four yugas

zamindar: landowner

Zee TV: a popular Hindi satellite TV channel

Appendix B: Useful Addresses

BUSINESS ADDRESS

Business Organizations in the United States

U.S. India Business Council
1615 H Street, N.W.
Washington, DC 20062–2000
Tel: (202)463–5492

India American Chamber of Commerce
P.O.Box 2110
Grand Central Station
New York, NY 10185–2110
Tel: (212)755–7181

U.S. Trade Department of Commerce
International Trade Administration
India Desk
Room 2308
14th & Constitution Avenues, N.W.
Washington, DC 20230
Tel: (202)482–2954

Business Organizations in India

American Business Council of India
U-50 Hotel Hyatt Regency
New Delhi 110 066
Tel: (11)688–5443

Associated Chambers of Commerce
Allahabad Bank Building
17 Parliament Street
New Delhi 110 001
Tel: (11)310–749

Chief Controller of Imports and Exports Ministry of Commerce
Udyog Bhawan
Maulana Azad Road
New Delhi 110 001
Tel: (11)301 1938/301 1275
(Deputy Chief Controller),
331–8857 (licensing)

Confederation of Indian Industries
23,26 Institutional Area
Lodhi Road
New Delhi 110 003
Tel: (11)462–9994

Export Import Bank of India
Centre One, Floor 21
World Trade Centre
Cuffe Parade
Mumbai 400 005
Tel: (22)218–5272, 218–6801

Foreign Investment Promotion Board
Prime Minster's Secretariat
South Block
New Delhi 110 011
Tel: (11)301–7839, 3040

India Investment Centre
Jeevan Vihar Building
Sansad Marg
New Delhi 110 001
Tel: (11)312–622

Indo German Chamber of Commerce
Maker Tower E, 1st Floor
Cuffe Parade
Mumbai 400 005
Tel: (22)218–6131

Indo-U.S. Joint Business Council
c/o Federation of Indian Chambers
of Commerce and Industry Federation House
Tansen Marg
New Delhi 110 001
Tel: (11)331–9251

**Industrial Credit and Investment
Corporation of India**
163 Backbay Reclamation
Mumbai 400 020
Tel: (22)202–2535
In Delhi: (11)331–9611, 12

Ministry of Commerce
Udyog Bhawan

New Delhi 110 011
Tel: (11)301–0261

Ministry of Finance
(Economic Affairs)
North Block
New Delhi 110 001
Tel: (11)301–4452 (Joint Secretary
for Investments)
301–2883 (Director)

Ministry of Industry
Udyog Bhavan
New Delhi 110 001
Tel: (11)301–1487 (Protocol),
301–0261 (Export Promotion),
301–4005, 1983 (Investment
Promotion and Project
Monitoring)

Secretariat for Industrial Approvals
Ministry of Industry
Udyog Bhavan
New Delhi 110 001
Tel: (11)301–0221, 1983

Banking and Financial Institutions

Reserve Bank of India (RBI)
New Central Office Building
Fort
Mumbai 400 023
Tel: (22)266–5726,
286–1602 (Approvals)

Reserve Bank of India
Central Office Building
Shahid Bhaqat Singh Road
Mumbai 400 023
Tel: (22)266–1602, 266–0604
Telex: 011–82318, 82455
Fax: (22)266–2105

**Export Credit Guarantee Corpora-
tion of India Ltd.**
Express Towers, 10th Floor
Nariman Point

Mumbai 400 021
Tel: (22)202–3023, 202–3046
Telex: 011–83231
Fax: (22)204–5253

Export-Import Bank of India
Centre One, Floor 21
World Trade Centre
Cuffe Parade
Mumbai 400 005
Tel: (22)218–5272
Telex: 011–85177 EXIM IN
Fax: (22)218–8075

General Insurance Corporation of India
Suraksha, 170
J.T. Road
Churchgate
Mumbai 400 020
Tel: (22)233–3046, 285–2041
Telex: 011–83833
Fax: (22)287–4129

Industrial Credit & Investment Corporation of India Ltd.
ICICI Building
163, Backbay Reclamation
Churchgate
Mumbai 400 020
Tel: (22)202–2535
Telex: 011–83062
Fax: (22)204–6582

Industrial Reconstruction Bank of India
19, N.S. Road
Calcutta 700 001
Tel: (33)209–941–45
Telex: 021–7197
Fax: (33)207 182

Industrial Development Bank of India
IDBI Tower
Cuffe Parade
Mumbai 400 005
Tel: (22)218–9111, 218–9121

Telex: 011–82193, 84812
Fax: (22)218–0411, 218–1294

Industrial Finance Corporation of India
Bank of Baroda Building
16, Sansad Marg
New Delhi 110 001
Tel: (11)332–2052, 332–1013
Telex: 031–65444, 66123
Fax: (11)332–0425

Life Insurance Corporation of India
Yoyaksnema
Jeevan Bima Marg
Mumbai 400 021
Tel: (22)202–8267, 202–2151
Telex: 022–82327

National Bank for Agriculture and Rural Development
Sterling Centre
Dr. Annie Besant Road
Mumbai 400 018
Tel: (22)493–8627
Telex: 011–73770 NAB IN
Fax: (22)493–1621

National Housing Bank
Hindustani Times House
18–20, Casturba Gandhi Marg
New Delhi 110 001
Tel: 371–2036–37
Telex: 031–66486
Fax: (22)371–5619

Security and Exchange Board of India
1st Floor, Mittal Court,
B Wing
24 Nariman Point
Mumbai 400 011
Tel: (22)223–886
Fax: (22)202–1073

Shipping Credit Investment Corporation of India
141, Maker Towers F

Cuffe Parade
Mumbai 400 005
Tel: (22)218–0800
Telex: 011–85721
Fax: (22)218–1539

Small Industries Development Bank of India
Nariman Bhavan
227 Vinay K. Shah Marg
Nariman Point
Mumbai 400 021
Tel: (22)202–7716
Telex: 011–85016
Fax: (22)204–4448

Unit Trust of India
13, New Marine Lines
Sir Vithaldas Thackersey Marg
Mumbai 400 020
Tel: (22)206–8468
Telex: 011–82365
Fax: (22)266–3673

Trade Service Organizations

All India Manufacturers Organisation
DHP Regional Board of AIMO
AIMO House
E1/11, Jhandewalan Extension
New Delhi 110 055
Tel: (11)528–848

All India Shippers Council
Federation House
Tansen Marg
New Delhi 110 001
Tel: (11)331–9251

Associated Chambers of Commerce and Industry (ASSOCHAM)
Allahabad Bank Building
17, Parliament Street
New Delhi 110 001
Tel: (11)310–704, 310–749, 310–779
Fax: (11)312 193

Confederation of Indian Industry (CII)
23–26 Institutional Area
Lodi Road
New Delhi 100 003
Tel: (11)615–693, 462–1874
Fax: (11)694–298

Directorate-General of Commercial Intelligence & Statistics
1 Council House Street
Calcutta 800 001
Tel: (33)283–111

Federation of Indian Chambers of Commerce and Industry (FICCI)
Federation House
Tansen Marg
New Delhi 110 001
Tel: (11)331–9251
Fax: (11)332–0714

Federation of Indian Export Organisations (FIEO)
PHD House, Opp. Asian Games Village
New Delhi 110 011
Tel: (11)686–4624, 686–1310
Fax: (11)686–3087

Indian Council of Arbitration
Federation House
Tansen Marg
New Delhi 110 001
Tel: (11)331–9251

Indian Investment Centre
Jeevan Vihar Building
Sansad Marg
New Delhi 110 001
Tel: (11)373–3673
Fax: (11)373–2245

India Trade Promotion Organisation (ITPO)
Pragati Bhavan
Pragati Maidan
New Delhi 110 001

Tel: (11)331–8143
Fax: (11)331–8143, 332–0855,
331–7896

World Bank India
P.O. Box 416
New Delhi 110 001

EXPORT COUNCILS AND COMMODITY BOARDS

**Agricultural and Processed Food
Products Export Development
Authority**
3rd Floor
Ansal Chambers II
Bhikaji Cama Place
New Delhi 110 066
Tel: (11)487–2141
Fax: (11)487–5016
Telex: 82061 FEDA IN

Apparel Export Promotion Council
15 NBCC Tower
Bhikaji Cama Place
New Delhi 110 066
Tel: (11)688–3351, 688–8300
Fax: (11)688–8584
Telex: 031 72196, 72442

**Basic Chemicals, Pharmaceuticals
& Cosmetics Export Promotion
Council**
Jhansi Castle
4th Floor
7 Cooperage Road
Mumbai 400 039
Tel: (22)202–1288, 202–1339
Fax: (22)202–6684
Telex: 011 84047 BCPC IN

**Cashew Export Promotion Council of
India**
P.B. No. 1709
Chitoor Rood
Ernakulam South

Cochin 682 016
Tel: (48)436–1459, 435–3357
Fax: (48)437–0973
Telex: 0885 6677 CPPC IN

Carpet Export Promotion Council
110-A/1 Krishna Nagar
Street No. 5
Safdarjung Enclave
New Delhi 110 029
Tel: (11)602–742, 601–024
Fax: (11)601–024

**Chemicals & Allied Products Export
Promotion Council**
World Trade Centre
14/1-B, Ezra Street
Calcutta 700 001
Tel: (33)258–216, 258–219
Fax: (33)255–070
Telex: 021 4368

Coffee Board
1, Dr. Ambedkar Veedhi
Bangalore 560 001
Tel: (80)262–917, 260–250
Fax: (80)226–5557
Telex: 0845 8281

Coir Board
P.O. Box No. 1752
M.G. Road
Ernakulam South
Cochin 682 016
Tel: (484)351–788, 354–397
Fax: (484)370–034
Telex: 0885 6363

**Cotton Textiles Export Promotion
Council**
Engineering Centre
5th Floor
9, Mathew Road
Mumbai 400 004
Tel: (22)363–2910, 361–1793
Fax: (22)363–2914
Telex: 011 75466 TCIL IN

Council for Leather Exports
Leather Centre
53 Sydenhams Road
Periamet
Chennai 600 003
Tel: (44)589–098, 582–041
Fax: (44)588–713
Telex: 041 7354 CLE IN

Electronics and Computer Software Export Promotion Council
PHD House
3rd Floor
Khelgaon Marg
New Delhi 110 016
Tel: (11)655–103, 655–206
Fax: (11)485–3412
Telex: 031 73333 ESC IN

Engineering Export Promotion Council
World Trade Centre
3rd Floor
14, 1B, Ezra Street
Calcutta 700 001
Tel: (33)250–442, 250–443
Fax: (33)258–968
Telex: 21 5109

Export Promotion Council for Handicrafts
6, Community Centre
1st & 2nd Floor
Basant Lok
Vasant Vihar
New Delhi 110 057
Tel: (11)600–871, 687–5377
Telex: 031 72315

Federation of Indian Export Organisations (FIEO)
PHD House
3rd Floor
Khelgaon Marg
New Delhi 110 016
Tel: (11)685–1310, 685–1312

Fax: (11)686–3087
Telex: 031 73194

Gem and Jewellery Export Promotion Council
Diamond Plaza
5th Floor
391-A, Dr. D. B. Marg
Mumbai 400 004
Tel: (22)385–6916, 388–8005
Fax: (22)386–8752
Telex: 011 75360

Handloom Export Promotion Council
18, Cathedral Garden Road
Nungambakkam
Chennai 600 034
Tel: (44)827–8879, 827–6043
Fax: (44)827–1761
Telex: 41 7168 HEPC IN

India Trade Promotion Organisation
Pragati Bhavan
Pragati Maiden
New Delhi 110 001
Tel: (11)331–9560, 331–7534
Fax: (11)331–8142

Indian Silk Export Promotion Council
62 Mittal Chambers
6th Floor
Nariman Point
Mumbai 400 021
Tel: (22)202–7662, 204–9113
Fax: (22)287–4606
Telex: 0118 3190 SILK IN

Marine Products Export Development Authority
P.B. No. 1663
MPEDA House
Panampilly Avenue
Cochin 682 015
Tel: (484)311–979, 311–901
Fax: (484)313–361
Telex: 0885–6288

Overseas Construction Council of India
H 118 (11th Floor)
Himalaya House
23, Kasturba Gandhi Marg
New Delhi 110 001
Tel: (11)332–7550, 332–2425
Fax: (11)331–1296
Telex: 031 65588 OCCI IN

Plastics and Linoleums Export Promotion Council
Centre 1, Unit 1, 11th Floor
World Trade Centre
Cuffe Parade
Mumbai 400 005
Tel: (22)218–4474, 218–4474
Fax: (22)218–4819
Telex: 011 83940

Rubber Board
P.B. No. 280
Sastri Road
Kottayam 686 001
Tel: (481)563–231
Fax: 481 564–639
Telex: 888 205

Shellac Export Promotion Council
World Trade Centre
4th Floor
14/1 b Ezra Street
Calcutta 700 001
Tel: (33)254–556, 255–725
Fax: (33)248–2070
Telex: 021 7622 23021

Spices Board
P.B. No. 1909
St. Vincent Cross Rd.
Cochin 682 018
Tel: (484)353–837, 353–578
Fax: (484)370–429
Telex: 0885 6534

Sports Goods Export Promotion Council
1-E/6, Swami Ram Tirath Nagur
New Delhi 110 055
Tel: (11)525–695, 529–255
Fax: (11)753–2147

Synthetic & Rayon Textiles Export Promotion Council
Resham Bhavan
78 Veer Nariman Rd.
Mumbai 400 020
Tel: (11)204–8797, 204–8690
Fax: (11)204–8358

Tea Board
14 Biplabi Trailokya
Maharaj Sarani
Calcutta 700 001
Tel: (33)260–210
Fax: (33)260–218
Telex: 021 4527

Tobacco Board
Srinivasa Rao Thota
G.T. Road
P.B. No. 322
Guntur 522 004
Tel: (863)30399, 32993
Fax: (863)33032
Telex: 071 264 TOBD IN

Wool & Woollens Export Promotion Council
612/714 Ashok Estate
24 Barakhamba Rood
New Delhi 110 001
Tel: (11)331–5512, 331–5205
Fax: (11)331–4625

EMBASSIES AND CONSULATES

American Embassy
Shantipath
Chanakyapuri
New Delhi 110021
Tel: (11)600–651

American Consulates
Lincoln House
78 Bhulabhai Desai Road
Mumbai 400026
Tel: (22)363–3611

5/1 Ho Chi Minh Sarani
Calcutta 700071
Tel: (33)242–3611

220 Mount Road
Chennai 600006
Tel: (44)827–3040

British High Commission
Chanakyapuri
New Delhi 110021
Tel: (11)601–371

Canadian Consulate
41/42 Maker Chambers VI
Jamnalal Bajaj Marg
Nariman Point
Mumbai 400021
Tel: (22)287–6027

Canadian High Commission
7/8 Shanti Path
Chanakyapuri
New Delhi 110021
Tel: (11)687–6500

French Consulate
Bacon
7th Floor
Madame Cama Road
Mumbai 400021
Tel: (22)202–1217

French Embassy
2/50E Shanti Path
Chanakyapuri
New Delhi 110021
Tel: (11)604–300

German Embassy
6/50G Shanti Path
Chanakyapuri

New Delhi 110021
Tel: (11)604–861

German Consulates
Hoechst House
10th Floor
Nariman Point
193 Backbay Reclamation
Mumbai 400021
Tel: (22)232–422

1 Hastings Park Road
Alipore
Calcutta
Tel: (33)711–141

22 Commander-in-Chief Road
Chennai
Tel: (44)471–747

SOCIAL AND CONVENIENCE ADDRESSES

Delhi

Hospitals and Clinics

Aashlok Hospital
25A Block AB
Safdarjung Enclave
New Delhi
Tel: (11) 609–629

All India Institute of Medical Sciences
Ansari Nagar
New Delhi
Tel: (11)661–123

Dr. Arya's Children's Clinic
19/1 Nizamudin East
New Delhi
Tel: (11)619–214

Sir Gangaram Hospital
Rajinder Nagar
New Delhi
Tel: (11)571–2389

Useful Addresses 257

Schools

The American Embassy School
Chandragupta Marg
Chanakyapuri
New Delhi
Tel: (11)605–949

The British School
San Martin Marg
Chanakyapuri
New Delhi
Tel: (11)602–183

The French School
184 Jor Bagh
Delhi
Tel: (11)698–077

The German School
B9 Maharani Bagh
Delhi
Tel: (11)631–581

Cultural Centers

India International Centre
40 Max Mueller Marg
Lodi Estate
New Delhi
Tel: (11)619–431

Triveni Kala Sangam
205 Tansen Marg
New Delhi
Tel: (11)388–833

Mumbai

Hospitals

Breach Candy Hospital
60-A Bhulabhai Desai Road
Mumbai
Tel: (11)822–3651

Hinduja Hospital
Veer Savarkar Marg
Mumbai
Tel: (22)467–575

Jaslok Hospital
15 Dr. Deshmukh Marg
Mumbai
Tel: (22)493–3333

Mumbai Hospital
13 Marine Lines
Mumbai
Tel: (22)266–3343

Schools

Campion School (for boys)
13, Cooperage Road
Mumbai

Mumbai International School
Gilbert Building
Babulnath, 2nd Cross Road
Mumbai
Tel: (22)828–2056

Mumbai Scottish School
Veer Savarkar Marg
Mumbai
Tel: (22)451–016

Department Stores

Akbarally's
45 Veer Nariman Road
Mumbai
Tel: (22)204–3921

Asiatic Departmental Store
73 Veer Nariman Road
Mumbai
Tel: (22)204–0892

Calcutta

Hospitals

The Bellvue Clinic
9 Loudon Street
Calcutta
Tel: 244–6925

Woodlands Nursing Home
8/5 Alipur Road

Calcutta
Tel: (33)453–951

Schools

La Martiniere (for boys)
11 Loudon Street
Calcutta
Tel: (33)244–2418

La Martiniere (for girls)
Rawdon Street
Calcutta
Tel: (33)244–3841

Loretta House (for girls)
7 Middleton Road
Calcutta
Tel: (33)244–3063

St. Xavier's (for boys)
30 Park Street
Calcutta
Tel: (33)244–2484

Chennai (Madras)

Hospitals

Apollo Hospital
21 Greams Lane
Chennai
Tel: (44)477–447

Devaki Hospital
148 Luz Church Road
Mylapore
Chennai
Tel: (44)777–07

The Tamil Nadu Hospital
439 Cheran Nagar
(off Old Mahabalipuram Road)
Perumbakkam
Chennai
Tel: (44)402–997

Willingdon Hospital
21 Pycrofts Garden Road

Chennai
Tel: (44)825–3552

Schools

Abacus Montessori School
38–39 Besant Avenue
Adyar
Chennai
Tel: (44)417–797

Harrington House School
21 Dr. Thirumurthi Nagar Main
Street
Nungambakkam High Road
Chennai
Tel: (44)472–546

Krishnamurthy Foundation International
The School
Damadar Garden
Adyar
Chennai
Tel: (44)415–645

Sishya
15 Second Street
Padmanabha Nagar
Adyar
Chennai
Tel: (44)412–652

Clubs

Indo American Association
10 Nandanam Main Road
Nandanam Extension
Chennai
Tel: (11)452–276

Udavum Karangal
Centre for Humane Services
460 N.S.K. Nagar
Chennai
Tel: (11)426–141

Working Women's Forum
55 Bhimasena Garden Streets

Mylapore
Chennai
Tel: (44)74553

Western-style Store

Nilgiris Dairy Farm
58 Dr Radhakrishnan Road
Chennai
Tel: (11)475–111

Boarding Schools

Hebron School
Lushington Hall

Kodaikanal International School
P.O. Box 25
Kodaikanal
Tamil Nadu 624101

Woodstock School
Musoorie
Uttar Pradesh
India

Appendix C: Additional Reading

WEB SITES

The Hindu:http://www.webpage.com/hindu/

India World Business Directory:http://www.indiaworld.com/open/biz/index.html

India Business Directory (gov't):http://www.webindia.com/india.html

IBIS (paints):http://www.indiaconnect.com/ibis/paintonl.htm

Software Technology Parks of India:http://www.stph.net

Gov't of India NYC office business facts:http://www.indiaserver.com/biz/dbi/MEA2.0html

How to Invest Info:http://www.indiaserver.com/biz/dbi/MEA3.0html

Doing Business with India:http://www.indiaserver.com/biz/dbi/dbi.html

Insider News:http://www.globalindia.com/index.htm(still sparse yet)

General Info:http://www.indiacomm.com/

Economic Times (daily news):http://www.economictimes.com/today/pagehome.htm(e-mail: times@giasd101.vsnl.net.in; Economic Times, Times House 7 Bahadurshah Zafar
Marg, New Delhi 110 002, India Phone: +91–11–3312277
Fax: +91–11–3715832

Business Services Syndicate consultants:http://www.indiagate.com/commerce/busi.html

Indian Economy:http://www.webcom.com/%7Eprakash/ECONOMY/ECONOMY.HTML

BUSINESS AND DOING BUSINESS IN INDIA

Books

India Fast Forward, 12 chapters aimed at foreign investors and overseas partners interested in commerce with India; a broad look at the effects of liberalization and the reforms undertaken since 1991. Mumbai: Business India Book Club (14th Floor, Nirmal, Nariman Point, Mumbai 400 021) (Fax: 91-22-287-5671).

India Means Business, a portfolio of brochures prepared by the Economic Co-ordination unit of the Ministry of External Affairs and Arthur Andersen & Co., Inc. Available through Indian trade affairs officers in Indian Embassies, and from Arthur Andersen & Co. and affiliated offices. Official propaganda versus real life, but highly information between the lines.

Balachandran, S., *Managing Ethics*, New Delhi, Sangeetha Associates. A comparison of the various management systems in general use in India and the ethical dilemmas they face.

Dandekar, V. M., *The Indian Economy: 1947–92*, New Delhi, Sage Publications. Analysis of the conditions that led to the 1991 liberalization program.

Kakar, Sudhir, *The Inner World: A Psychoanalytic Study of Childhood and Society in India*. Oxford: Oxford University Press. Mainly of use to business people in the advertising and marketing communities, this is also a good background read for anyone doing business in India.

Ninan, Sevanti, *Through the Magic Window: TV and Change in India*, New Delhi: Penguin. From tool of the government to satellite dishes, CNN, and MTV, television has influenced India in incalculable ways. This is a populist book rather than a serious study, but it's the only one on the subject available and at least an introduction to India's TV scene.

Pant, Manoj, *Foreign Direct Investment in India: The Issues Involved*, New Delhi: Lancers Books. Based on interviews with academics, government officials, and expatriate business people, this is a thorough and balanced look at the issues involved in investing in India.

Singh, Mina, *Business Etiquette, A Book of Modern Manners for the Indian Office*, New Delhi: Rupa & Co.

Vakil, Tarjani, *Achieving Excellence: Case Studies of 6 Indian Export Companies*, New Delhi: Tata McGraw-Hill.

Business Periodicals That Will Airmail Overseas

Business India, B-24 Maheshwari Towers, Road No. 1, Banjara Hills, Hyderabad 500 034. Fax: (91)842 390-233. (Airmail: US$ 110/yr.)

Business Today, Subscriptions, Post Box 247, New Delhi 110 011. Fax: (91)11 331-6180/331-08385. E-mail:btoday@giasd101.vsnl.net.in (Airmail:$125/yr.)

Business World, 10th Floor, New Delhi House, Barakhamba Road, New Delhi 110
    001. Tel: (91)11 372–2684–85. (Airmail: US$110/yr.)
India Today, Post Box 115, New Delhi 110 001. Fax: (91)11 331–6180. Telex:
    31–62634 INTO IN. (Airmail US$120/yr.)

HISTORY AND POLITICS

Brown, Judith M., *Gandhi: Prisoner of Hope*. New Haven: Yale University Press.
Crossette, Barbara, *India—Facing the Twenty-First Century*, Bloomington: Indiana
    University Press. Reflections by one of America's most astute journalists,
    a long-time New York Times correspondent in India. This is probably
    the most important and informative book on life in India after Liberali-
    zation.
Embree, Ainslie T., *Sources of Indian Tradition, Vol. 1; From the Beginning to 1600*.
    New York: Columbia University Press.
Galbraith, John Kenneth, *Ambassador's Journal*. Boston: Houghton Mifflin.
Gandhi, Mohandas, *The Essence of Hinduism*. New Delhi: The Navjivan Trust.
Kapoor, Sanjay, *Bad Money: Bad Politics: The Hawala Story*, New Delhi: Alka
    Paperbacks (Har-Anand Publications).
Naqvi, Saeed, *The Last Brahmin Prime Minister of India*, New Delhi: Har-Anand
    Publishers.
Radhakrishnan, Sarvepalli, *The Hindu View of Life*. London: Unwin Paperback.
    London.
Salgaocar, Ranjana, *The Pleasure of Your Company*, Pyramid Books.
Sisson, Richard, and Leo E. Rose, *War and Secession: Pakistan, India and the
    Creation of Bangladesh*. Berkeley and Los Angeles: University of Califor-
    nia Press.
Thapar, Romila, *A History of India*, (2 vols). London: Penguin Books. A broad,
    non-academic history covering cultural subjects as much as political and
    religious ones.
Zakaria, Rafiq, *The Widening Divide: An Insight into Hindu-Muslim Relations*, New
    Delhi: Viking Penguin. A painstaking analysis of the tempestuous rela-
    tions between these two religious groups.

TRAVELING IN INDIA

Alberuni, *Alberuni's India*, New York: Norton. Fascinating account by the trav-
    eler, adventurer and chronicler in 13th-century India.
Al Rasham, *The Wonder that was India*, London: Sidgwick & Jackson. Survey of
    Indian history, society, music, art and literature from 400 BC to the
    coming of the Muslims.
Bose, Sunil, *Indian Classical Music*, New Delhi: Vikas Publishing House. The
    emotions and history behind Indian classical music.

Boyce, Mary, *Zoroastrians: Their Religious Beliefs and Practices*, London: Routledge. A survey of Zoroastrian secular and religious history.

Cole, W. O., and P. Singh Sambhi, *The Sikhs: Their Religious Beliefs and Practices*, London: Routledge.

Crann, Roy, *Indian Art*, London: Thames & Hudson. The most reasonable and concise general introduction to Indian art, from Harappan seals to Moghul miniatures.

Davidson, Robyn, *Desert Places*, New York/New Delhi: Viking Penguin. A thrilling account of the life of the desert nomads of Gujarat and Rajasthan.

Fishlock, Trevor, *India File*, London: John Murray. The latest edition of this now classic analysis of contemporary Indian society brings the picture up to date with essays on the Golden Temple siege and the rise of Rajiv Gandhi.

Frater, Alexander, *Chasing the Monsoon*, New Delhi: Penguin. Frater's wet-season jaunt up the west coast and across the Ganges plains is a great monsoon read for those who don't like being wet all day long.

Gombrich, Richard. *Theravada Buddhism*, London: Routledge & Kegan Paul. A history of Theravadin beliefs and practices from their beginnings to the present.

Khokar, Mohan, *Traditions of Indian Classical Dance*, New Delhi: Clarion Books. Detailing the religious and social roots of Indian dance, this lavishly illustrated book, with sections on regional traditions, is an excellent introduction to the subject.

Lewis, Norman, *A Goddess in the Stones*, London: Pan Macmillan. This veteran English travel writer's account of his trip to Calcutta and around the backwaters of Bihar and Orissa includes some vivid insights into tribal India. One of the more accomplished travelogues of recent years.

Naipaul, V. C., *India; A Wounded Civilisation*, New Delhi: Penguin. Naipaul, A Trinidadian Indian indicts India for narrow-mindedness and barbaric selfishness amid debilitating poverty and misguided faith.

O'Flaherty, Wendy, *Hindu Myths*, New Delhi: Penguin. Translations of popular Hindu myths, providing on insight into the foundations of Hinduism.

Reat, Noble Ross, *Buddhism, A History*, Fremont, California: Asian Humanities Press. A thorough account of the history of Buddhism from the historical perspective.

Rippin, Andrew, *Muslims: Their Religious Beliefs and Practices*, London: Routledge. The essential guide to Islamic history and religious beliefs.

Spear, Percival, *History of India Volume II*, London: Penguin. Covers the period from the Moghul era to the death of Gandhi.

Tagore, Rabindranath, *Selected Works*, London: Penguin. Poems, prose, and mystical verse by the Bengali Nobel Laureate.

Thapar, Romila, *History of India Volume I*, London: Penguin. Concise paperback account of early Indian history, ending with the Delhi Sultanate.

Tully, Mark, *No Full Stops in India*, London: Penguin. Personal anecdotes and first-hand accounts of political events over the past twenty years by an almost lengendary BBC correspondent.

Wade, Bonnie, *Music in India: The Classical Traditions*, New Delhi: Manmohar. A thorough catalogue of Indian music, outlining the most commonly used instruments, with excellent illustrations and musical scores.

Zashner, R. C., *Hinduism*, Oxford: Oxford University Press. Lively, accessible and often amusing catalogue of Hinduism and Indian society.

THE DAILY AND WEEKLY PRESS

Economic and Political Weekly, Mumbai
Frontline, Chennai
India Abroad, New York
India Magazine, Mumbai
India Today, New Delhi
Inside-Outside (architecture and landscape design), Mumbai
Mainstream, New Delhi
New Quest, Mumbai
Sunday, Calcutta
The Illustrated Weekly of India, Mumbai

Index

1 Up Ads Agency, 184
1991 liberalization, 1, 6, 16, 17, 64
1991 population, 62
1991 reforms, 3, 5
1991 restructuring, 2
1991–1995 retail revolution, 64
1992 *Second Upmarket Media Survey*, 91
1996 elections, 3, 6
1996 internal survey by LS Electronics, 116
1996 Lok Sabha election, 47

Abby (Advertising Club of Bombay) Awards for Excellence, 203
Accounting practices, 20
Acquisitions, 113
Action, 191
Ad agency growth rates, 180; penetration/cost-efficiency, 186; relevancy, 179; strategies, 173
Adhikari, Gautam, 43
Adidas, 191, 192, 210
Administered prices, 38
Administrative and political services, 149

Adspend, 115, 169, 207
Advanit, Ashok, 44
Advertising, 89, 145; billings, 89; costs, 63; expenditure on press and TV, 92; regulations, 90
Advertising Avenues, 174
Advertising Standards Council of India (ASCI), 90
Affluence, 70
Africa, 113, 166
After-sales operations, 196; service, 118
Agarwal, Rajiv, 177
Agarwalla, Arvind, 48
Agni, 155
Agriculture, 5
Ahmedabad, 181
Ahmedabad Electricity, 23
Ahura-Mazda, 155
AIDS, 9, 11, 232
Aid to poor countries, 10
AIG Insurance, 123
Air conditioners, 67, 102, 118, 220
Airfreight, 202
Airlines, 103

Ajay Home Products, 204, 205
Akai, 110, 113
Akashwani Radio, 90
Akbar, 165
Alayn Soap, 137
Alexander the Great, 164
Allah, 160
Allahabad, 223
Allgemeine Frankfurter, 41
Allied Signal, 122
All India Dental Association, 187
All-India Radio, 48
All-natural drinks, 235
Aloofness, 152
Ambassador automobiles, 121
Ambiance, 176
Ambedkar, Dr., 159
America, 10
American Express, 82, 201
America Online, 50
Aminodrip, 232
Ammirati Puris Lintas, 173
Amtrex, 118
Amul Butter, 49, 224
Amul Company, 225
Amway Corporation, 227, 229
Anagram Finance, 124
Ananda Bazar Patrika, 43
Anand Group, 121, 122
Andhra Pradesh, 24, 95
Andromeda Communications, 187
Anthem Communications, 203
Anti-consumerism, 64
Anti-perspirant, 207
Apollo Tyres, 168
Apple Computers, 118, 119, 135
Appy apple drink, 234
Aptiva, 119
Arabia, 164
Argentina, 36
Ariel, 189, 190
Arjuna, Prince, 157
Armani, Giorgio, 78, 188

Arms Communications, 203
Arthur Andersen Co., 97
Artificial flavoring, 206
Arvand Mills, 78
Arvin, 122
Aryan invaders, 155
ASCI Consumer Complaints Council, 90
Asia, 1
Asian cultures, 152
Asiasat-3, 56
Asia's Consumer Markets, 99
Asoka, 16
Aspire, 119
Assam, 95
Association of Indian Automobile Manufacturers (AIAM), 121
Astrology, 16, 155
AT&T, 41
Atman, 157
Audiovisual ads, 236
Auditing practices, 17
Australia, 12
Austria, 86
Authority, 154
Authority figures, 152
Authorized capital, 24
Auto components industry, 33, 120
Auto manufacturers, 106
Automobiles, 105
Automotive Component Manufacturers' Association (ACMA), 120
Auto parts and supplies, 120
Avon, 227

Babus (traders), 10, 149, 208
Baby care, 83
Bait-un-Nas'r Bank, 108
Bajaj, 22, 106, 178, 184, 207
Bajaj, Rahul, 178
Bakeries and confectionery stores, 78
Ballapur Industries, 22
Balsara, Sam, 173

Bandhej premium clothing, 200

B&W (black-and-white) television, 112

Bangalore, 44, 103, 125, 130, 143, 169, 170, 180, 181, 201, 220, 223, 237

Bangkok, 100

Bangladesh, 56, 138

Banking controls, 2

Bank of America, 186

Bankruptcy, 16

Banque Paribas, 31

Baroda, 180, 181

Baskin Robbins, 78

Basu, Sanat, 191

BAT (British-American Tobacco), 95, 123

Bata Bazaars, 190

Bata Family Stores, 190

Bata For Her, 191

Bata Power, 210

Bata Sandaks, 191

Bata Shoe Company, 190

Bata Signors, 191

Bata Super Stores, 190

Bausch & Lomb, 168, 202

BBC World, 53

BBDO, 89

Beanstalk computers, 102

Beer, 145

Behr of Germany, 122

Bell Atlantic, 40

Benetton, 78, 192

Bengal, 165

Bengali Banal, 148

Bengali language, 43

Bennett, Coleman & Co., 42, 47

Berne Convention, 87

Bhagavad Gita, 157

Bhandar, Kendriya, 79

Bhandar, Sahakari, 79

Bhandarkar, Usha, 173

Bharatiya Janata Party (BJP), 54

Bharat Petroleum Corp. Ltd. (BPCL), 29

Bhartia, Shobhana, 43

Bhikkhu, 159

Bicycles, 63, 83

Bihar, 71, 95

Birla, 21, 22

Birla Group, 117

Birla-3M, 223, 225

Birla, K. K., 42, 43

Biscuits, 96

BITV, 54

BJP, 13

Black-and-white (B&W) television, 218

Black markets, 85

Black money, 7

Blue Star, 184

Body spray, 207

Bombay, 31, 41, 47, 48, 49, 57, 63, 66, 166. *See also* Mumbai

Bombay Dyeing, 32, 123

Bombay Stock Exchange (BSE), 25, 32, 35, 73

Bournvita, 93

Boutique markets, 188

Bozell, 89

BPL, 113, 114; "BPL Corners," 169; BPL Galleries, 222; BPL India, 110; BPL Ltd., 169; BPL Mobile, 104

Brahma, 156

Brahman, 157

Brahmins, 16, 149, 157, 165; Brahminism, 155

Brainstorm, 202

Brand: boutiques, 222; "brand stick," 188; conflict, 29; failures, 80, 205; image, 190; ownership, 88; preferences, 6; relationship, 141

Branded goods, 223

Braun, 104, 225

Brazil, 36, 86

Britain, 53, 165
Britannia, 210
Britannia beverage supplements, 223
Britannia Industries, 207
British administration, 149
British Airways, 186
British hegemony, 166
British Raj, 223
Broadcast Media., 28
Brooke Bond Lipton, 197, 208
Buddha, 156, 158
Buddhism, 16, 155, 157, 159, 165
Built-in obsolescence, 96
Bullion, 167
Bundling products, 105
Bureaucracy, 7, 14, 74
Business and economic reporting, 43
Business and Political Observer, 44
Business India, 44, 46, 148
Business Standard, 43, 48
Business Today, 77, 143, 173
Business World, 143
Buying behavior of television customers, 127

Cable television, 30, 43, 55, 135
Cablewallahs, 53, 55, 58
Cadbury, 93, 175, 179, 223
Calcutta, 41, 43, 44, 49, 63, 73, 166, 190
Caliph, 161
Caltex, 29
Canara Bank, 102
Capacity constraints, 96
Capel, James, 32
Capital-account convertibility, 4
Capital appreciation, 20
Capitalism, 14
Capital markets, 2, 44
Carlton Communications, 22
Carlton Media Group, 53
Carona, 210
Carrier, 116, 118

Cars, 67
Carteling, 88
Cash flow, 20
Casteism, 7
Caste purchasing patterns, 188
Caste system, 3, 5, 7, 9, 163
Castrol, 30, 31
Casual wear from California, 145
C-DoT, 203
Cellular telephones: licenses, 41; phones, 186; providers, 41; service, 40
Cement industry, 27
Central Asia, 163
Centralized power, 14
Centralized purchasing, 213
Centre, the, 5, 6, 124
"The Centre" (the cabinet), 42
Centre for Monitoring Indian Economy (CMIE), 101
Chadha, Rajesh, 37
Chain-store outlets, 218
Chaiwallah ("tea hawker"), 197, 211
Chandigarh, 44
Chandragupta period, 159
Chang Yun of Korea, 122
Channel A, 202
Charpoi bed, 147
Chase Manhattan, 34
Chemists, 78
Chennai, 41, 63, 66, 70, 72, 73, 92, 124, 135, 200. *See also* Madras
Chettiar, P. G. Chengalvaraya, 235
Chettiars, 149
Chidambaram, P., 3
Child labor, 43
Child rearing, 151
Children, 11, 14
China, 2, 6, 14, 33, 91, 164, 165
Chinese, 13
Christianity, 156, 162
Christmas, 236
Chrysler Motors, 120

Cibaca lime gel toothpaste, 205
Ciba Vision, 168
Cielo automobile, 122, 189
Cifran, 231
Cigarettes, 80, 176; shops, 78
CII Task Force on Corporate Governance, 19
Cinema, 89
Cipla Company, 88, 232
CitiBank, 103, 106, 185, 187
City congestion, 219
Civil servants, 149
Clive, Lord, 165
Clothing, 38
CNN, 28, 110
Co-branded credit card, 106
Coca Cola, 15, 22, 102, 148, 184, 193
Coca Cola-Parle alliance, 194
Code for Commercial Advertising on TV, 90
Cogentrix, 20
Coimbatore, 127, 181
Colawallahs, 211
Colgate-Palmolive, 81, 187
Collection agencies, 106
Collective discipline, 14
Colonial India, 164
Color television, 12, 220; market, 109; outlook, 112
Co-marketing, 88
CommerceNet, 50
Common Minimum Programme, 123
Communist, 237; political influence, 107
Community affairs, 11
Companion TV, 125
Company newsletters, 201
Company registrations, 24
Competition, 82; strategies, 101
Competitive Strategies company, 103
CompuServe, 50
Computer and office equipment, 134
Computer software, 87

Confederation of Indian Industry (CII), 18
Congress Party, 55, 150
Conscientiousness at work, 14
Consumer and consumerism: credit, 105; demand, 67; durables, 67, 69, 70, 75, 149, 218, 220; electronics, 109; electronics companies, 113; finance, 82, 221; market, 63, 218; market seasonality, 112; nondurables, 229; panels, 97; products, 82; spending, 12, 63; surveys, 12
Consumer-durables boom, 175, 217
Consumer-goods imports, 64
Consumerism, 6, 75
Consumer Pulse, 97
Consumers, 18, 30, 62
Consumer's product mix, 67
Consumer's sophistication cycle, 169
Contact lenses, 168
Contract Advertising, 176
Contract Agency, 178, 203
Contract distribution, 223
Convenience items, 63, 69
Conviron TR iron capsules, 233
Cooking, 13
Cookware, 63
Cool Cats, 204
Coorg filter coffee, 198
Copyright Act, 1957, 87
Copyrights, 86, 87
Core competencies, 23
Core value in advertising, 141
Corporate governance, 17; corporate strategies, 82
Corruption, 7, 9, 11
Cosmetics market, 207
Cosmopolitan, 52
Cotton, 167
Countrywide Finance, 106, 111
Credit, 22

Credit cards: 82, 186; companies, 106; histories, 221; segment, 102; to farmers, 105; worthiness, 221

Credit management processes, 106

Credit rating agencies, 106

Credit Rating Information Service of India Limited (CRISIT), 39

Crime, 9, 11, 12

Criminal Bureau of Investigation, 40

Crore (defined), 59

Cross-product conflicts of interest, 226

Crunch candy bars, 208

Crusades, the 161

CTVS, 110; marketing, 111

Culture and customs, 151

Current account deficits, 4, 5

Current and capital accounts, 2

Curtis, Helene, J. K., 209

Dabral, Sonal, 175

da Cunha Associates, 178

da Cunha, Rahul, 178

Daewoo Electronics, 22, 34, 116, 117, 189

Daewoo Precision Industries, 122

da Gama, Vasco, 166

Dalits, 157

Damodar Valley Corporation, 59

Dana Corp., 122

DCM, 22

DCM Daewoo, 122

DCM Ltd., 134

D'Cold, 206

Dealer advisory panels, 221

Deccan Herald, 44

Declining birth rates, 62

Delhi, 23, 24, 41, 44, 63, 73, 77, 79, 92, 95, 103, 180, 206, 227

Delhi decadent, 148

Delphi Automotive, 120

Demand Assigned Multiple Access (DAMA), 59

Demand for capital, 34

Democracy, 1, 3, 9, 16, 17

Demographic replacement, 112

Demographics, 61, 65, 71; profiles, 147

Denial, 81

Deodorant, 207

Department of Telecommunications (DOT), 27, 59

Department stores, 78

Depository systems, 26

Designer Coffee, 197

Dhar, Abhinav, 174

Dhara refined oil, 209

Dharma (the path to freedom and enlightenment), 153

Dhobi (washerwomen caste), 104, 138

Diesel automotive segment, 102

Digambara sect of Jainism, 159

Digital compression technology, 57

Dignity Professionals, 182

Diners Club, 82

Dingorub, 206

Direct-mail campaigns, 221; catalogs, 230

Direct marketing (DM), 83, 185, 186

Direct-to-home (DTH) digital transmission, 55

Direct TV, 57

Disclosure, 17

Discovery Channel, 28, 57

Discretionary income, 61

Dishwashers, 65

Disposable incomes, 67

Distribution: 63, 208, 211; channels, 213; houses, 213; network margins, 213; overheads, 215; territories, 214

Distributors, 105, 214

Diwali, 236

D'Mart supermarket, 79

Dolphin Group, 79

Domestic investment, 2

Donaldson, Lufkin & Jenrette, 34
Doordarshan (DD), 10, 28, 30, 52, 53, 55, 56, 58, 81, 90, 92, 172, 175
Downpurchasing trends, 78
Dravidians, 165
Drug abuse, 9
Drugs, 82
DSP Financial Consultants, 31
D'Tach, 205
Dual-pricing systems, 84
Durables, 12, 96; durables credit, 106
Durrani, Tara, 139
Dutch, the, 166
Duty-free shops, 188

E-Times, 43
Eagle Star Insurance, 123
East Asia, 17, 33, 91
East Coast, 63
East West Airlines, 103
Economics: fundamentals, 4; growth, 9; liberalism, 1; poverty, 5; reform, 3, 10, 13, 16, 37; vested interests, 10
The Economic Times, 43, 51
Economies of scale, 96
The Economist, 41, 53
Edible oils, 96, 209
Editors, 42
Editor's Choice tea, 81
Education, 8, 9, 11
Edutainment, 202
Eenadu, 46
Election campaigns, 183
Electrical machinery, 38
Electrical power, 237
Electrolux, 116
Electronic media, 30
Electronics market, 113
Elf petrol and lubricants, 30
Emotional layering, 141
Employees, 18

Employment, 5; of women in media, 173
Emporio, 78, 188
England, 166
English-language papers, 42; press, 42
English publications, 91
Enron, 6, 20
Entertainment electronics, 96
Entrepreneurialism, 5, 24, 238
Environment, 11, 12, 13
Equity: financing, 33; futures and options, 26; structures of ventures, 37
Escapism, 153
Escorts Group, 79
ESPN, 56
Ethnic-specific brands, 83
Ethnic values, 83
European, 11
European fashion and beauty accessories, 188
Eutelsat, 57
Evita soap, 83
Exchange rate reform, 4
Exclusive dealership, 222
Exclusive distributors, 219
Exide battery company, 184
Exit policies, 4
Export restrictions, 38
External debt, 5
Extrinsic value, 189
Exxon, 29

Fa, 207
Face, psychology of, 15
Factory training, 221
False product information, 83
Family Fiefdoms (not a TV sitcom but should be) 21
Family planning, 95
F&N Coca-Cola (Pvt.), Ltd., 194
Fanta, 195
Far East Computers, 135

Fashion: based on traditional garments, 136; retailing, 199
Fast Lane, 202
Fast-Moving Consumer-Goods (FMCG), 92, 213, 219
FDI-to-GDP ratio, 3
Federation of Indian Chambers of Commerce and Industry (FICCI), 23
Federation of Medical Representatives Association of India (FMRAI), 231
Feedback Marketing Services, 97
Feminism, 151
Fertilizer, 38; seed and pesticide retailers, 105
Ffolio in Bangalore, 199
Films, 13; and television, 10
Finance Ministry, 18
Finance-Related Companies (FRCs), 24
Financial institutions, 18; markets, 19; services, 49
Financial Times, 41, 46
Fire Temple at Udvada, 156
First Leasing, 124
Five Pillars of Islam, 160
Flexipack marketing, 206
Folklore, 50
Footwear, 38
Forbes magazine, 77
Ford Motors, 34
Foreign: financial institutions (FFIs), 33; institutional investors (FIIs), 19; newspaper investments, 52; press, 6; television programs, 10; trade, 4
Foreign Bank, 31
Foreign investment, 2, 4; capital investment, 5; direct investment (FDI), 18; exchange regulations, 28; in print media, 52; reserves, 2, 4

Fortis Financial Services, 124
Four Noble Truths of Buddhism, 158
France, 53
France Telecom, 41
Frequent-flier programs, 103
"Fridgies" (refrigerators), 148
Friends of Universal Civil Society, 46
Frooti, 80, 234
Fudged, 3
Fujitsu, 186

Gabriel (Shock Absorbers) India, 121
Gandhi, Indira, 135, 154, 195
Gandhi, Mahatma, 6, 42, 149, 157
Gandhi, Rajiv, 52
Ganges Delta, 63
Gangetic plain, 63
Gau-mata ("nation-mother"), 154
GDP, 1, 2, 5; growth, 38, 62
GE Capital, 82, 111
GEEP Industrial Syndicate, 223, 224
Gender bias, 171
Gender Images, 171
General Accident, 123
General Electric, 22, 39
General Foods, 66
General-purpose magazines, 44
Genesis Marketing, 187
German patent law, 86
Ghost shoppers, 130
Giftware, 63
Gillette, 225
Glass products, 38
Glaxo, 95, 232
Global depository receipts (GDRs), 19, 31
Global Trust Bank, 102
Goa, 95
Godbole, Prashant, 178
Godrej, 80, 156, 225
Godrej Foods, 184, 233
Godrej's Jumping-brand mango drink, 234

Godrej Soaps, 83, 184
Gods, 23
Goenka, Vivek, 43
Gokaldas Exports, 237
Golden Roast coffee, 198
Goldman Sachs, 31
Goldstar (LG Electronics), 113, 116
Government, 13; interference in local affairs, 6; -run shops, 84
Gowda Administration, 110
Gowda, Deve, 16
Great Britain, 166
Greenfield plants, 113
Green Revolution, 70, 148
Grey, Trikaya, 173, 176
Grundig, 110
Guardian Royal, 123
Gujarat, 24, 107, 156, 166, 181
Gulf States, 85
Gupta period, 157
Gupta, Ravi, 173
Gurgaon, 120
Gurudwara, 162
Guru Granth, 161
Guru Nanak (1469–1539), 161
Guru worship, 153

Hadlee dried peas, 206
Hair-care products, 83
Hajj, 160
Hallmark Cards, 187
Hamara newsletter, 202
Hamsa Research Group, 97
Hand-held vacuum cleaners, 228
Harijans, 157
Haryana state, 120
HCL Corp., 135; America, 135; Comnet, 59; Frontline, 102, 103; India, 134
HDFC, 82
Health care, 33
Health tonics, 83
Hegira, 160

Henkel KGmA of Germany, 207, 208
Henko detergent, 208
Hero Cycles, 83
Hewlett-Packard, 135
Hidden income, 221
Hidden takeovers, 22
High-end white goods market, 116
High Definition TV (HDTV), 112
High-value durables, 229; merchandise, 191
Himachal Pradesh, 71
Hindi language, 45; dailies, 42; publications, 91
The Hindu, 47, 51
Hinduism, 54, 155, 156, 159, 165, 199
Hinduja family, 56
Hinduja, Rajendra, 237
Hindu nationalism, 45, 148; nationalist parties, 195; revivalists, 54; self-identity, 154; temples, 23
Hindustan Ciba-Geigy, 205, 210
Hindustan Lever, 59, 69, 81, 167, 169, 173, 185, 202, 208
Hindustan Petroleum Corp. Ltd. (HPCL), 29
Hindustan Thompson Associates (HTA), 173
The Hindustan Times, 42, 43, 46, 53, 173
Hindutva, 45, 154
"Hindutva Middle Class," 54
Hire-purchase (leasing), 75, 82
Hiring local employees, 194
Historical craftsmanship, 148
Hitachi, 117
Hoardings (billboards), 146, 183
Hobbies, 13
Holidays, 10
Home: appliances, 168; PC Market, 118
Home TV (Hindi entertainment channel), 53

Hong Kong: television broadcasts, 52; city of, 46, 99
Hongkong & Shanghai Banking Co., 34
Hoover Co., 116
Horlicks, 93, 223
Household equipment, 104; products consumer dynamics, 140
Housing Development Finance Corp. (HDFC), 111, 123
"Hoysala" sari designs, 137
HTA, 174
Hughes Communications, 57
Hughes Escorts Communications Limited (HECI), 59
Humanists, 12
Human rights, 151
Humans turned into legends, 158
Hush Puppies, 210
Hutchinson, Max, 104, 186
Hyderabad, 24, 46, 181, 200
Hydrogenated fats, 96

Ice cream, 206
Iced tea, 206
Illustrated books, 228
Illustrated Weekly of India, 43–44
Image magnet, 66
Image migration, 188
Imagination, 14
Imam, Syeda, 176
Immigrants, 13
Immorality, 153
Import barriers, 2; reform, 64; restrictions, 38
Impotence, 154
Impulse purchases, 167
IN Cablenet, 56
Income classes, according to average annual income, 71
Independence, 6, 224
Independent small retailers, 217

India, 5, 7, 8, 14, 33, 34, 37, 38, 40, 41, 52, 88, 95, 104, 107, 118, 123, 158, 161, 166, 179, 189
India Government Business Directory, 51
India Link, 182
Indian: feeling of superiority, 30; society, 151
Indian Airlines, 30, 103
The Indian Express, 43, 48, 52
Indian Institute of Management, 143
Indian Institute of Technology (IIT), 48
Indian-language newspapers, 42, 45
Indian Market Research Bureau (IMRB), 97
Indian Medical Association (IMA), 232
Indian Newspaper Society (INS), 181
Indian Space Research Organization (ISRO), 57
Indian Trade and Merchandise Marks Act, 1958, 87
Indian TV, 57
Indian women, 171; women's exposure to media, 93
"India on Internet," 48
India's earliest culture, 13, 163
India's retailing world, 217
India Today, 8, 44, 46, 47, 77, 148
India web sites, 51
IndiaWorld, 47, 48, 49
IndiaWorld Business Directory, 51
Indirect taxes, 38, 67
Indo-British Petroleum (IBP), 29
Indo-Japanese bike segment, 195
Indonesia, 138
Indra, 158
Indus River, 156, 158
Industrial Credit & Investment Corporation of India (ICICI), 21, 124
Industrial Development Bank of India (IDBI), 25

Industrial families, 149
Industrialists, 149
Inefficient enterprises, 4
Inexpensive software specialists, 135
Infiniti, 189
Inflation, 2, 3, 4, 9, 11, 17
Information economy, 151
Information highway, 48
Infrastructure industries, 2
Inquiry, 14
Insat-2E, 57
Insider News, 51
Installment-plan, 107
Institutional investors, 18
Institutional structures, 1
Insurance companies: 187; premiums, 123; sector, 123
Integrated Hoarding Plan (IHP), 185
Intellectual property rights, 77, 86
International: money markets, 22; relations, 10; TV, 1, 55
International Apparel Park, 237
International development agencies, 18
International Finance Corp., 36
International Institute for Population Studies, Bombay, 93
International Management Institute, 102
International Monetary Fund (IMF), 5
International Research Associates (INRA), 8
Internet, 47, 56; commercial connections, 48
Intersputnik satellite, 57
Interstate competitiveness, 39
Intranets, 50
Inventions, 13
Investment, 6
Investment Information and Credit Rating Agency (IICRA), 39
Investor flight, 20

IPO and shares markets, 23
Irani, Farhad, 102
Iron and steel products, 38
Ishikawa Gasket Co., 122
Islam, 155, 160, 165
Islamic Banking, 107; terms, 108
ISO 9000 levels of quality, 122
ITC, 124, 199

J. W. Thompson, 89
Jacquard, 136
Jaffrey, Jaaved, 177
Jain, Praveen, 49
Jain, Samir, 42, 43
Jainism, 149, 159
Jainsons, 77, 220
Jaipur, 180, 182
Jaisalmer cigarettes, 206
Jambudipa ("Flower of the Rose-apple Tree"), 158, 210
James I, 165
Jammu, 71, 95
Japan, 14, 99, 123, 165
Jardine Fleming, 32
Jataka ("occupation"), 163
Jati ("lineage"), 152, 163
Jeep automobiles, 22
Jesus, 161
Jet Fighter, 209
JF Electra Ltd., 33, 34
Jina, 159
JK Tyres, 168
Jobs: 9, 10; redundancies, 4; -related education, 13
Joint ventures, 1, 36, 82, 83, 113
Joly Jely, 234
Joseph, Denis, 177
Journalists, 42
Joy Visual Products, 125
Judiciary, 1
Joint-venture (JV) agreements, 37
JVC, 110

Kakkar, Prahlad, 177
Kalinga, 16
Kalra, Satish, 210
Kalyani Brakes, 122
Kanoi, Francis, Marketing, Research, 97
Kanpur, 72
Karma, 153, 156, 159
Karnataka, 136, 237
Karnataka State Industries Corporation (KSIC), 137
Kashmir, 10, 71
Kellogg Co., 169
Kelvinator, 85, 116, 223
Kerala Industrial Infrastructure Development Corporation (KINFRA), 237
Kerala state, 46, 71, 91, 95, 107, 162, 237
Kerala State Electricity Board, 237
KFC (Indian name for Kentucky Fried Chicken Co.), 6, 148
Khanna, Mike, 173
Khazana Shops, 77
Kickbacks, 33
Kinetic, 106
Kinetic Engineering, 204
KINFRA Textiles and Apparel Park, 237
Kirana (corner-store) merchants, 78, 211, 217
Knock-offs, 85
Kochi, 200
Kodambakkam art deco, 235
Koran, 160
Korea, South, 164
Kotak Mahindra, 31, 49
Kothari General Foods, 225
Kottayam, 45
Krishnamurthy, A. G., 173
Krishna Valley Development Corporation (KVDC), 39
Ksatriya, 149, 157

Kuala Lumpur, 101
KU-band transponders, 56, 57
Kukde, Gopi, 174
Kumar, S., Ramesh, 143
Kumaran Silks, 235

Labor laws, 21; reform, 4
Lakh, 59
Lakhani, 191
"Lalitaji" campaign for Surf, 173
Lamipack marketing, 206
Language and content in the public media, 172
Lard, 96
Large multibrand stores, 219
Lawlessness, 11
Layoffs (of workers), 4
Lazard Credit Capital, 32
Leadership, 15
Learning by rote, 14
Leasing, 82
Leather products, 38
Lee Gram Agency, 137, 138
Leisure and personal interests, 12
Le Monde, 41
Leo Burnett Advertising, 89
Le Sancy soap, 169
Letters to editors, 11, 15
Levack, John, 33
Levis 501s, 78
Levi's jeans, 189
Lexus automobiles, 189
LG Electronics, 110, 113. *See also* Goldstar
Liberalization, 26, 34, 37, 42, 64, 80, 110, 174, 188
Liberty, 191
License Raj, 7
Licensing databases, 135
Life expectancies, 61, 62
Life Insurance Corp., 124
Lintas India, 89, 173, 175, 178
Lipstick, 168

Lipton, 69; Treetop brand, 233
Liquefied petroleum gas (LPG), 26
Liril soap, 175
Lite Bite potato wafers, 206
Literacy rates, 62
Little Hearts, 210
Little's Big Hug Sipper, 204
LML Vespa, 178
London, 167
Loral Space Systems, 57
Lord Cromer, 164
Lotto Shoes, 191
Lotus, 87
Lotus Book House, 107
Louis Farouk, 148
Lower income classes, 12
Lubricants, 30, 102; industry, 29
Lucknow, 44
Lucky GoldStar, 110
Lunel, Karen, model, 176
Lupin Company, 232
Lux, 95
Luxuries, 63
Luxury Market, 78

Maa Bozell Advertising, 170
McCann Ericsson, 89
McKinsey & Co., 22, 97
Mac OS, 119
Madison-D'arcy Masius, Benton &
    Bowles (DMB&B), 173
Madras, 41, 56, 63, 66, 220. *See also*
    Chennai
Madras Stock Exchange, 35
Maggi Hot and Sweet Sauces, 177;
    Noodles, 208
Mahabharata, 68, 157
Maharajah appliances, 65
Maharaja International, 116
Maharashtra, 24, 39, 71, 93, 107, 237
Mahavira, 159
Mahindra, 22
Mahindra, Sona, 121

Major economic regions, 63
Majorub, 206
Makruh (defiling), 199
Malayala Manorama, 45, 46
Malayalam language, 46
Malaysia, 56, 101, 123, 150; Measat
    satellite, 56
Malhotra Committee, 123, 124
Manchester, 166
Manila, 100
Manorama, 46
Manufactured consumer goods, 6
Manufacturer-controlled retail shops,
    219
Manufacturer-owned stores, 217
Margarine, 205
Marie Claire, 191
Market: differences between Indian
    and Western, 29; economics, 5,
    14; economy, 1, 7; intermediaries,
    214; for Internet services, 47;
    R&D, 110; research, 80, 97
Marketing, 145, 167, 186; budgets,
    63; mix, 179; strategies, 27, 83,
    188
Marketing and Business Associates,
    97
Marketing and Research Group
    (MARG), 6, 8, 70, 97
Marriage: 151; counseling, 151
Maruti, 106, 121, 146
Maruti Auto's *Gatirang*, 202
Maruti Class Indians, 147
Maruti, Jay Bharat, 120
Maruti Udyog, 120
Marwaris, 42
Mass market penetration, 224
Mass merchandisers, 217
Mattel, Leo, 186
Mauritius, 31, 49
Maurya Sheraton Hotel & Towers,
    199
Maytag, 117

Mealmaker, 225

Mecca, 160

Media, 6, 8; culture, 42; industry, 52; penetration, 91

Medina, 160

Medline, 232

Megacities, 73

Mehta, Prem, R., 173

Mehta, Vinod, 44

Menezes Cosmetics, 207

Men's toiletries, 207

Merchandising, 167; defined, 168

Merchandising Specialists, 170

Mergers, 113

Merrigold Margarine, 205

Merrill and Goldman, 32

Merrill Lynch, 31, 32

Mesco, 191

Me-too products, 30, 231

Metromedia Technology, 184

Mexico, 36

Microsoft, 87

Microwave ovens, 85

Middle class, 7, 8, 71, 147

Middle East, 113, 155

Middle Path, 159

Military, 70

Milkfood Yogurt, 206

Milkybar, 208

Mill cloth, 236

Mining, 38

Ministry of Health and Family Welfare, 93

Minorities, 8

Mirc Electronics, 114, 175

Mistrust of the world, 154; of women, 154

Mithraism, 156

Mixer-blenders, 104, 147

Mixie Class Indians, 147

Mobil, 29

MODE Research, 97

Modern symbols and rituals, 142

Modi, 21

Modi Care, 227, 228; just-enough mentality, 229

Modi Entertainment Network, 56, 57

Modi Hoover, 117, 118

Modi, K. K., Group, 227

Modi Xerox, 187

Mohammed, 156, 160

Moksha, 159

Money for value (MEV), 188

Moneylenders, 106

Monica Electronics, 174

Monopolies, 83

Monopolies and Restrictive Trade Practices Act, 214

Monotheism, 155

"Monsoon fade," 112

Moody's, 39

Morality, 153

Morgan Stanley, 31, 32

Moscow, 54

Moses, 161

Mote, Chotu, and The World Of Electricity, 201

Mother-child relationships, 152

Mothers, working, 13

Motorcycles, 8, 12, 67

Moulinex, 104

Mount Everest mineral water, 223

MRAS—Burke, 97

MRTP Act, 83

MTV, 28

Mudra Communications, 173

Mughal, 165

Multibrand, multilocation chain stores, 219

Multibrand Stores, 220

Multilevel Marketing (MLM), 226

Multimedia PC, 119

Multinational Corporations (MNCs), 36, 64, 82, 116, 186

Multiple-location stores, 219

Mumbai, 23, 24, 31, 41, 63, 66, 72, 73, 77, 79, 92, 107, 116, 130, 135, 156, 179, 187, 188, 206. *See also* Bombay
Murdoch's News Corp., 52
Murdoch, Rupert, 52
Murshidalvad, 165
Muslims, 45, 107, 199
Mutual funds, 19, 33
Mysore, 136
Mythic features, 158

Nabco, 122
Nadar, Shiv, 134
Nagpur, 181, 182
Nalli's, 235
Nanji, Elsie, 176
Nanz of Germany, 79
Narasimha, Pradeep, 207
NASDAQ, 25
National Council for Applied Economic Research (NCAER), 6, 12, 37, 68, 70, 74, 97
National culture, 55
National Dairy Development Board, 49, 209
National Family Health Survey, 3, 93, 95
National Institute of Fashion Technology (NIFT), 238
National Institute of Information Technology (NIIT), 135, 201
National psychology, 1
National Readership Survey, 97, 184
National Stock Exchange (NSE), 25, 35, 58
National Thermal Power Corporation (NTPC), 201
Navakal, 44
Nehru, 6, 52
Nehru, Jawaharlal, 6, 54, 150
Nehruvian socialism, 10
Nehruvian vision, 7

Nepal, 54, 138
Nescafe, 197
Nestea, 206
Nestle, 167, 177, 197, 206, 208
Netherlands, 86
New-age spiritual ideas, 57, 155
New Delhi, 70
New Delhi Television, 52
New India Assurance, 123
Newports, 78
New Products, 95
News Corporation, 53
Newsletters, 201
News programming, 12
Nexus, 224
Nexus Equity, 177
Nexus Logistics, 223, 224
NIIT Times, 201
Nike, 193, 210
Nilgiris, 79
Ninan, T. N., 43
Nippon Telegraph & Telephone, 40
Nirma, 79, 173; detergent, 190
Nirvana, 158
Nissan, 189
Noble Eightfold Path, 158
Nonalignment, 7
Nonbanking financial companies, 82
Nondurable consumer products, 62, 96
Nonelectrical machinery, 38
Nonferrous metals, 38
Non-Hindi regional newspaper groups, 46
Nonmanufacturing Companies, 23
Nonmetallic mineral products, 38
Nonperforming assets, 21
Non-Resident Indians (NRIS), 49
Non-soap detergent, 137
North versus South debate, 7
Norway, 86
Notre Advertising, 180
Nurturing mother, 152

Nutrition, 7

Obedience and loyalty, 14
"Offtake" purchases, 167
Ogilvy & Mather, 175, 177, 179
OHM Advertising Agency, 185
One Day at . . . , ad series, 178
One-person advertising agencies, 181
Onida, 110, 113, 114, 115, 174; Arcades, 222; TV, 175
Operation Ghost Shopper, 130
Operations Research Group (ORG), 97
Opium, 167
"Organized credit," 105
Oriflame International, 227; Natural Cosmetics, 203
Orissa, 71, 95
Outdoor Site Classification & Audience Research Survey (OSCAR), 185
Outlook, 44
Overbuying, 228
Over-the-Counter Exchange of India (OTCEI), 58

Packaged goods, 69, 84
Packaging, 206
Padamsee, 173
Padamsee, Alyque, 175
Padmasalyar weaving community, 235
Pagelink, 187
Pagers, 186
Pakistan, 138
Paloma, 206
Pamper-the-customer marketing, 199
Panamsat-4, 56, 58
Pan-Asian advertising, 92
Panasonic, 110
Pande, Mrinal, 173
Pandey, Piyush, 175
Paper products, 38

Parallel imports, 85
Paras Pharma, 206
Parker fountain pens, 189
Parle Agro, 81, 234; Exports, 176, 194
Parrys Sweets, 223, 224, 225
Parsees, 155, 156
Partnership, 1
Patent Law, 85, 86
Patents Act of 1970, 86
Pathfinders India, 98
Pathfinders Investment, 34
"Paul Newman" market, 199
Pearson and Carlton Communications, 52, 56
Pearson Group, 46
Peenya Industrial Park, 237
Peerless Group, 123, 124
Pennzoil, 30
PepsiCo, 22, 69, 102, 167, 169, 184, 208, 22; "silent salesman," 170
Pepsi distribution system, 208
Pepsi Foods, 169, 174, 194
Per capita GDP, 2; GNP, 2; income, 62
"Perceived Good Deal," 189
Peregrine, 32
Perfect Circle, 121
Performa, 119
Persia, 155, 163
Personal consumption, 67
Personal/power relationships, 222
Pertech Computers, 101, 104
Petroleum industry, 30; products, 29
Pharmaceutical companies, 33, 88; product distribution, 230
Phased roll-outs, 204
Philippines, 36, 100
Philips, Godfrey, India, 206
Philips India, 59, 106, 110, 111, 113, 114, 115, 168
Phoenix, 191
Piggybacking, 224
Pillai, G. C., Gopala, 237

Pingo, 234
Pinkcity Agency, 182
The Pioneer, 44
Pistra, 163
Plantains (bananas), 211
Plant closures, 4
Pluralism, 17
Pohit, Sanjib, 37
Point-of-purchase sales, 168
Polar Industries, 204
Political: discussion, 12; freedom, 1; history, 14; linkages, 150; stability, 2
Political Activities, 11
Politicians, 3, 6, 55
Politics, 11
Pollution, 11
Population pressure on the school system, 62
Populism, 16, 17
Populist spending, 3
Pornography, 154
Portfolio investment, 34
Portu, 165
Portuguese, 166
Positioning, 65
Post-Independence Generation, 5
Post-Purchase Behavior, 129
Poverty, 5, 12, 74; levels, 62
Power: pollution, 15; relationships, 221
Prabhu, A. G., 49
Practicality, 65
Pragmatists, 12
Premium-goods distribution, 224
Press, 1
Prester John myth, 155
Prestige, 65; -enhancing items, 63
Prestige Brand pressure cookers and kitchenware, 223
Price, 209; controls, 96; sensitivity, 219
Pricing, 65, 84; psychology, 83

Primary education, 7
Private banks, 31, 102; broadcasters, 30; companies, 24; enterprise, 2; sector, 1, 10
Privatizations, 32
Process-patent approach, 231
Proctor & Gamble, 59, 80, 81, 167, 184, 189, 208; *Moonbeams*, 202
Product: awareness, 221; bundling, 119; innovators, 218; life cycles, 81; naming, 206; piracy, 85, 87; positioning, 79
Production bases for multinationals, 83
Proprietary showrooms, 222
Public companies, 18
Public-company shareholders, 18
Public health, 7
Publicis, 89
Public sector, 3; monopolies, 4; reform, 4; units, 4; (PSUs), 26
Puja (devotional) shrine, 145
Puma shoes, 210
Pune, 24, 72, 117, 127, 180, 187, 188, 200, 234
Punjab, 10, 71, 95, 162
"Pure Order of Men" (*Khalsa*), 162
Purgatory, 155
Purie, Aroon, 44
Purolator, 121

Quality control methods, 169
Quantum Market Research, 98
Quarrying, 38
Qur'an, 160

Racks, dispensers, and storage packs, 168
Radio, 89
Raheja, Rajan, 44
Raising capital, 22
Rajadeva (god-king), 15
Raj and Mati, 145, 167

Rajarathinam, P., 44
Rajasthan, 95
Rajasthan Industrial Development Corporation, 39
Rajya Sabha (parliament's upper house), 42
Rakshit, Gautam, 174
Ramadan, 160
Ramayana, 68, 157
Ramms India, 170
Ramzan, 236
Ranbaxy, 124, 203, 231, 232
R&D companies, 115
Ranee, Alina, 171
Ranga Reddy, 24
Rao, Narasimha, 46
Rao/Singh reforms, 5, 21
Rasna, 66, 224, 225
Rawana, 157
Ray-Ban Sunglasses, 66, 168
Ray, Bharati, 172
Raymond Textiles, 177
Ready-mades market, 130
Readymoney, 79
Recession, 10, 11
Recruitment ads, 203
Recruitment and tender ads for public-sector undertakings, 181
Reddys, Dr., 88
Rediffusion, 48
Redif on the Net, 48
Reebok, 184, 192, 193, 210, 224; distribution, 223
Reference-point retailing, 221, 222
Reforms, 6; in domestic policy, 38; from 1996 to 2000, 4
Refrigerators, 8, 67, 85, 116
Regional and rural advertising, 180
Regional language press, 44
Registrar of Restrictive Trade Agreements, 83
Reinz of Germany, 122
Reliance Group, 59; Industries, 26, 44

Religion, 9, 13, 15, 155
Religious differences, 9; training, 153
Resale prices, 84
Research and academic infrastructure, 1
Research costs, 97
Research International (India), 80, 98
Resentment against the urban middle class, 149
Reserve Bank of India, 49, 87, 102
Retail audits, 97
Retail Barometer, 81
Retail chain stores, 217
Retail Design & Merchandising, 170
Retailers, 66, 214
Retailing, 217; community, 218
Retail market, 78
Retail outlet types, 218
Revlon, 168
Rich/poor disparities, 3
Rickshawallah (rickshaw puller), 236
Rico, 122
Rituals, 153
Ritz Bits, 207, 210
R. K. Swamy/BBDO, 183
Rolex, 78
Rollscon India, 227
Roman Empire, 164
Rome, 156
Roy, Ashok, 174
Roy, Someshwar, 130
RPG Telecom, 27
Ruffles chips, 208
Rupee, 70
Rural: consumer market, 62; consumers, 63; electricity, 149; fairs and festivals, 69; market, 67–69, 75; marketing, 69; middle class, 69, 148; purchasing power, 70; retailers, 221; retailing, 222; sector, 5
Russia, 54

Sacred Book, 161

Saffron brigade, 54
Sales, 211
Same-branded products, 228
Sampath, Suresh, 131
Samsung, 110, 113, 116, 118
Sandesh, 44
Sanitation, 7
Sardar Sarovar Narmada Nigam Ltd.,
    39
Sari market, 136
Sarkar, Anita, 173
Sarkar, Aveek, 43
Satellite and cable TV, 41
Satellite Management Group
    (SMG), 57
Satellite television, 64, 110
Sati (widow's self-immolation), 154
Savings, 2; as a proportion of the
    GDP, 68
Sawant, P. B., Chairman of the Press
    Council, 47
Scat Media Consultancy, 57, 58
Scent-familiar, 228
Schaeffer fountain pens, 189
Schroders (Capital Partners (Asia)
    Ltd., 33, 53
Scientology, 57
Scooter market, 8
"Scooty," 195
Scotch Brite, 223, 225
Seasat, 57
Seasonal cycles, 220
Secunderabad, 24
Securities and Exchange Board of In-
    dia (SEBI), 19, 21
Seiko, 85
Self-regulation in advertising, 90
Shakun Advertising, 180
Shamanism, 155
Shareholders, 17
Shares markets, 35; purchases, 2
Shariyah law, 107, 160
Shaving systems, 205

Sheaffer pens, 223
Shell, 29
Shell Agency, 182
Shia, 161
Shinawatra Satellite group, 56
Shipping Credit Investment Corpora-
    tion of India (SCICI), 124
Shirtings (fabric for shirts), 236
Shiva, 156
"Shoehorn-with-toothbrush" prod-
    ucts, 205
Showroom appearance, 196
Shriram family, 22
Shudras, 157, 165
Shyam Microsat Communications, 59
Siddhartha Gautama, 157
Sikhism, 155, 161
Singapore, 2, 48, 78, 100, 150, 194
Singer Company, 107
Singh, J. D., 102
Singh, Gobind (1675–1708), 161
Singh, Manmohan, 5
Singh, Reena, 224
Singhania, 21
Single-tier pricing, 88
Sinha, Tara, 173, 189; Associates,
    173
Sita, 157
"Sleeping" partners, 32
Small office/home office (SOHO)
    market, 118
Small retailers, 219
SmithKline Beecham Consumer
    Brands, 93, 95
Smith New Court, 32
Smuggling, 64, 85
Snack food, 207
Snob appeal, 65
Snowcem, 187
Soap, 96
Social: critics, 171; development,
    150; expectations, 63; freedom, 1;
    issues, 13; poverty, 5; protection,

3; reform, 8; safety net, 3; strata, 163; unrest, 3
Social/religious conservatives, 64
Socialism, 7, 14
Socialist intelligentsia, 151
Software Technology Parks of India, 51
Sona Steering Systems, 121
Sony, 52, 57, 110, 113
Sony Entertainment TV, 57
Sonys, 113
Soros, George, 34
"South Block" (Ministry of External Affairs), 42
Southeast and East Asia, 41
Southeast Asia, 85, 91, 105, 157, 161, 165
Southeast Asians of Indian Ancestry, 234
Southeast Coastal belt, 63
South Korea, 2, 100, 117
Soya milk drinks, 234
Specialized merchandising businesses, 167
Specialty chemicals, 33
"Speed money," 40
Spencer & Co. refrigerators, 223
Spencer's, 223
Spending power, 61
Spiritual adviser, 16
Spiritual dualism, 156
Spoilage, 228
Spredit Margarine, 205
Sri Lanka, 10, 56, 138
"Srimati India," 93, 147
Stagflation, 16
Stakeholder interests, 17
Standard Chartered, 103, 130
Standard Life of the U.K., 123
Star, 30, 31
Star TV, 56, 92, 110
State Bank of India (SBI), 25, 82, 124
State creditworthiness, 39

State government advertising, 45
State governments, 4, 25
Stateless languages, 45
Statesman, 43
Steel Authority of India, 27
Sterling Holiday Resorts, 186
Stickers, danglers, and posters, 168
Stock Exchanges, 25
Stockists, 105, 214, 215
Stock-Keeping Units (SKUs), 226
Stores specializing in extended-payment credit, 218
Stoves, 63
Strategic alliances, 82
Strategic retention, 219
Subscribed capital, 24
Subsidiary municipalities, 39
Subsidies, 16, 38
Subsidized sectors of the work force, 70
Suburban growth, 219
Suburbanites, 8
Sufis, 155, 161
Suitings (fabric for suits), 236
Sumeet, 104
Sundaram Finance, 124
Sunglasses, 168
Sunni, 161
Sun TV, 56
Superbazar, 79
Superjumbo deals, 228
Supermarket retailing, 79
Supermarkets, 79
Super-rich market, 76
Suppliers, 18
Surat, 189
Surf, 173
Surf/Persil, 190
Survival strategies, 113
Suzuki Motorbikes, 195
Svetambara, 159
Swami role, 15–16
Syngal, Brijendra, 50

Syriac Christians, 155, 162

Taboos, 153
Taiwan, 100
Taj Hotels, 77
Taj Mahal, 150
Takeovers, 19–20
Talbros, Reinz, 122
Tallow, 96
Tamil-language, 46
Tamil Nadu, 24, 27, 71, 93, 95, 220
Tang, 66, 225
Tarang, 130; Textiles, 130
Taste testing, 198
Tata, 21, 59, 123, 124, 156; Cafe, 197; family, 123; Information Systems Ltd., 118; Steel, 27
Tata's flavor database, 198
Tax reform, 4; structure, 2
TCS, 203
Technologists, 12
Technology transfer, 37
Telcos, 106
Telecommunications, 2, 20, 33, 40, 82; Minister, 50; Ministry, 40
Telecom privatization, 40
The Telegraph, 43
Telephone connections, 8
Television, 12, 69, 89, 92, 96; advertising, 67; advertising revenues, 53; distribution, 113; market, 125; ownership, 110; rating points (TRPs), 28; rating services, 97
Telstra of Australia, 41
Terrorism, 10, 11
Tetrapak, 80, 233
Textile imports, 34; industry, 34, 166
Textiles, 33
Thaicom-3, 56
Thailand, 2, 56, 100, 150
Thane, 24
Thapar, 21
Thapar, Lalit, 44

Thapar, Romila, 165
Third-party distribution, 223; agreements, 216
Third world, 10
Thomson, 110
Thugs, 6
Thums-Up, 176
Time Magazine, 46
The Times, 41, 42, 43
The Times of India, 44
Times of India group, 42, 81
Tires, 168
Titan Watch Co., 78, 167, 179, 195
Toilet soap, 80
Tomyas Advertising, 180
Toothbrushes, 205
Toothpaste, 83
Top Ramen, 208
Toshiba, 110
Toyota, 189
Trade and Merchandise Marks Act, 87
Trade liberalization, 38
Trademarks, 86, 87
Trade promotions, 83
Trading practices, 83
Tradition, 14
Transparency, 6, 17
Transport equipment, 38
Transport infrastructure, 212
Travel, 9, 12, 13
The Tribune, 44
Trichur, 180
TRW, 106
TTK, 223, 226; Distribution, 216; Prestige-brand cookers, 225
Tungusic tribes, 163
Turkey, 36
TV, 7, 8, 44, 47; ads, 180, 182; financing, 111; home shopping, 230; market, 30, 53; pricing, 111; product features, 112; program

quality, 111; replacement market, 112; retailing, 111
TV Ads Agency in Baroda, 181
TV5, 46
TV-owning family, 6
TVS India, 195

UCB Belgium, 88
Undeclared income, 76
Underdeveloped marketing areas, 194
Underprivileged, 8
Unemployment, 5, 10, 11, 12
Unfair trading practices, 83
Unilever, 69, 95, 233
Union action, 231; restriction, 233
Unionization among sales representatives, 231
United Front government, 123
United Nations, 87
United States, 9, 10, 11, 12, 13, 14, 34, 50, 100, 120, 122, 135
Unit Trust of India, 31
Unit trusts, 2
Universal Convention (copyrights), 87
University of Michigan, 37
University of Pennsylvania, 205
Untouchables, 157, 159
Upanishads, 157
Up-market fashion outlets, 191
Up-Marketing, 195
Upper middle-class market, 109
The Urban Market, 69
Urban Demographics, 72
Urbanization, 54
Urban India, 5; market, 63, 65, 68; women, 95
Urdu, 45
US$/Rupee conversion rate, 59
Usha, 168
"Usha Corners," 169
Usha Group, 59
Usha International, 169

U.S. West, 41
Uttar Pradesh, 71, 95
UUNet, 50

Vacuum cleaner, 104
Vaishyas, 157, 165
Value-added ladder, 150–51
Value for money (VFM), 188
Vama, 77
Vanitha, 47
Vantage Agency, 183
Varnas (paleo-castes), 146, 156, 163
Vasisht, Rudra, 137, 138
Vedas, 156
Vernacular regional media, 6
Vested interests, 26
Videocon International, 110, 113, 114
Videocon Plazas, 222
Videocon TV, 189
Video magazines, 202
Vihara, 158
Vikram, Jitendra, 125
Visa International, 77, 82
Vishnu, 156, 159
Visibility, 169
Vivek & Co., 220
Volfarm, 225
Voltas, 117, 204, 216, 223, 224, 225
Voltas World, 222
Volume Fabric Retailing, 235
VSAT Communications, 58
VSNI(public-sector controller of India's electronic gateways), 50
Vutek, 184

wallah, 44
Walls Ice Cream, 209
Wall Street Journal, 48
"Wall Street Walk," 17
Warburg Pincus, 34
Warehouse high-discount operations, 217

Warrior-king, 16
Washing machines, 96; market, 116
Wealth, 70
Wearhouse, 237
Web site costs, 47
Weddings, 63
The Week, 46
Weekender, 237
Welcomgroup, 199
West Bengal, 24, 71, 107
West Coastal Belt, 63
Western Europe, 12, 13
Western Region consumer market, 138
Westinghouse, 117
Weston Elecroniks, 117
West versus East debate, 7
Wharton School of Business, 205
"Wheaten-skinned," 148
Whirlpool, 116
White goods, 96, 113
Wholesale and retail trade, 38
Wholesalers, 105, 214, 215
Windows: 3.1, 119; 95, 119
Wine, 145
Wipro, 135, 225
Wipro-Acer, 118, 119
Wockhardt, 232

Wood, Ernest, 139
Women, 93; in the electronic media, 172; as entrepreneurial types, 172; figures, 172; in India, 151
Women's shoes, 191
Working mothers, 13
World Bank, 5
World Cup Cricket, 194
World Wide Web, 47
Wrigley's chewing gum, 223–25
Wristwatches, 67

Xenophobia, 32

Yahoo port, 51
Yahoo search using the keywords "India" and "India and Business," 49
Young & Rubicam, 89

Zarathustra, 155
Z-Axis, 181
Zee Cinema, 28
Zee TV, 28, 30, 31, 52, 53, 56, 92, 93
Zen Communications, 207
Zend-Avesta, 155
Zenter India, 137; Worldwide, 139
Zoroastrianism, 155

About the Author

DOUGLAS BULLIS is a writer, editor, and currently owner of Atelier Books, a full-service book production firm serving international publishers with interests in the Southeast Asian market. His clients include major publishers here and abroad. Mr. Bullis has written and published more than 200 articles on topics ranging from art and cultural history to business, country investment, and technology transfer. He also is author of *Doing Business in Today's India* (Quorum, 1998).